LORCAN COLLINS

1916

THE RISING

HANDBOOK

THE O'BRIEN PRESS
DUBLIN

First published 2016 by
The O'Brien Press Ltd,
12 Terenure Road East, Rathgar, Dublin 6, D06 HD27, Ireland.
Tel: +353 1 4923333; Fax: +353 1 4922777
E-mail: books@obrien.ie. Website: www.obrien.ie
The O'Brien Press is a member of Publishing Ireland.

ISBN: 978-1-84717-599-1

8 7 6 5 4 3 2 1
20 19 18 17 16

Printed and bound in Poland by Białostockie Zakłady Graficzne S.A.
The paper used in this book is produced using pulp from managed forests.

Picture Credits: The author and publisher thank the following for permission to use
photographs and illustrative material: p18 (17PD-1A11-30), p22 (17NO-1A66-01), p34
(17PC-1B14-19), p75 (top), p76 (top, 17PD-1A14-22), p76 (bottom, 17PD-1A14-25),
p77 (top, 17PC-1B52-07a), p78 (bottom, 17PD-1A13-01), p101, p104 (17PD-1A12-15),
p145 (17PC-1A44-01), p150 (17PC-1A54-25), p160 (17PD-1A14-15) courtesy of the
Kilmainham Gaol Collection; p30, p41, p61, p63, p67 courtesy of Lorcan Collins; p58, p72
(top), p73 (bottom), p75 (bottom), p77 (bottom), p78 (top), p79 (bottom), p80 courtesy
of the National Library of Ireland; p106 courtesy of Philip Tardif and the family of Bryant
Hamilton; p71 courtesy of Tom Stokes; p72 (bottom) courtesy of the Pearse Museum; p73
(top) courtesy of the MacDonagh family); p74 courtesy of the Plunkett family.

LORCAN COLLINS was born and raised in Dublin. He
founded the 1916 Walking Tour in 1996. He co-authored
The Easter Rising: A Guide to Dublin in 1916 (O'Brien Press,
2000) with Conor Kostick. He wrote the biography of James
Connolly (O'Brien Press, 2012) for the 16 Lives series of
books which he co-edited with Ruan O'Donnell. Lorcan
lectures on Easter 1916 in the United States and is a regular
contributor to radio, television and historical journals.

DEDICATION

For my Mam and Dad, Treasa and Dermot.

ACKNOWLEDGEMENTS

Special thanks to the love of my life, Trish Darcy, for carrying everything on her shoulders, including taking care of our loving children, Fionn and Lily May, who I thank for being very patient and understanding while I wrote and researched this book.

The following people are deserved of special gratitude: Nicola Reddy for her eagle-eyed editorial skills and constructive suggestions, which really shaped the book. Emma Byrne for her brilliant design work. Michael O'Brien, Ivan O'Brien, Íde Ní Laoghaire, the late Mary Webb and all at The O'Brien Press including Claire, Kunak, Helen, Susan, Erika, Bex, Jamie, Brenda, Sarah, Ruth, Fionnuala and Carol.

Joe Connell was particularly helpful and kind. Ray Bateson was always happy to share his knowledge. Dr Conor McNamara, whose kindness shall not be forgotten. Lar Joye in Collins Barracks, many thanks. Fr Joe Mallin in Hong Kong. Aidan Murphy from Met Éireann. Special thanks to Jonathan Rossney. Gerry Kavanagh, Colette O'Flaherty, Glenn Dunne, Berni Metcalfe and Keith Murphy at the National Library of Ireland. Jordan Goffin, Special Collections Librarian, Providence, Rhode Island. Hugh Beckett, Lisa Dolan, Commandant Victor Laing, Noelle Grothier, Captain Stephen MacEoin, Adrian Short and all at the Bureau of Military Archives. Dr John Gibney, Dr Shane Kenna, Joe Duffy, Rory O'Donnell, Dr Conor Kostick, Dr Brian Hughes, Dr Angus Mitchell, Derek Molyneux and Darren Kelly. Patrick Collins from the National Motor Museum Trust in England. Dr Ann Mathews, Liz Gillis, Dr Mary McAuliffe and Micheál Ó Doibhilín. Maeve O'Leary. The *16 Lives* authors including Helen Litton, Brian Feeney, Mary Gallagher, Roisín Ní Ghairbhí, Meda Ryan, John O'Callaghan and my comrade and co-editor Dr Ruan O'Donnell. Donal Collins. Rachel Breen. Prof. Mary McCay, Prof. Andrew Hazucha, Prof. Shawn O'Hare, Prof. John Wells, Prof. Scott Hendrix. Enda Grennan at the *Asgard*. Stew Bradfield. For German translations Larissa Thome, Susanne Morgan and Elisabeth Thom. All at Kilmainham Gaol especially Aoife Torpey and Conor Masterson.

(ctd. over)

Malachaí Duddy. George McCullough and Mervyn Colville and all at Glasnevin Trust. Francis McGuigan. Ronnie Daly, Paul Callery, Rod Dennison, Jim Langton and all the Volunteers. Rita O'Hare. Gordon Kennedy. Patrick Finlay. Liam Cowley. Cecelia Hartsell. Honor O'Brolchain, Barry Lyons, Jim Connolly Heron, Matt Doyle, Terry Fagan, Padraig Yeates, Aengus Ó Snodaigh, Muriel McAuley, Kieran McMullen, Pádraig Óg Ó Ruairc, Dave Kilmartin, Seán O'Mahony, Nora Comiskey, Padraig Beirne, Colette Palsgraaf and Henry Fairbrother. Richard Boyd Barrett. Malvina Walsh and the Laois 1916 Commemoration Committee. Cara and Con O'Neill. John Murphy. Brian Crowley at the Pearse Museum. Seán Quinlan of North Kerry Museum.

For all their constant encouragement, thanks to Mam, Dad, Orla Collins, Diarmuid Collins, Mark Childerson, Eibhlis Connaughton, Gerry Walsh, Rory Dunne, Colin Duffy, the Collins Clan. Carmel Darcy, Pat, Eoin, Barry and all the Darcy Clan. All the Farrell Clan. Aoife, Oisín, Ferdia, Roisín and Nora. Paul Quinlan, Fiona Fairbrother, Denise Keoghan, Liam Wynne, Ciara & Hank Gallagher, Gary Quinn, Davorka Naletilic, Frank Allen, Tom Stokes, Carol Murphy, Peter Reid. John Donoghue, James Donoghue, Alan Martin, Kenny Whelan, John Francis, Rock-on Tommy, Joey, Eugene, Shane, Matt and all the great people at the International Bar. Mannix Flynn. Pat Ingoldsby. The Kennedy sisters and all the Moore Street Traders. Dec Mills. Lar & Elaine. Anna McHugh and all the lads in the GPO including Alan Murphy, George Ellis, Anthony Snedker, Paul Lynch, Phil Freer, John Holland, Richie Hyland, Frank Robinson, Dave Holland, Dave M'Cormack, Michael Sheehan, Dave O'Rourke, Helen Flaherty, Michael Tracey, Joe Cogan, John Power, Jim Spillane and B. O'Connell. All at Fáilte Ireland on Suffolk Street, thanks for the constant support. Ciarán Murray, Sam McGrath, Donal Fallon and the Fallon Clan. Tony Nicoletti, Stew Reddin, Bas Ó Curraoin, Jack Gleeson and Conor Ó Mearáin.

Finally my aul' pal Shane MacThomáis, who'd have loved going through this book looking for errors; gone but not forgotten.

CONTENTS

Section One: Timeline

1798, May to September Rebellion of United Irishmen against British rule in Ireland

1801, 1 January Two Acts of Union come into force. The Parliament is removed from Dublin and the United Kingdom of Great Britain and Ireland comes into existence

1803, 23 July Robert Emmet's uprising in Dublin

1803, 20 September Emmet is hanged and then beheaded on Thomas Street

1823 Daniel O'Connell establishes the Catholic Association to campaign for Catholic emancipation

1829 Catholic emancipation is delivered with the passing of the Roman Catholic Relief Act

1840 Repeal Association founded by O'Connell to repeal the Acts of Union

1843 O'Connell's 'Monster Meetings' attended by hundreds of thousands

1845–52 The Great Hunger in Ireland. At least one million people die and an estimated one million emigrate

1848 Young Ireland uprising inspired by the Year of Revolutions. Leaders banished to Van Diemen's Land (now Tasmania)

1858, 17 March The Irish Republican Brotherhood (IRB), also known as the Fenians, is formed with the express intention of overthrowing British rule in Ireland by whatever means necessary

1867, February & March Fenian uprising

1870, May Home Rule movement founded by Isaac Butt, who previously campaigned for amnesty for Fenian prisoners

1879–82 The Land War: agrarian agitation against English landlords

1884, 1 November The Gaelic Athletic Association (GAA) is founded. Immediately infiltrated by the IRB

1886, 8 April First Home Rule Bill for Ireland introduced in the House of Commons but fails to gain a majority

1893, 13 February Second Home Rule Bill introduced. House of Lords vetoes Bill later that year

1893, 31 July Conradh na Gaeilge (the Gaelic League) founded by Douglas Hyde and Eoin MacNeill

1900, September Cumann na nGaedheal (Irish Council) founded by Arthur Griffith

1905 Cumann na nGaedheal, the Dungannon Clubs and the National Council are amalgamated to form Sinn Féin ('We Ourselves')

1909, August Countess Markievicz and Bulmer Hobson organise nationalist youths into Na Fianna Éireann ('Warriors of Ireland'), a kind of boy-scout brigade

1912, 11 April Prime Minister H. H. Asquith introduces the Third Home Rule Bill to the British Parliament. It is later rejected by the House of Lords, but the Parliament Act of 1911 had removed their right of veto. Home Rule expected to be introduced for Ireland by autumn 1914

1913, January Edward Carson and James Craig set up Ulster Volunteer Force (UVF) with the intention of defending Ulster against Home Rule

1913, August Jim Larkin, founder of the Irish Transport and General Workers' Union (ITGWU), calls for a strike for better pay and conditions

Police attacking strikers during the 1913 Dublin Lockout.

1913, 26 August The Dublin Lockout begins

1913, 30 August James Nolan and James Byrne are beaten by police. Both die of their injuries within a few days. Widespread rioting in Dublin city

1913, 31 August Jim Larkin is arrested at a banned rally on Sackville Street. In the ensuing police attacks, hundreds are injured and John McDonagh, beaten in his home, dies a few days later. This day becomes known as Labour's 'Bloody Sunday'

1913, 23 November James Connolly, Jack White and Jim Larkin establish the Irish Citizen Army (ICA) in order to protect strikers

1913, 25 November The Irish Volunteers founded in Dublin to 'secure and maintain the rights and liberties common to all the people of Ireland'

1914, 20 March British Army officers threaten to resign if ordered to act against the UVF and enforce Home Rule, an event known as the 'Curragh Mutiny'

1914, April Cumann na mBan founded as a Volunteer army for women

1914, 24 April A shipment of 25,000 rifles and three million rounds of ammunition is landed at Larne for the UVF

1914, 26 July Irish Volunteers unload a shipment of 900 rifles and 29,000 rounds of ammunition in Howth, freshly arrived from Germany aboard Erskine Childers's yacht, the *Asgard*. British troops fire on a crowd on Bachelors Walk, Dublin, and three citizens are killed. A few days later, a further shipment of 600 rifles and 20,000 rounds of ammunition is landed in Kilcoole, Co. Wicklow

1914, 4 August Britain declares war on Germany

1914, 9 September Meeting held at Gaelic League headquarters between IRB and other republicans and socialists. Initial decision made to stage an uprising while Britain is at war

1914, 18 September Home Rule for Ireland shelved for the duration of the First World War

1914, September 170,000 leave the Volunteers and form the National Volunteers or Redmondites. Only 11,000 remain as the Irish Volunteers under Eoin MacNeill

1915, May to September Military Council of the IRB is formed

1915, 1 August Pearse gives a fiery oration at the funeral of Jeremiah O'Donovan Rossa, an old Fenian who died in the US and was buried in Glasnevin Cemetery

1916, 19–22 January James Connolly meets the IRB Military Council and is informed of the plans for an uprising at Easter. He is also sworn into the IRB, thus ensuring that the ICA shall be involved in the Rising

1916, 20 April (Thursday)

4.15pm The *Aud* arrives at Tralee Bay laden with 20,000 German rifles for the Rising. Captain Karl Spindler waits in vain for a signal from shore

1916, 21 April (Friday)

2.15am Roger Casement and his two companions go ashore from *U-19* and land on Banna Strand in Kerry. Casement is arrested at McKenna's Fort at Carrahane Strand

6.30pm The *Aud* is captured by the British Navy and forced to sail towards Cork Harbour

1916, 22 April (Saturday)

9.30am The *Aud* is scuttled by her captain off Daunt's Rock

10pm Chief of Staff of the Irish Volunteers Eoin MacNeill issues a countermanding order in Dublin to try to stop the Rising

1916, 23 April (Easter Sunday) MacNeill places an advertisement in the *Sunday Independent* halting all Volunteer operations. The Military Council meets to discuss the situation. The Rising is put on hold for twenty-four hours. Hundreds of copies of the Proclamation of the Republic are printed in Liberty Hall

1916, 24 April (Easter Monday)

12 noon The Rising begins in Dublin. Volunteers, Irish Citizen Army, Fianna Éireann and Cumann na mBan occupy key buildings in the city:
• The Mendicity Institution occupied by Seán Heuston
• Commandant Edward Daly of the Irish Volunteers' First Battalion occupies the Church Street area around the Four Courts
• The Second Battalion under Commandant Thomas MacDonagh occupies Jacob's Biscuit Factory
• Constable James O'Brien is killed at Dublin Castle. A detachment of the ICA under Seán Connolly occupies City Hall
• Éamon de Valera, commanding the Third Battalion, takes over Boland's Mills. A section occupies 25 Northumberland Road and Clanwilliam House at Mount Street Bridge
• Commandant Michael Mallin of the ICA occupies St. Stephen's Green
• Commandant Éamonn Ceannt of the Fourth Battalion occupies the

South Dublin Union (SDU). A large contingent of Volunteers under Captain Seamus Murphy occupy Jameson's on Marrowbone Lane

12.17pm Attack carried out on the Magazine Fort in Phoenix Park

12.45pm Patrick Pearse reads the Proclamation outside the GPO, Headquarters of the Army of the Irish Republic

1.15pm Lancers fired upon from the GPO and repelled

4.15pm British troops arrive from the Curragh. Looting around Sackville Street

7.30pm British attack City Hall

1916, 25 April (Tuesday)

3.45am British reinforcements arrive from the Curragh. General William Lowe assumes command of British forces in the city

4am British occupy the Shelbourne. Using a machine gun, they rake the lower ground in Stephen's Green. Most ICA escape to College of Surgeons

8am Ceannt and his men barricade the Nurses' Home of South Dublin Union. Volunteers in Marrowbone Lane continue sniping at the British

2pm ICA at City Hall and Mail & Express Office surrender

2.15pm HMS *Helga* fires two shots into Boland's Mills

3.15pm British attack Irish positions near Phibsborough. Barricades at North Circular Road and Cabra Road destroyed

5pm Pearse reads a manifesto from the Provisional Government to the citizens of Dublin. Martial law proclaimed by Viceroy Wimborne

1916, 26 April (Wednesday)

8am HMS *Helga* shells Liberty Hall, backed up by British 18-pounders and machine guns

9am Con Colbert and his section, having abandoned Watkins' Brewery for Roe's Distillery, join forces with those in Marrowbone Lane

10.05am Francis Sheehy-Skeffington, Patrick McIntyre and Thomas Dickson executed in Portobello Barracks

12.15pm HMS *Helga* shells a distillery building beside Boland's Mills. Surrender of the Mendicity Institution under Seán Heuston

12.25pm Reinforcements from England, Sherwood Foresters, suffer huge casualties as they advance up Northumberland Road towards Mount Street Bridge

Afternoon Starry Plough hoisted above the Imperial Hotel. Section 1 of the Defence of the Realm Act – which gives the right of a British subject charged with an offence to be tried by civil court – is suspended

Evening Fires on Sackville Street spread

9pm Gen. Sir John Grenfell Maxwell ordered to Dublin to suppress Rising

1916, 27 April (Thursday)

10am British 18-pounder field guns shell Sackville Street

1pm James Connolly wounded in shoulder and later in foot

3–9pm Close combat fighting in Nurses' Home. Cathal Brugha severely wounded. The British abandon the SDU to Volunteers

5pm British troops leave Dublin Castle and engage the Four Courts. Using improvised armoured cars, they make incursions into Church Street area

1916, 28 April (Friday)

1am British troops shoot civilians in their homes in North King Street

2am General Maxwell arrives and assumes command of British Army in Ireland

3am Clerys and the Imperial Hotel are burned to the ground

5am Constant artillery fire directed at the Metropole and the GPO

9.30am Pearse issues another manifesto from GPO explaining that the HQ is isolated

10.30am Thomas Ashe and Fifth Battalion go into action in Ashbourne

7pm GPO roof in flames

8.10pm The O'Rahilly charges down Moore Street with a company of men and is killed in action

8.40pm Evacuation of the GPO. Garrison spend the night in Moore Street and surrounding laneways

1916, 29 April (Saturday)

12.45pm Provisional Government holds meeting in HQ at 16 Moore Street. Elizabeth O'Farrell approaches British under a white flag

3.45pm Patrick Pearse surrenders to General Lowe and signs surrender order

6pm Edward Daly surrenders Four Courts

1916, 30 April (Sunday)

Thomas MacDonagh surrenders Jacob's and Second Battalion. Éamonn Ceannt surrenders South Dublin Union and Fourth Battalion. Michael Mallin surrenders Stephen's Green. Éamon de Valera surrenders Third Battalion. Thomas Ashe surrenders Fifth Battalion

1916, 1 May (Monday) Prisoners in Richmond Barracks are sorted into categories by G Division of Dublin Metropolitan Police (DMP)

1916, 2 May (Tuesday)

Morning Shootout in Bawnard House, Castlelyons, Co. Cork. Head

Constable W.C. Rowe shot dead. Thomas and William Kent arrested

Afternoon Courts-martial of Patrick Pearse, Thomas Clarke and Thomas MacDonagh

1916, 3 May (Wednesday)

3.25am Pearse, Clarke and MacDonagh executed

Afternoon Courts-martial of Edward Daly, Michael O'Hanrahan, Joseph Plunkett and Willie Pearse. Dublin streets returning to normality: shops open, trams begin to run and the DMP resumes control of policing

1916, 4 May (Thursday)

4–4.30am Daly, O'Hanrahan, Plunkett and Willie Pearse executed

Afternoon Courts-martial of John MacBride, Con Colbert, Seán Heuston and Éamonn Ceannt in Dublin, and of Thomas Kent in Cork

1916, 5 May (Friday)

4.30am MacBride executed

Afternoon Court-martial of Michael Mallin

1916, 8 May (Monday)

4–4.30am Colbert, Heuston, Ceannt and Mallin executed

1916, 9 May (Tuesday)

4.30am Thomas Kent executed in Cork Detention Barracks

Afternoon Courts-martial of Seán MacDiarmada and James Connolly

1916, 12 May (Friday)

4–4.30am MacDiarmada and Connolly executed

Section Two: Documents & Newspapers

EASTER MANOEUVRES: GENERAL ORDERS

Orders for Irish Volunteers, which were published in *The Irish Volunteer*, 8 April 1916.

1. Following the lines of last year, every unit of the Irish Volunteers will hold manoeuvres during the Easter Holidays. The object of the manoeuvres is to test mobilisation with equipment.

2. In Brigade Districts the manoeuvres will be carried out under the orders of the Brigade Commandants; ... in the case of the Dublin Brigade, the manoeuvres will, as last year, be carried out under the direction of the Headquarters General Staff.

3. Each Brigade, Battalion or Company commander, as the case may be, will, on or before 1st May next, send to the Director of Organisation a detailed report of the manoeuvres carried out by his unit.

P. H. Pearse, Commandant,

Director of Organisation.

Headquarters, 2 Dawson Street,

Dublin, 3rd April, 1916

THE CASTLE ORDER

Eugene Smith, a Dublin Castle official, passed a document to Seán MacDiarmada's IRB intelligence group, and they transcribed it into an agreed code. MacDiarmada then passed it to Joseph Plunkett. The document was most likely written by General L.B. Friend to the Chief Secretary, Augustine Birrell; it discusses how any trouble over the introduction of conscription in Ireland would be dealt with. Plunkett translated the code – perhaps adding a few lines of his own – then asked his brother George, Rory O'Connor and Colm O'Lochlainn to print the document on a small hand press in Larkfield, Kimmage.

Dublin Castle were quick to label the document as 'bogus', but it was certainly based on something authentic. They pointed out that it was amateurish as it lacked punctuation (there was a shortage of capital letters for the small hand press); however it did cause anger at the proposed treatment of some prominent citizens. Francis Sheehy-Skeffington passed a copy to Alderman Tom Kelly, who read it into the minutes of a Dublin Corporation meeting on Wednesday, 19 April 1916.[1]

Secret Orders issued to Military Officers.

The cipher from which this document is copied does not indicate punctuation or capitals.

'The following precautionary measures have been sanctioned by the Irish Office on the recommendation of the General Officer Commanding the Forces in Ireland. All preparations will be made to put these measures in force immediately on receipt of an Order issued from the Chief Secretary's Office, Dublin Castle, and signed by the Under Secretary and the General Officer Commanding the Forces in Ireland. First, the following persons to be placed under arrest: – All members of the Sinn Fein National Council, the Central Executive Irish Sinn Fein Volunteers, General Council Irish Sinn Fein Volunteers, County Board Irish Sinn Fein Volunteers, Executive Committee National Volunteers, Coisde Gnotha Committee Gaelic League. See list A3 and 4 and supplementary list A2.

'Dublin Metropolitan Police and Royal Irish Constabulary Forces in Dublin City will be confined to barracks under the direction of the Competent Military Authority. An order will be issued to inhabitants of city to remain in their houses until such time as the Competent Military

Authority may otherwise direct or permit. Pickets chosen from units of Territorial Force will be placed at all points marked on Maps 3 and 4. Accompanying mounted patrols will continuously visit all points and report every hour. The following premises will be occupied by adequate forces and all necessary measures used without need of reference to Headquarters. First, premises known as Liberty Hall, Beresford Place; No. 6 Harcourt Street, Sinn Fein Building; No. 2 Dawson Street, Headquarters Volunteers; No. 12 D'Olier Street, 'Nationality' Office; No. 25 Rutland Square, Gaelic League Office; No. 4 Rutland Square, Foresters' Hall; Sinn Fein Volunteers premises in city; Trades Council premises, Capel Street; Surrey House, Leinster Road, Rathmines.[2] THE FOLLOWING PREMISES WILL BE ISOLATED AND ALL COMMUNICATION TO OR FROM PREVENTED: — PREMISES KNOWN AS ARCHBISHOP'S HOUSE, DRUMCONDRA; MANSION HOUSE, DAWSON STREET; No. 40 Herbert Park; Larkfield, Kimmage Road; Woodtown Park, Ballyboden; Saint Enda's College, Hermitage, Rathfarnham; and in addition premises in list 5D, see Maps 3 and 4.'

EOIN MACNEILL'S REACTION TO THE 'CASTLE ORDER'

On 19 April, MacNeill issued this order to Irish Volunteer Commanders:

Your object will be to preserve the arms and the organisation of the Irish Volunteers … In general you will arrange that your men defend themselves and each other in small groups so placed that they may best be able to hold out.

Upon learning of the plans on Good Friday, MacNeill initially agreed with the inevitability of the Rising. However, he changed his mind on Holy Saturday when he heard about the loss of the arms shipment from Germany. He therefore issued this command:

Volunteers completely deceived. All orders for special action are hereby cancelled and on no account will action be taken.

Jim Ryan went to Cork city with this message. The O'Rahilly went to Limerick by taxi. He also went to Kerry, West Cork and Tipperary. MacNeill's countermanding order was printed in a Sunday newspaper:

> *Sunday Independent*, 23 April, 1916
>
> Owing to the very critical position, all orders given to Irish Volunteers for tomorrow, Easter Sunday, are hereby rescinded, and no parades, marches, or other movements of Irish Volunteers will take place. Each individual Volunteer will obey this order strictly in every particular.
>
> MacNeill

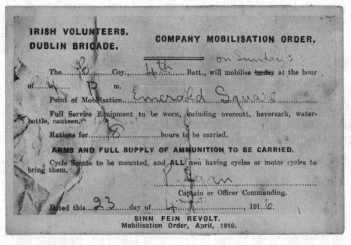

This mobilisation order gives the start time of the Rising as Sunday at 4pm.

MEETING IN LIBERTY HALL, EASTER SUNDAY

The Military Council of the IRB met in Liberty Hall at 9am on Easter Sunday to discuss the situation. The meeting lasted for four hours.[3] A decision was made to send out dispatches confirming MacNeill's countermanding order, to avoid confusion and to stop the rest of the country rising up before Dublin. They also decided to postpone the Rising to the following day, Easter Monday, 24 April 1916, at 12 noon.

PATRICK PEARSE'S LETTER TO MACNEILL ON THE AFTERNOON OF EASTER SUNDAY

To Eoin MacNeill, Woodtown Park.

Commandant MacDonagh is to call on you this afternoon. He counter-manded the Dublin parades today with my authority. I confirmed your countermand as the leading men would not have obeyed it without my confirmation.

PEARSE'S DISPATCH TO VOLUNTEER COMMANDERS

A number of couriers were present in the Keating Branch of the Gaelic League on North Frederick Street at 8pm on Easter Sunday. Patrick Pearse issued them with small slips of paper that read:

We start operations at noon today. Monday. Carry out your instructions.

P H Pearse

THE FENIAN PROCLAMATION OF 1867

On 10 February 1867, the Fenians issued a Proclamation. It is included here to help the reader compare and contrast it with the 1916 Proclamation.

The Irish People of the World

We have suffered centuries of outrage, enforced poverty, and bitter misery. Our rights and liberties have been trampled on by an alien aristocracy, who treating us as foes, usurped our lands, and drew away from our unfortunate country all material riches. The real owners of the soil were removed to make room for cattle, and driven across the ocean to seek the means of living, and the political rights denied to them at home, while our men of thought and action were condemned to loss of life and liberty. But we never lost the memory and hope of a national existence. We appealed in vain to the reason and sense of justice of the dominant powers.

Our mildest remonstrances were met with sneers and contempt. Our appeals to arms were always unsuccessful.

19

Today, having no honourable alternative left, we again appeal to force as our last resource. We accept the conditions of appeal, manfully deeming it better to die in the struggle for freedom than to continue an existence of utter serfdom.

All men are born with equal rights, and in associating to protect one another and share public burdens, justice demands that such associations should rest upon a basis which maintains equality instead of destroying it.

We therefore declare that, unable longer to endure the curse of Monarchical Government, we aim at founding a Republic based on universal suffrage, which shall secure to all the intrinsic value of their labour.

The soil of Ireland, at present in the possession of an oligarchy, belongs to us, the Irish people, and to us it must be restored.

We declare, also, in favour of absolute liberty of conscience, and complete separation of Church and State.

We appeal to the Highest Tribunal for evidence of the justness of our cause. History bears testimony to the integrity of our sufferings, and we declare, in the face of our brethren, that we intend no war against the people of England – our war is against the aristocratic locusts, whether English or Irish, who have eaten the verdure of our fields – against the aristocratic leeches who drain alike our fields and theirs.

Republicans of the entire world, our cause is your cause. Our enemy is your enemy. Let your hearts be with us. As for you, workmen of England, it is not only your hearts we wish, but your arms. Remember the starvation and degradation brought to your firesides by the oppression of labour. Remember the past, look well to the future, and avenge yourselves by giving liberty to your children in the coming struggle for human liberty.

Herewith we proclaim the Irish Republic.

The Provisional Government

THE 1916 PROCLAMATION

The Proclamation of Irish Independence was printed on Easter Sunday in Liberty Hall. It is the document that was used by the Military Council of the IRB to declare or proclaim an Irish Republic.

POBLACHT NA HÉIREANN

'Poblacht na hÉireann' means 'Republic of Ireland'. It does not mean 'Proclamation of Independence' – that would be 'Forógra na Saoirse'. 'Ríocht' means 'kingdom'; 'pobal' means 'people'. By extracting the word for 'king' ('rí') from 'ríocht' and replacing it with 'pobal', an invented word for 'republic' was devised: 'poblacht'.

AUTHOR OF THE PROCLAMATION

The Proclamation was composed on behalf of the seven members of the Military Council of the IRB – Thomas J. Clarke, Seán Mac Diarmada, Thomas MacDonagh, P. H. Pearse, Éamonn Ceannt, James Connolly and Joseph Plunkett – and, having consented to the insertion of their names at the end of the document, they are known as the 'Signatories of the Proclamation'. They also became the Provisional Government of the new Irish Republic.

As regards an author, no one knows for sure, but Patrick Pearse is the most obvious candidate. Doubtless there was some input from the other Military Council members – especially James Connolly – and it's hard to imagine that poets Thomas MacDonagh and Joseph Plunkett did not add to the content. Christopher Brady, who printed the Proclamation, mused over this in his witness statement: 'Although I read the manuscript I could not say in whose hand-writing it was. It certainly was not Connolly's as I was familiar with his scrawl.' [4]

APPROVAL OF PROCLAMATION

Kathleen Clarke, wife of Thomas, recalled how on 'Tuesday of Holy Week' (18 April), he had told her 'that a Proclamation had been drawn up to which he was first signatory … Some time before, Pearse had been asked to draft it on lines intimated to him and submit it to the Military Council. He did, and some changes were made … The meeting had been held in Mrs. Wyse Power's house in Henry Street.' [5]

POBLACHT NA H EIREANN.

THE PROVISIONAL GOVERNMENT
OF THE

IRISH REPUBLIC
TO THE PEOPLE OF IRELAND.

IRISHMEN AND IRISHWOMEN : In the name of God and of the dead generations from which she receives her old tradition of nationhood, Ireland, through us, summons her children to her flag and strikes for her freedom.

Having organised and trained her manhood through her secret revolutionary organisation, the Irish Republican Brotherhood, and through her open military organisations, the Irish Volunteers and the Irish Citizen Army, having patiently perfected her discipline, having resolutely waited for the right moment to reveal itself, she now seizes that moment, and, supported by her exiled children in America and by gallant allies in Europe, but relying in the first on her own strength, she strikes in full confidence of victory.

We declare the right of the people of Ireland to the ownership of Ireland, and to the unfettered control of Irish destinies, to be sovereign and indefeasible. The long usurpation of that right by a foreign people and government has not extinguished the right, nor can it ever be extinguished except by the destruction of the Irish people. In every generation the Irish people have asserted their right to national freedom and sovereignty ; six times during the past three hundred years they have asserted it in arms. Standing on that fundamental right and again asserting it in arms in the face of the world, we hereby proclaim the Irish Republic as a Sovereign Independent State, and we pledge our lives and the lives of our comrades-in-arms to the cause of its freedom, of its welfare, and of its exaltation among the nations.

The Irish Republic is entitled to, and hereby claims, the allegiance of every Irishman and Irishwoman. The Republic guarantees religious and civil liberty, equal rights and equal opportunities to all its citizens, and declares its resolve to pursue the happiness and prosperity of the whole nation and of all its parts, cherishing all the children of the nation equally, and oblivious of the differences carefully fostered by an alien government, which have divided a minority from the majority in the past.

Until our arms have brought the opportune moment for the establishment of a permanent National Government, representative of the whole people of Ireland and elected by the suffrages of all her men and women, the Provisional Government, hereby constituted, will administer the civil and military affairs of the Republic in trust for the people.

We place the cause of the Irish Republic under the protection of the Most High God, Whose blessing we invoke upon our arms, and we pray that no one who serves that cause will dishonour it by cowardice, inhumanity, or rapine. In this supreme hour the Irish nation must, by its valour and discipline and by the readiness of its children to sacrifice themselves for the common good, prove itself worthy of the august destiny to which it is called.

Signed on Behalf of the Provisional Government,

THOMAS J. CLARKE.

SEAN Mac DIARMADA.   THOMAS MacDONAGH.
P. H. PEARSE,   EAMONN CEANNT,
JAMES CONNOLLY.   JOSEPH PLUNKETT.

Jenny and John Wyse Power had a restaurant at 21 Henry Street, just around the corner from the GPO. Their daughter recalled a different date for the meeting: 'On Wednesday [19 April] I was asked by Bulmer Hobson to take a message to Terence MacSwiney in Cork ... Before I left home for the afternoon train Sean MacDermott came in to ask for the use of a room for a meeting that evening ... I was gone before the meeting but my mother told me that six or seven people attended, including Pearse and Tom Clarke. The presence of the latter, who was not on the Volunteer Executive, and the small number present suggests that the meeting consisted of the signatories of the Republican Proclamation.' [6]

THE FATE OF THE HANDWRITTEN PROCLAMATION

The original handwritten manuscript of the Proclamation has never been found. Printer Christopher Brady said he gave it to James Connolly along with the first copy of the Proclamation: 'I gave the first proof to James Connolly at 9pm and he checked it with the manuscript and I never saw the manuscript after that.' [7]

PROCLAMATION WITH SIGNATURES OF THE MILITARY COUNCIL

Éamonn Ceannt told one of his men that he did not sign. William T. Cosgrave, future President of the Executive Council of the Irish Free State, wrote in his witness statement: 'Prior to Ceannt's trial, certainly before its conclusion, he told me he had not signed the Proclamation. He had been unable to attend at the time the signatures were being put to the Proclamation; but the naked fact is that he did not write his name to the Proclamation.' [8]

There is no copy of the Proclamation with the actual signatures of the Signatories.

THE PIECE OF PAPER WITH THE NAMES OF THE SIGNATORIES

Michael Molloy maintained that there was a piece of paper with the signatures of the Military Council attached to the handwritten manuscript of the Proclamation: 'I do not know what became of the manuscript of the Proclamation but the signatures of the Proclamation were appended on a separate piece of paper in the order in which they were required. I took this with me and put it in my pocket and had it on my person when I was later a prisoner in Richmond barracks. Realising how dangerous it would be if the document containing actual signatures of the Proclamation was found, I destroyed it by chewing it up into small pieces and spitting it out on the floor.' [9]

PRINTERS OF THE PROCLAMATION

Christopher Brady was the printer of the Proclamation. The compositors were Michael Molloy and Liam O'Brien. These men were the printers of James Connolly's newspaper the *Workers' Republic*, and they also printed various ITGWU-related items.

SIZE OF THE PROCLAMATION

20" x 30" (508mm x 762mm) normally, but it can vary. [10]

PRINTING MACHINE FOR THE PROCLAMATION

Double Crown Wharfedale, manufactured in Otley in the Yorkshire Dales, England. This was the machine that was usually used to print James Connolly's newspaper the *Workers' Republic*.

PAPER USED FOR THE PROCLAMATION

Double Crown, poster size, 20" x 30". It was purchased specifically for the job from Saggart Paper Mill.

FONTS

The larger type is made of wood. On original copies of the Proclamation, the first 'R' in IRISH REPUBLIC is broken at the tail. This was 'fixed' in facsimile editions of the document. The font used is mostly Antique No. 8, made by Miller & Richard of Edinburgh, and the most common size is Two-line Great Primer.

HORIZONTAL INK LINES

Lead strips, four points in size, were used to separate each line of type. These are sometimes visible as horizontal lines of ink on Proclamations and can be quite random.

TURNING AN F INTO AN E

In the line 'TO THE PEOPLE OF IRELAND', the 'E' in 'THE' was an 'F' that was fashioned into an 'E' by Christopher Brady.' [11]

WRONG TYPE FONTS

The compositors ran out of the letter 'e' and used a different type, which has been identified variously as Abbey Text or Tudor Black. In the last sentence of the third paragraph, a number of these incorrect 'e's appear.

MISTAKE IN THE PROCLAMATION

In the first line of the last paragraph, there is an upside down 'e'. It would appear that the word 'protection' is misspelled with a double 'e' – as 'proteetion'.

NUMBER OF COPIES PRINTED

Printer Christopher Brady recalled putting together two bundles of 1,250 each: 'The machine was ready for first printing at about 8.30pm on Easter Sunday night and the job was finished between 12 and 1 on Easter Monday morning. We had then run off 2,500 copies.'[12] Michael Molloy, the compositor, thought the number was around 1,000.

PRINTED IN TWO HALVES

Compositor Michael Molloy recalled: 'At about 11am we set about work on setting the type and when we had the top portion of it set half way down, even to complete that half we had to treat letters with sealing wax. We could not go any further for the moment. So we sent up a message to Connolly that we would have to print the Proclamation in two halves. And the answer was, "Go ahead."'[13]

The first half consisted of the first three paragraphs and ended with the line, '… of its welfare, and of its exaltation among the nations'.

BOTTOM-HALF PROCLAMATIONS

The bottom half was still in the printing machine as the British soldiers broke into Liberty Hall – they printed some off as souvenirs. There is a 'half-Proclamation' in Kilmainham Gaol, and every now and then they come up for auction. Generally they are poorly printed, as it required great skill to use the Wharfedale.

'SIX TIMES DURING THE PAST THREE HUNDRED YEARS'

The question is often asked as to what specific 'uprisings' this line refers: 'six times during the past three hundred years they have asserted it in arms'. Three hundred years before the Rising would have been 1616, so the first event we come to after that is the rebellion of 1641. The next logical candidate might be the Williamite Wars of 1689–91; although they may be seen as a conflict between kings, Patrick Sarsfield ranks as an iconic nationalist leader. The 1798 United Irishmen rebellion is a must, as is the 1803 uprising of Robert Emmet. The 1848 Young Ireland uprising was short-lived but a clear attempt to assert national freedom. The Fenian uprising of 1867 surely deserves inclusion too. A compelling argument can be made to include the Irish National Invincibles of 1882, who carried out the Phoenix Park assassinations, but the Williamite Wars had a greater impact.

NUMBER OF PROCLAMATIONS IN EXISTENCE TODAY

There may be as few as thirty Proclamations left, but no count is available for those in private hands. A number are with institutions including the GPO, Collins Barracks,[14] Kilmainham Gaol,[15] the Jackie Clarke Collection, Liberty Hall, Trinity College and Leinster House. There is one in the American Irish Historical Society, New York, and one in Providence Public Library in Rhode Island.

PEARSE'S MANIFESTO

Patrick Pearse read out the following manifesto to a large crowd at Nelson's Pillar on Tuesday evening, 25 April 1916.

The Provisional Government
TO THE CITIZENS OF DUBLIN
The Provisional Government of the Irish Republic salutes the Citizens of Dublin on the momentous occasion of the proclamation of a Sovereign Independent Irish State now in course of being established by Irishmen in Arms.

The Republican forces hold the lines taken up at Twelve noon on Easter Monday, and nowhere, despite fierce and almost continuous attack of the British troops, have the lines been broken through. The country is rising in answer to Dublin's call, and the final achievement of Ireland's freedom is now, with God's help, only a matter of days. The valour, self-sacrifice, and discipline of Irish men and women are about to win for our country a glorious place among the nations.

Ireland's honour has already been redeemed: it remains to vindicate her wisdom and her self-control.

All citizens of Dublin who believe in the right of their Country to be free will give their allegiance and their loyal help to the Irish Republic. There is work for everyone: for the men in the fighting line, and for the women in the provision of food and first aid. Every Irishman and Irishwoman worthy of the name will come forward to help their common country in this her supreme hour.

Able bodied Citizens can help by building barricades in the streets to oppose the advance of the British troops. The British troops have been firing on our women and on our Red Cross. On the other hand, Irish Regiments in the British Army have refused to act against their fellow countrymen.

The Provisional Government hopes that its supporters – which means the vast bulk of the people of Dublin – will preserve order and self-restraint. Such looting as has already occurred has been done by hangers-on of the British Army. Ireland must keep her new honour unsmirched.

We have lived to see an Irish Republic proclaimed. May we live to establish it firmly, and may our children and our children's children enjoy the happiness and prosperity which freedom will bring.

Signed on behalf of the Provisional Government,

P. H. PEARSE

Commanding in Chief the Forces of the Irish Republic, and President of the Provisional Government.

MARTIAL LAW DECLARATION ON WEDNESDAY, 26 APRIL 1916

A PROCLAMATION

Regulations to be observed under MARTIAL LAW

I, Major-General, the Right Hon. L. B. Friend, C.B., Commanding the Troops in Ireland hereby Command that

1. All persons in Dublin City and County shall keep within their houses between the hours of 7.30 p.m. in the evening and 5:30 a.m. on the next morning, on all days until further notice: unless provided with the written permission of the Military Authorities: or, unless in the case of fully qualifies medical practitioners or medical nurses in uniform in the discharge of urgent duties.

2. All persons other than members of His Majesty's Forces or Police, or acting in aid of said forces, who are seen carrying arms, are liable to be fired upon by the military without warning.

3. All persons shall give all information in their possession as to stores of arms, ammunition or explosives, or of the movement of hostile bodies to

the nearest military authority, or to the nearest police barracks.

4. All well disposed persons are hereby warned and advised to keep away from the vicinity of all places where military operations are in progress or where hostile bodies are moving, and persons that enter such areas do so at their own risk.

Dated at Headquarters, Irish Command, Park Gate, Dublin.

26th April, 1916.

L. B. Friend, Major General, Commanding Troops, Ireland.

PATRICK PEARSE'S ADDRESS TO THE ARMY OF THE IRISH REPUBLIC

Headquarters, Army of the Irish Republic,

General Post Office, Dublin,

28th April, 1916, 9.30 a.m.

The Forces of the Irish Republic, which was proclaimed in Dublin, on Easter Monday, 24th April, have been in possession of the central part of the capital, since 12 noon on that day. Up to yesterday afternoon Headquarters was in touch with all the main outlying positions, and, despite furious and almost continuous assaults by the British Forces all these positions were then still being held, and the Commandants in charge were confident of their ability to hold them for a long time.

During the course of yesterday afternoon, and evening, the enemy succeeded in cutting our communications with our other positions in the city, and Headquarters is today isolated.

The enemy has burned down whole blocks of houses, apparently with the object of giving themselves a clear field for the play of artillery and field guns against us. We have been bombarded during the evening and night by shrapnel and machine gun fire, but without material damage to our position, which is of great strength.

We are busy completing arrangements for the final defence of Headquarters, and are determined to hold it while the building lasts.

I desire now, lest I may not have an opportunity later, to pay homage

STOP PRESS!

THE IRISH REPUBLIC

(Irish) "War News" is published to-day because a momentous thing has happened. The Irish Republic has been declared in Dublin, and a Provisional Government has been appointed to adminster its affairs. The following have been named as the Provisional Government :—

Thomas J. Clarke.
Sean Mac Diarmada
P. H. Pearse.
James Connolly.
Thomas Mac Donagh.
Eamonn Ceannt.
Joseph Plunkett.

The Irish Republic was proclaimed by a poster, which was prominently displayed in Dublin.

At 9.30 a.m. this morning the following statement was made by Commandant-General, P. H. Pearse :—

The Irish Republic was proclaimed in Dublin on Easter Monday, 24th April, at 12 noon. Simultaneously with the issue of the proclamation of the Provisional Government the Dublin Division of the Army of the Republic, including the Irish Volunteers, Citizen Army, Hibernian Rifles, and other bodies, occupied dominating points in the city. The G.P.O. was seized at 12 noon, the Castle was attacked at the same moment, and shortly afterwards the Four Courts were occupied. The Irish troops hold the City Hall and dominate the Castle. Attacks were immediately commenced by the British forces and were everywhere repulsed. At the moment of writing this report, (9.30 a.m., Tuesday) the Republican forces hold all their positions and the British forces have nowhere broken through. There has been heavy and continuous fighting for nearly 24 hours, the casualties of the enemy being much more numerous than those on the Republican side. The Republican forces everywhere are fighting with splendid gallantry. The populace of Dublin are plainly with the Republic, and the officers and men are everywhere cheered as they march through the streets. The whole centre of the city is in the hands of the Republic, whose flag flies from the G.P.O.

Commandant General P. H. Pearse is commanding in chief of the Army of the Republic and is President of the Provisional Government Commandant General James Connolly is commanding the Dublin districts. Communication with the country is largely cut, but reports to hand show that the country is rising, and bodies of men from Kildare and Fingall have already reported in Dublin.

---◆◆---

MORE PIRACY.

The condition of affairs illustrated in the following comment from " The Advocate," a New York Irish Redmondite paper, is not at all unlike piracy on the high seas. In its latest issue to hand " The Advocate " says :—

"Since the British Government began to seize the mails we have been informed by some of our Swedish acquaintances that the little cheques they have sent to the old folks at home have never reached their destination. If this be true, and we have no reason to doubt it, then the British Government stands convicted of the most contemptible kind of petty larceny which the criminal annals of the world can show. Sweden is just now experiencing a depression in all kinds of business owing to being cut off from other neutral nations by Great Britain, and consequently a little help from their exiled brethren is much needed in countless Swedish households. Now, it may be asked what Great Britain hopes to accomplish by preventing the exiled Swedes from helping their suffering kindred at home ? The reason is not far to seek. The Socialist party is very strong in Sweden, and is growing stronger in proportion to the increase in the difficulty of the masses to make ends meet. Now, Great Britain knows that were it not for the opposition of the Socialists Sweden would long since have entered the war on the side of Germany, hence it is to her interest to add by every means at her disposal to the Socialists' power. Therefore in robbing the mails of these little cheques he is robbing deserving people of the means of tiding over the dull season, and expects that, driven by necessity, many will turn to the Socialists in their extremity, and thus Sweden's continued neutrality will be secured. This is the explanation our Swedish acquaintances give of England's thieving conduct in this regard. For the honour of our poor human nature, let us hope the case is not as bad as it is said to be."

•---◆◆---•

A page from Irish War News, *the newspaper issued by Republican forces on Tuesday, 25 April, 1916.*

to the gallantry of the soldiers of Irish Freedom who have during the past four days been writing with fire and steel the most glorious chapter in the later history of Ireland. Justice can never be done to their heroism, to their discipline, to their gay and unconquerable spirit in the midst of peril and death.

Let me, who has led them into this, speak in my own, and in my fellow commanders' names, and in the name of Ireland present and to come, their praise, and ask those who come after them to remember them.

For four days they have fought and toiled, almost without cessation, almost without sleep, and in the intervals of fighting they have sung songs of the freedom of Ireland. No man has complained, no man has asked 'why'. Each individual has spent himself, happy to pour out his strength for Ireland and for freedom. If they do not win this fight, they will at least have deserved to win it. But win it they will, although they may win it in death. Already they have won a great thing. They have redeemed Dublin from many shames, and made her name splendid among the names of cities.

If I were to mention the names of individuals, my list would be a long one. I will mention only that of Commandant-General James Connolly, Commanding the Dublin Division. He lies wounded, but is still the guiding brain of our resistance.

If we accomplish no more than we have accomplished, I am satisfied. I am satisfied that we have saved Ireland's honour. I am satisfied that we should have accomplished more, that we should have accomplished the task of enthroning, as well as proclaiming, the Irish Republic as a Sovereign State, had our arrangements for a simultaneous rising of the whole country, with a combined plan as sound as the Dublin plan has been proved to be, been allowed to go through on Easter Sunday. Of the fatal countermanding order which prevented those plans from being carried out, I will not speak further. Both Eoin MacNeill and we have acted in the best interests of Ireland.

For my part, as to anything I have done in this, I am not afraid to face either the judgement of God, or the judgement of posterity.

(Signed) P. H. Pearse, Commandant-General.

GENERAL LOWE'S LETTER TO PATRICK PEARSE

From Commander of Dublin Forces

To P.H.Pearce [sic]

29.April/16 1.40 P.M.

A woman has come in and tells me you wish to negotiate with me. I am
prepared to receive you in BRITAIN ST at the North End of MOORE
ST provided that you surrender unconditionally.

You will proceed up MOORE ST accompanied only by the woman
who brings you this note under a white flag.

W.M. Lowe, B. Gen.

DRAFT SURRENDER DOCUMENT

A draft surrender document in Patrick Pearse's distinctive handwriting
was pencilled onto a piece of cardboard in 16 Moore Street, HQ of the
Army of the Irish Republic, during the dying hours of the Rising on
Saturday 29 April. The text reads as follows:

H.Q. Moore St.

Believing that the glorious stand which has been made by the soldiers
of Irish freedom during the past five days in Dublin has been sufficient
to gain recognition of Ireland's national claims at an international peace
conference, and desirous of preventing further slaughter of the civil
population and to save the lives of as many as possible of our followers,
the members of the Provisional Government here present have agreed by
a majority to open negotiations with the British Commander.

P. H. Pearse, Commandant General, Commander in Chief, Army of
the Irish Republic, 29 April 1916.[16]

GENERAL LOWE'S SECOND LETTER TO PATRICK PEARSE

From Commander of Dublin Forces

To P.H. Pearce [sic]

I have received your letter. Nothing can be considered until you surrender unconditionally.

On your surrender to me I will take steps to give every one acting under your orders sufficient time to surrender before I recommence hostilities which I have temporarily suspended.

You will carry out instructions confirmed in my last letter as regards approaching me.

29.4.16, 2.40 PM

W.M Lowe, Brg. Gen.

THE SURRENDER DOCUMENT SIGNED BY PEARSE, CONNOLLY AND EVENTUALLY MACDONAGH ON SATURDAY 29 APRIL, 1916

In order to prevent the further slaughter of Dublin citizens, and in the hope of saving the lives of our followers, now surrounded and hopelessly outnumbered, the members of the Provisional Government at present at Headquarters have agreed to an unconditional surrender, and the Commandants of the various districts in the City and Country will order their commands to lay down arms.

P. H. Pearse, 29th April 1916, 3:45 p.m.

I agree to these conditions for the men only under my own command in the Moore Street District and for the men in the Stephen's Green Command.

James Connolly, April 29/16

On consultation with Commandant Ceannt and other officers I have decided to agree to unconditional surrender also.

Thomas MacDonagh

PHOTOGRAPH OF SURRENDER

The famous image of Pearse surrendering to General William Lowe causes a little controversy. It has been mooted that Elizabeth O'Farrell,

who accompanied Pearse to meet Lowe, was 'airbrushed' out of the image. Close inspection reveals that her boots are visible in one version of the photograph, while in another, it seems they have been 'removed'. What purpose this would serve is left to the reader's imagination – perhaps the most benign explanation is that a printer wanted a cleaner image.

There are three versions in existence: in the first, the British officer facing Pearse – John Lowe, son of General Lowe, who later became a Hollywood actor under the name John Loder – is lighting a cigarette. In the second, the cigarette is gone and the faces have been 'touched up'. In the third, O'Farrell has been removed. In early published versions, her boots were always present. As late as 1966, the *Capuchin Annual* published the picture as it was … with O'Farrell's boots and dress clearly visible.

Section Three: Weapons & Barracks

RIFLES

HOWTH MAUSERS

It is often stated that the same arms dealer who sold weapons to the Ulster Volunteers also sold them to the Irish Volunteers, but this is not true.

The UVF purchased over 200 tons of guns and ammunition in 1914 from Bruno Spiro, son of the founder of the arms dealing company 'Benny Spiro'.[1]

Fifteen hundred German Mausers Model 1871 were purchased on behalf of the Irish Volunteers from Moritz Magnus Jr., an arms dealer in Hamburg.[2] The rifles and 49,000 rounds of ammunition were landed in late July 1914 in Howth and early August in Kilcoole (see pp45–46).

The Mausers were 11mm, single-shot, bolt-action weapons, the most common rifle used by the Volunteers during the Rising. They fired a centre-fire necked cartridge with a .43 calibre lead bullet. The Mauser weighed 9.92 pounds, and had a barrel length of over 33 inches and an overall length of 53 inches. A manually actuated bolt gave it a low rate of fire of four or five rounds per minute; any more would see the barrel heating up. They were engraved in Gothic script with the words 'I.G. Mod. 71' – I.G. means 'Infanterie-Gewehr' or 'Infantry Rifle'.

LEE-ENFIELD RIFLES

Various models of Lee-Enfield rifles and carbines were used during the

Rising. The standard weapon the British soldiers had was the SMLE or Short Magazine Lee-Enfield No. 1 Mark I. The SMLE was introduced in 1904. It weighed 8.82 pounds and had a barrel length of 25 inches. It had a ten-round capacity and fired a British Cartridge MK VII .303, the same cartridge used for the Lewis Machine Gun. The SMLE had a muzzle velocity of 2,441 feet per second and could fire around 20 rounds per minute with a range of 1,640 feet.

LONG LEE-ENFIELD

James Grace smuggled his weapon for the Rising all the way from Canada. He brought it to Mount Street Bridge, where he fought at 25 Northumberland Road. 'I was in uniform also and had my long Lee-Enfield rifle and about fifty rounds of .303 ammunition. I also had an automatic pistol and 200 rounds of ammunition for it.'[3]

MARTINI-ENFIELD RIFLES

Seamus Kavanagh, who also fought at Mount Street Bridge during the Rising, recalled with clarity the economics of getting a rifle: 'An Arms Fund was set up which was known as the G.P. (General Purpose) Fund, into which we paid our sixpences and shillings every week, and when we had paid ten shillings we got a Howth rifle ... Those of us who were at Howth got a Howth gun free. We continued to pay into the G.P. Fund and when I had paid fifteen shillings I received a Martini-Enfield rifle in exchange for the Howth gun for which I was allowed ten shillings, the price of the Martini being twenty-five shillings. In this way I also got a .38 revolver for twenty-five shillings.'[4]

GARIBALDI AND LEE-METFORD RIFLES

Captain Bernard McAllister of the Fifth Battalion (Fingal) Dublin Brigade stated that in 1914 he 'had the only rifle the company got. It was the type known as Howth Mauser. Subsequently the Company purchased six or seven Italian (Garibaldi) rifles.' On Easter Monday McAllister said he procured a Lee-Metford from another Volunteer.[5]

MARTINI-HENRY RIFLE

Charles Saurin of F Company, Second Battalion, was well armed: 'I weighed myself down with all equipment and impedimenta that had been listed for us in *An tÓglách* from time to time, together with my Martini-Henry single-shot rifle, about 4 feet in length, and a sword bayonet which would add about another 2 feet to it, not to mention a bare 28 rounds of ammunition for the rifle. I also had a .38 revolver and about 30 rounds of ammunition for it, and a large sheath knife. Apart from leather ammunition pouches, belt, full pack, haversack with food, filled water bottle and metal canteen.'[6]

FIVE-SHOT BSA

Captain Liam Tannam wrote in his witness statement that he used a Birmingham Small Arms rifle on Tuesday of Easter Week: 'I had taken a 5-shot B.S.A. .303 rifle from the G.P.O. in place of the Lee-Enfield I had brought in (because the Lee-Enfield had disappeared). While I was taking this B.S.A rifle a man named Murray, a close friend of big John O'Mahony, called out for O'Mahony. O'Mahony came and said, "that's my rifle". Then somebody else whom I forget said, "Leave it with Liam. I happen to know he is an excellent shot."' [7]

VETTERLI-VITALI RIFLES

A shipment of Vetterli-Vitali Model 1870/87 rifles were imported by the Irish Parliamentary Party for the National Volunteers after the split. It is eminently possible that a few of these were used in 1916 by the Irish Volunteers, but there was no specific mention of them in the witness statements.

SHOTGUNS AND PIKES

Double-barrelled and single-barrelled shotguns were also used during the Rising. James Coughlan, C Company, Fourth Battalion, remembered: 'There was at least one Volunteer in the party between the church and the main gate of the South Dublin Union who was armed with a shotgun. He was an oldish man, Gibson, I think, was his name, and he was enthusiastic on the merits of the shotgun for close quarter engagements.'[8]

It wasn't just the occasional Volunteer who brought his own shotgun, as Seán O'Keeffe, who fought with de Valera during the Rising, recalled. 'I was instructed by Captain Seán MacMahon to report … at the Columcille Hall to collect some shotguns and shotgun ammunition. It was handed to me by Michael Staines and I brought it back to 144 Pearse Street … As far as I can remember we got altogether between 40 and 50 shotguns and about 1,400 shotgun cartridges.'[9]

Many men also armed themselves with pikes. Irish Volunteer Michael Knightly, a member of F Company, First Battalion, Dublin Brigade, was stationed in the GPO during the Rising. He later stated: 'Though I hated the idea of shooting, I was determined to hold my window at all costs and I thought if it came to quick action my shotgun would be useless. I treasured my pike which I kept on a ledge at the side of the window on which I could stand and fight.'[10]

PISTOLS

C96 'BROOMHANDLE' MAUSER

The C96 or 'Peter the Painter'[11] proved very effective during the Rising and is particularly associated with the Battle of Mount Street Bridge. Countess Markievicz and Cathal Brugha had C96s, as did Mick Malone at 25 Northumberland Road. The C96 had a wooden holster that doubled as a stock and turned it from a pistol into a carbine. It had a ten-round internal magazine fed by a stripper clip or a removable magazine. It weighed a little over a kilo (40oz) and had an effective firing range of up to 200 metres.

COLT .45

Donal O'Hannigan, who was appointed to take charge of the Dundalk and Louth Volunteers during the Rising, recalled in his witness statement that he had 'a Service Lee-Enfield rifle and a .45 Colt revolver which I got from [Michael] O'Hanrahan. We did our drills with dummy rifles. We got together a number of shotguns which were collected from various sources.'[12]

SMITH & WESSON .38

Volunteer James Coughlan of C Company, Fourth Battalion, who fought in the SDU, recalled in his witness statement that he had 'a Smith & Wesson .38 revolver, with 75 rounds of ammunition.'[13]

BROWNING PISTOL

Patrick Pearse owned a Browning and famously a sword-stick. Major de Courcy-Wheeler of the British Army presented Pearse's Browning 7.65mm automatic pistol to President Seán T. O'Kelly at a special function in Dublin Castle on 29 April 1949.

.32 SAVAGE

On their journey to Cahirciveen in Kerry to dismantle the wireless station and bring it to Tralee to broadcast to the *Aud*, Denis Daly and Colm O'Lochlainn encountered two RIC men who blew a whistle and swung lamps in the darkness. O'Lochlainn stated: 'I remember grasping the .32 Savage I had borrowed from Joe Plunkett (my own Webley being a bit heavy for travelling) while I heard Denny say "Will we shoot?" "No," says I, "let someone else start the war. Talk will do these fellows." And so it did.'[14] (See pp112–113 for more on this mission.)

The Savage Model 1907 Automatic weighed 19 ounces, was 6.5 inches in length, and used a .32 calibre (7.65 x17mm) with a capacity of 10 rounds.

WEBLEY REVOLVER

A standard British side arm, also used by some of the Army of the Irish Republic. It would eject all six empty cartridges once it was folded open, allowing the user to quickly reload. It fired a .455 calibre round.

BAYONETS

French Model 1874 Gras rifle bayonets and French Model 1866 Chassepot were altered to fit the Howth Mausers. Those who had long Lee-Enfields tended to have the correct Model 1888 knife bayonet.

HOMEMADE BOMBS

Liverpool Volunteer Patrick Caldwell remembered: 'The Kimmage garrison was full time employed by Captain Plunkett on the filling of cartridges with buckshot and also the making of crude bayonets and home-made bombs.'[15] Liberty Hall was used for some time before the Rising as a bomb factory. For three months, a number of the Citizen Army had been engaged in full-time munitions work making grenades and bombs.[16]

WEAPONS ON THE *AUD*

The *Aud*, which was scuttled off Daunt's Rock near Cobh Harbour, had 20,000 captured Russian Model 1891 Mosin-Nagant rifles, 10 Maxim machine guns and at least 3 million rounds of ammunition on board. (See pp46–53 for more.)

ORDNANCE QF 18-POUNDER

The 18-pounder field artillery gun first came into service in 1904. Weighing in at over a ton (2, 822 pounds), it had a range of up to four miles. The 18-pounder had an overall length of 7 feet 8 inches, which is quite compact. QF 18-pounders are often mistakenly called howitzers, but they were in fact field guns.

Four 18-pounders were transported from Athlone on Tuesday, 25 April, and brought into action the following day. Two were placed at Tara

CARTRIDGE, Q.F. 18 P.ᴿ SHRAPNEL, MARK I.

SCALE = ⅓.

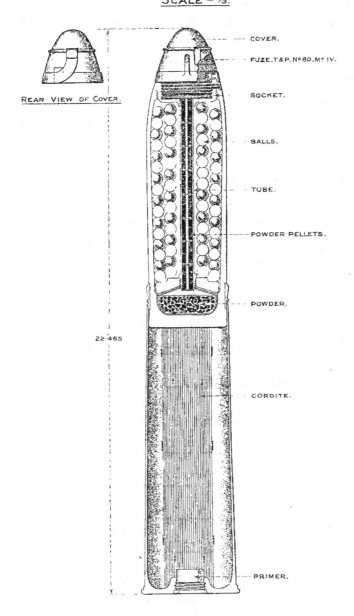

REAR VIEW OF COVER.

COVER.

FUZE, T & P, Nº 80, Mᵏ IV.

SOCKET.

BALLS.

TUBE.

POWDER PELLETS.

POWDER.

22·465

CORDITE.

PRIMER.

Street, where they were aimed at Liberty Hall on the other side of the Liffey. 'The two 18-pounders opened fire almost simultaneously. At the first report every pane of glass in the street was shattered, and even in Trinity College the solid buildings seemed to quake.'[17] The 18-pounders shelled the GPO from the southside and the northside.

There were no high explosives used in the 18-pounders, as the only type of shells available were shrapnel shells. The shrapnel was made up of about 9 pounds of small balls of lead-antimony (7:1 mix). The Mark I shell usually contained 364 bullets, about 41 per pound.

BRITISH ARMOURED VEHICLES

During the Rising a number of trucks were fitted out with armoured protection in the Inchicore Rail Works. The order for the work came under the direction of the British Army and consisted of mounting loco-motive boiler barrels on to road lorries. British soldiers then entered the boilers and fired their weapons through small holes cut into the metal. False holes were also painted on the boilers to confuse the enemy. There is an entry in the accounts ledger for the Inchicore Works that reads: 'Military Account, War Office. Armouring Motor Cars £365.'[18]

BRITISH LEWIS MACHINE GUN

A light, portable machine gun that used the British .303 calibre round. The Lewis gun was gas operated, air-cooled, weighed about 28 pounds and was a little over 50 inches in length. In 1916 it had a 47-round cir-cular pan magazine and a muzzle velocity of 2,440 feet per second. It had a range of 2,624 feet and fired 550 rounds per minute.

BRITSH ARMY BARRACKS IN DUBLIN IN 1916

The Royal Barracks (1706), Benburb Street, Dublin 7. Handed over to General Richard Mulcahy on 17 December 1922 and immediately renamed Collins Barracks.[19] In 2001, handed over to the National Museum.

Richmond Barracks (1814), Inchicore, Dublin 8. Named after the Lord Lieutenant Charles Lennox, 4th Duke of Richmond. Handed over to Commandant Dan Coughlan on 15 December 1922 and renamed Keogh Barracks.[20] In 1924 it was handed over to Dublin Corporation, who converted it into a housing scheme.

Islandbridge Barracks (1850), Islandbridge, Dublin 8. In 1942 it was renamed Clancy Barracks, and in 2001 it was sold to a developer.

Portobello Barracks (1815), Dublin 8. Handed over to General Eoin O'Duffy and Commandant Tom Ennis on 18 May 1922. In 1952 it was renamed Cathal Brugha Barracks.[21]

Beggar's Bush Barracks (1827), Haddington Road, Dublin 4. Handed over to Commandant General Paddy Daly on 31 January 1922. Closed in the 1920s.

Ship Street Barracks (1811), Dublin Castle, Dublin 2. Built for Army engineers but quartered British soldiers in 1916.

Wellington Barracks (1813), South Circular Road, Dublin 8. Former Bridewell Prison (closed 1877) became Wellington Barracks in 1891. Handed over to Commandant Tom Ennis on 12 April 1922 and later named Griffith Barracks.[22] Became Griffith College in 1991.

Marlborough Barracks (1892), Blackhorse Avenue, Dublin 7. First named Grangegorman Barracks. Handed over to Free State on 17 December 1922. Later named McKee Barracks.[23]

Linenhall Army Pay Corps Barracks (1728), Coleraine Street, Dublin 7. Originally built as a trade hall, it was only occupied temporarily by soldiers in the 1870s. By 1916 a small number of army clerks worked there. They were taken prisoner by the Volunteers, who then set fire to the barracks.

Section Four:
The Sea &
the Easter Rising

SUMMARY OF BOATS AND SHIPS ASSOCIATED WITH THE EASTER RISING

SUBSECTION I

The *Asgard*, landed weapons in Howth in 1914.

The *Kelpie*, smuggled weapons and transferred them to the *Chotah*.

The *Chotah*, landed weapons in Kilcoole in 1914.

SUBSECTION II

The *Aud*, attempted to land weapons off the Kerry Coast in 1916.

U-20, the undersea boat that broke down with Roger Casement on board.

U-19, the undersea boat that brought Casement to Ireland.

Dinghy from *U-19*, the boat that landed Casement on Banna Strand.

HMT *Setter II*, the scout vessel whose crew boarded the *Aud*.

HMT *Lord Heneage*, the trawler that chased the *Aud*.

HMS *Zinnia*, spotted the *Aud* but left her alone.

HMS *Bluebell*, the ship that captured the *Aud*.

SUBSECTION III

HMS *Helga*, the vessel that bombarded Dublin.

SUBSECTION I

THE *ASGARD* AND THE HOWTH GUNRUNNING

On 26 July 1914, the *Asgard* yacht sailed into Howth Harbour with 900 Mausers on board. This gaff-rigged ketch was 51 feet in length, 27½ tons in weight, and was built and designed in Norway by the Scottish-Norwegian Colin Archer. She was owned by Erskine Childers and Molly Childers née Osgood. They received delivery of the yacht from Larvik in August 1905, a present from Molly's family. [1]

CREW OF THE *ASGARD*

Erskine Childers, Gordon Shephard (yachtsman and member of the Royal Flying Corps), Molly Childers, Mary Spring Rice, and two men from Gola Island, Donegal: Patrick McGinley and Charles Duggan.

DETAILS OF GUNRUNNING

On the morning of 10 July 1914, the *Kelpie*, followed later in the afternoon by the *Asgard*, departed Cowes on the Isle of Wight for the coast of Belgium. They planned to rendezvous with Darrell Figgis and a tug-boat called the *Gladiator*, which had come from Hamburg laden with weapons for the Irish Volunteers. All vessels would meet near the Ruytingen Light-ship in the English Channel, close to the mouth of the River Scheldt.

The *Kelpie* got to the tug on 12 July and loaded up with 600 Mausers and 20,000 rounds (twenty boxes). The *Asgard* later packed 900 Mausers and 29,000 rounds onboard. Both yachts made their way back to the Irish Sea and waited off the coast of Wales.

The *Asgard* had plenty of time to make it across the Irish Sea. Shephard had to be put ashore at Plymouth, but Childers was a capable sailor. Back in Dublin, Bulmer Hobson, Darrell Figgis and Thomas MacDonagh had planned the operation carefully. On the three Sundays preceding the 26 July, the Irish Volunteers had marched out to Howth for drill instruction; by the third Sunday, the police had lost interest in them. So on 26 July

1914, hundreds of Volunteers and Fianna boys with handcarts unloaded the boat within half an hour.

THE *CHOTAH*, THE *KELPIE* AND THE KILCOOLE GUNRUNNING

As a ruse to avoid the capture of her cargo, on 25 July 1914, the 26-ton *Kelpie* transferred her load of weapons and ammunition onto the 48-ton *Chotah* twenty miles west of Bardsey Island, in Cardigan Bay, Wales, directly across the Irish Sea from Arklow, Co. Wicklow.

On 28 July the *Kelpie* arrived off Bray Head, near where the authorities had expected her to arrive in Dalkey Harbour; rumours and false stories had been spread in advance of the gunrunning. The *Kelpie* was empty, having given her load to the *Chotah*, thus throwing the authorities off the scent.

On Saturday, 1 August, the *Chotah* left the Welsh coast and made her way to Kilcoole, Co. Wicklow. A convoy of vehicles and Volunteers awaited her arrival, and in the early hours of Sunday, 2 August, the shipment was unloaded onto smaller boats and brought ashore.

CREW OF THE *KELPIE*

Conor O'Brien (owner; cousin of Mary Spring Rice), Kitty O'Brien (Conor's sister), Diarmuid Coffey, Thomas Fitzsimons and George Cahill.

CREW OF THE *CHOTAH*

Sir Thomas Myles (owner), James Creed Meredith, George Cahill, Thomas Fitzsimons and Hervey de Montmorency.

SUBSECTION II

THE *AUD*

In April 1916, the *Aud* was laden with 20,000 rifles, 3 million rounds of ammunition and 10 machine guns in Lübeck, Germany, bound for the coast of Kerry and the Army of the Irish Republic. The ship sailed north between Sweden and Denmark then along the coast of Norway as far as the Arctic Circle. She then sailed southwest of the Faroe Islands down towards Rockall and then along the coast of Ireland.

CASEMENT

Sir Roger Casement was never on board the *Aud*. He travelled to Ireland on the submarine *U-19*. However, Casement did meet her captain, Karl Spindler, on 7 April 1916 in Berlin.

DISGUISING THE *LIBAU* AS THE *AUD*

This ship was built in 1911 and originally named the *Castro*. She was owned by Thomas Wilson & Son Co. Ltd. When the First World War broke out, she was captured in Kiel Canal, converted into an auxiliary naval cruiser, and renamed SMS *Libau*.

Once at sea with her Kerry-bound cargo, she was renamed the *Aud*, after an existing Norwegian ship of similar appearance. The German crew lowered themselves over the sides on ropes and planks and painted 6-feet high letters, by torch-light in the dark: AUD-NORGE.

The *Aud* was 250 feet in length and 35 feet in breadth. She had a nominal speed capability of 9.5 knots and a total dead weight (the amount a ship can carry) of 2,000 tons. Her total gross tonnage (internal volume) was 1,228.36 tons.

THE *AUD'S* CARGO

Captain Robert Monteith was responsible for packing the rifles for the *Aud* in Berlin. 'The rifles were packed five in a case, complete with bayonets, belts and ammunition pouches. In each case, in addition, were packed seven hundred and fifty rounds of ammunition – one hundred and fifty per rifle. A reserve of this ammunition was packed in cases of 1,000 rounds … In short, each case contained complete equipment for five men.' [2] According to Monteith, they also had on board 'ten machine guns, ammunition for the Howth rifles, together with a supply of explosives and incendiary bombs'.

THE CREW OF THE *AUD*

Captain Karl Spindler, Officer Otto Hess, Officer Walter Düsselmann, Machinist Paul Rost, Karl Hauenschild, Wilhelm Augustin, Wilhelm Bruns, Rudolph Strehlau, Peter Mathiesen, Signalman Friedrich Schmitz, Albert Schabbel, August Hoffmann, Karl Battermann, Christian Meyer, Haver Schildknecht, Paul Gutzmer, Jans Dunker, George Pöhlmann, Joseph Kuligowski, Adolf Böthling, Gustav Schmidt and Herrmann Brod.

TIMELINE

The *Aud* left Lübeck at 6pm on Sunday, 9 April 1916. At 4pm on Holy Thursday, 20 April 1916, she arrived off the coast of Kerry.

ORDERS FOR THE *AUD*

Leave port in such due time that the vessel arrives in Fenit Harbour in the days from April 20th at the earliest and April 23rd at the latest. In accordance with arrangements a vessel to pilot the steamer is to lie in wait in the days from April 20th to April 23rd at the entrance to Tralee Bay near the Island of Innistooskert. This vessel to be recognized by day by one of the crew wearing a green sweater and at night by two green lanterns shown intermittently, so that they are not visible from the shore.[3]

CONFUSED ORDERS

The arms deal was organised with the Germans through John Devoy, head of Clan na Gael in the US. Messengers had to travel from Dublin to New York by steamship to speak with Devoy, who sent word to the German Embassy in Washington, which was then relayed to Berlin.

The IRB Military Council wanted the weapons to arrive just as the Rising broke out on Easter Sunday, 23 April, when the Kerry Volunteers would be in command of the area. The German Foreign Office in Berlin sent a message on 1 March 1916 saying they would land the weapons between 20 and 23 April. Without consulting the Military Council, John Devoy replied: 'Irish agree. Will follow instructions.

The journeys of the Aud, U-20 and U-19.

Details sent to Ireland by messenger.' The Military Council sent Philomena Plunkett to New York with the reply: 'Arms must not be landed before the night of Sunday 23rd. This is vital. Smuggling impossible. Unloading must occur promptly.' This message arrived after the *Aud* had sailed, and the ship had no radio. The IRB Military Council in Dublin assumed the *Aud* would land no earlier than Easter Sunday; the ship's captain, meanwhile, was aiming to arrive between 20 and 23 April.

RIFLES ON BOARD THE *AUD*

20,000 Russian Mosin-Nagant M91 rifles. These may have been some of the weapons captured after the Russian surrender at the Battle of Tannenberg in 1914.

AMMUNITION ON THE *AUD*

There were five distinct cartridges on the *Aud*:[4] M91 (Mosin-Nagant) 7.62x54mmR; M91 (Mosin-Nagant) 7.62x54mmR (Snub-nosed) (M1908 'spitzer');[5] M98 (Mauser) 7.92x57mm; M71 (Mauser) 11x60mmR;[6] 9mm Parabellum. If there were 20,000 rifles and they were packed into cases of five, it follows that there were 4,000 cases with 750 rounds per case, which adds up to 3 million rounds for the Mosin-Nagant M91s. There were also additional rounds for the Howth Mausers.

HMT *SETTER* II

106 feet long, weighing 171 tons and armed with a 6-pounder, the *Setter* II was a British scout vessel whose crew boarded the *Aud* as she lay in wait in Tralee Bay. The crew were not traditional Navy seamen, so it was easy for Captain Karl Spindler to convince them that the *Aud* was having engine trouble. In fact, Spindler invited them all for drinks, and the skipper let it slip that they were told to be on the lookout for a German ship.

HMT *LORD HENEAGE*

153 feet long, weighing 421 tons and armed with a 12-pounder and two

machine-gun nests, the *Lord Heneage* came bearing down on the *Aud* as she manoeuvred around Tralee Bay. Spindler gave orders to steam south at full speed. For several hours, the *Lord Heneage* managed to keep the *Aud* within sight and broadcast her coordinates to the Navy.

HMS *ZINNIA* AND HMS *BLUEBELL*
Acacia Class Sloops, both 1,200 tons, with an average speed of 16 knots. The ships had two 12-pounder guns and two 3-pounder guns.

HMS *ZINNIA*
On 21 April, the HMS *Zinnia*, under Lieutenant Commander Wilson, sighted the *Aud*. However, after a quick visual, they thought her harmless and left the *Bluebell* to investigate.

HMS *BLUEBELL*
The HMS *Bluebell*, under Lieutenant Martin Hood, spotted the *Aud* a few minutes after the *Zinnia*, 18 miles west of Skellig Rock. At 6.45pm, the *Aud* was ordered to sail under her escort. Spindler tried to pretend he had engine trouble, but a shot across the bow from the *Bluebell* forced him to proceed at 8.30pm. Between 6.45pm on 21 April and 9.28am on 22 April, the *Aud* covered a distance of only about 100 miles, vindicating Spindler's claim that he delayed the enemy as much as possible.[7]

SCUTTLING OF THE *AUD*
As the *Aud* sailed towards Cobh Harbour, she scuttled herself (by detonating explosives in the ship's hull) off Daunt's Rock at 9.28am on 22 April.

WRECK OF THE *AUD*
The *Aud* wreck is at Latitude 51 42.680 N and Longitude 08 14.423 W.

U-20
Captained by Walther Schwieger, she was the U-boat that sunk the RMS

Lusitania off the Old Head of Kinsale in May 1915.[8] She was initially assigned to bring Roger Casement, Robert Monteith and Daniel Bailey (also known as Daniel Beverly) to Ireland on the same night the *Aud* would arrive, but she broke down in the North Sea.

TRANSFER FROM *U-20* TO *U-19*

On 12 April, *U-20* left for Ireland. A day and a half out to sea, the crank actuating the diving fins broke and *U-20* was forced to return to dock in Helgoland (a small island 29 miles off the German coast). *U-20* arrived in Helgoland at 5am on 15 April. The three Irishmen were transferred to another submarine, *U-19,* which set off from Helgoland at 1.26pm on 15 April.[9] *U-19* was commanded by Raimund Weisbach.

U-19 SPECIFICATIONS

Weight: 650 tons. Displacement: 837 tons submerged. Length: 64.15 metres. Height: 8.10 metres. Speed: 15.4 knots (at surface), 9.5 knots (submerged). Range: 7,600 miles (at surface), 80 miles (submerged). Torpedoes: 6. Crew: 35. Max Depth: 50 meters (164 feet).

NOT ALWAYS 'UNDERSEA'

U-19 could travel 80 miles under sea before needing to resurface. Most of the journey to the Kerry coast was made on the surface, with a couple of test dives.

CAPTAIN OF *U-19*

Raimund Weisbach was also the officer who fired the torpedo from *U-20* (commanded by Schwieger) that sunk the *Lusitania* in 1915.

COMING ASHORE

Casement and his two companions rowed the final two miles on the *U-19*'s semi-collapsible dinghy.[10] They were capsized, so they waded ashore and walked south on Banna Strand. A farmer watching proceedings alerted his nephew, who went to the RIC at Ardfert. The police arrived around 1pm and arrested Roger Casement at McKenna's Fort at Carrahane Strand on Good Friday, 21 April 1916.[11]

GERMAN NAVAL DEMONSTRATION AGAINST EAST ANGLIA

The IRB Military Council asked the Germans to provide some kind of naval diversion at the time the Rising was scheduled to begin. This came as an attack on East Anglia beginning at noon on 24 April. Norwich, Lincoln, Harwich and Ipswich were bombed, as was a military base at Lowestoft. A number of British and German ships were destroyed, and there were dozens of casualties on both sides.

SUBSECTION III

HMS *HELGA*

The ship that bombarded Dublin was built as a patrol vessel and belonged to the Fisheries Department until war broke out. She is sometimes referred to as HMY *Helga* due to her reclassification in 1915, when she was taken over by the British Admiralty and became an 'armed auxiliary patrol yacht'.[12] However, her correct name is HMS *Helga*.[13]

SPECIFICATIONS FOR THE *HELGA*

The *Helga* was built in 1908 by the Dublin Dockyard. She was 155 feet in length and 24 feet 6 inches in breadth and weighed 328 tons. She had two sets of triple expansion engines, which gave her a speed of a little over 12 knots. After she was taken over in 1915 she was armed at the bow with a quick-firing (QF) 12-pounder coastal defence gun, which had a range of 10,700 metres and could fire 15 rounds per minute using only two gun crew. At the stern, she was armed with a QF 3-pounder Vickers (anti-torpedo boat weapon) known as a Pom-Pom.

HELGA FIRING AT LIBERTY HALL

At 8am on the Wednesday of Easter Week, 26 April, the *Helga* anchored beside the Custom House and commenced bombarding Liberty Hall. British military 18-pounders were also aimed at Liberty Hall from the southside of the Liffey at Tara Street.

According to the *Sinn Féin Rebellion Handbook*, one of Guinness's steamers was lying close to Butt Bridge, and the Loop Line Railway Bridge was also an obstruction: 'It was impossible under these conditions to bring direct fire to bear upon the objective. The gunners of the *Helga* were accordingly obliged to adopt a plan of dropping fire.'[14] The log of the *Helga* does not mention the need to 'drop fire' and simply states: '26 April. Proceeded up River. Stopped near Custom House. Opened fire on Liberty Hall in conjunction with Military. Fired 24 rounds (8.00am).'

HELGA FIRING AT BOLAND'S MILLS

According to the log of the *Helga*, at 2.15pm on Tuesday, 25 April, two rounds from her gun were fired into Boland's Mill. The *Helga* also fired 14 rounds on the buildings of the distillery beside Boland's Mills at 12.15pm on Wednesday, 26 April.

In a clever ruse, de Valera ordered a green flag to be hoisted on top of the distillery tower at Grand Canal Quay; the *Helga* gunners aimed at that, which saved Boland's Mills from being bombarded. In all, the *Helga* only fired 40 rounds from her 12-pounder during the Rising.

THE *HELGA* BECAME THE *MUIRCHÚ*

In 1923 the Free State purchased the *Helga* and renamed it *Muirchú* ('Hound of the Sea'). She was used as an Irish fisheries vessel. On her final voyage to be scrapped, having been sold to the Hammond Lane Foundry, she accidentally sank on 8 May 1947 near the Saltees.[15]

Section Five: Organisations, Flags & Banners

IRISH REPUBLICAN BROTHERHOOD (IRB)

Founded: 17 March 1858 by James Stephens.
Members in 1916: Bulmer Hobson estimated 2,000 in Ireland.[1]
Structure: The IRB was initially established along military lines, with the first four letters of the alphabet denoting rank: A for Colonel, B for Captain, C for Sergeant, D for Private.

IRB Circles were groups of sworn members in certain districts; they were led by a Centre. A group of Circles formed a District, which was under the control of a District Centre. Further up the chain there was a County Circle, under the command of a County Centre, who in turn was under the control of Representatives on the Supreme Council, e.g. Leinster, South England, Scotland.

SUPREME COUNCIL AT TIME OF RISING

Executive: President, Denis McCullough; Treasurer, Thomas Clarke; Secretary, Seán MacDiarmada.

Representatives: Ulster, McCullough; Leinster, Sean Tobin; Munster, Diarmuid Lynch; Connaught, Alex McCabe; South England, Dick Connolly; North England, Joseph Gleeson; Scotland, Pat McCormick. Two other members: Patrick Pearse and Dr Pat McCartan.[2]

MILITARY COUNCIL OF THE IRB AT TIME OF RISING

The Military Council, who signed the Proclamation on behalf of the Provisional Government, were: Thomas J Clarke, Seán MacDiarmada, Thomas MacDonagh, P. H. Pearse, Éamonn Ceannt, James Connolly and Joseph Plunkett. Note that Supreme Council president Denis McCullough was out of the way in Belfast; Clarke, MacDiarmada and the rest of the Military Council were really in control of the IRB.

IRB OATH

I, A. B., in the presence of the Almighty God, do solemnly swear allegiance to the Irish Republic, now virtually established, and that I will do my very utmost, at every risk, while life lasts, to defend its independence and integrity; and, finally, that I will yield implicit obedience in all things, not contrary to the laws of God, to the commands of my superior officers. So help me God. Amen.

ALTERNATIVE IRB OATH

I, A.B., in the presence of Almighty God, do solemnly swear allegiance to the Irish Republic, now virtually established; and that I will do my very utmost, at every risk, while life lasts, to defend its independence and integrity; that I will bear true allegiance to the Supreme Council of the Irish Republican Brotherhood and Government of the Irish Republic and implicitly obey the Constitution of the Irish Republican Brotherhood and, finally, that I will yield implicit independence in all things, not contrary to the laws of God, to the commands of my superior officers and will preserve inviolable the secrets of the organization. So help me God! Amen.[3]

THE HIBERNIAN RIFLES

Founded: 1907.
Members in 1916: 30.

Structure: The Hibernian Rifles were formed after a split within the Ancient Order of Hibernians (AOH). They were effectively the military wing of the AOH Irish-American Alliance, who felt that the AOH Board of Erin were too sectarian and were behaving like a nationalist version of the Orange Order. The Hibernian Rifles had a headquarters at 28 North Frederick Street, Dublin. Although they were under the direct influence of Clan na Gael, they were also friendly with the Irish Citizen Army. They published a weekly journal called *The Hibernian*, edited and published by John J Scollan, who fought in the GPO alongside a small number of his comrades.

FIANNA NA HÉIREANN OR NA FIANNA ÉIREANN

Founded: 16 August 1909 at a meeting in 34 Camden Street [4] by Bulmer Hobson and Countess Markievicz. Hobson was elected first President and Markievicz Vice-President; Padraig O'Riain was elected Secretary.[5]
Objective: To re-establish the Independence of Ireland.
Means: The training of the youth of Ireland, mentally and physically, to achieve this object by teaching, scouting and military exercise, Irish history and the Irish language.

UNIFORM, FLAG AND SALUTE

Kilt Uniform. Green jersey, with sage colour cuffs, collar and shoulder straps, brass buttons, dark green kilt with saffron brat caught by broach at left shoulder; white haversack carried on the left side, leather belt; shoes and stockings.

Knicks Uniform. Olive Green shirt (double-breasted, no pockets on outside, high collar, brass buttons, shoulder straps), navy blue knicks, dark green felt hat.

Dress Regulations. Haversacks to be worn from shoulders to back knapsack fashion when empty or otherwise; axes to be fixed to belt at left side; knives on right side; coats strapped to belt at back. No badges,

Countess Markievicz and Na Fianna, 1913.

ribbons or emblems of any description to be worn except Fianna ones. The Fianna badge to be worn in front of hat.

Regulation Flag. The Fianna flag, which must be carried on all public parades and demonstrations shall be a likeness of a rising sun on a blue background, with the words 'Na Fianna Éireann' in golden letters on top. Size of flag about 6 feet by 4 ½ feet; pole about 9 feet.

The Fianna shall salute the National song concluding any public meeting by standing to attention and remaining at the salute during the final chorus of the song. The uniforms and other articles used by the Fianna shall be of Irish manufacture as far as possible.[6]

NA FIANNA OATH

I promise to work for the independence of Ireland, never to join England's armed forces and to obey my superior officers.

HEADQUARTERS STAFF

Appointed by the Ard Coiste in August 1915, they held office until Easter 1916.[7]

Chief of the Fianna: Padraig O'Riain

Chief of Staff: Bulmer Hobson

Adjutant General: A P Reynolds

Director of Training: Seán Heuston

Director of Organisation: Eamon Martin[8]

Director of Equipment: Leo Henderson

Deputy Director of Equipment: G Houlihan[9]

Director of Finance: H B Mellows[10]

NA FIANNA OFFICERS

They formed the Dublin Battalion before the Easter Rising 1916:[11]

(a) Battalion Staff

Commandant: E. Martin (wounded in action 1916)[12]

Vice-Commandant: S. Heuston (executed 1916)[13]

Adjutant: P. Cassidy

Quartermaster: J Pounch

(b) Sluagh Commanders

1. An Cead Sluagh: P. Cassidy

2. Brian Boru: H. Mellows[14]

3. Inchicore: E. Murray

4. Blackhall Street: S. McLoughlin

5. Merchants Quay: G. Holohan

6. North Frederick Street: S. Heuston

7. Ranelagh: N. MacNeill

8. Fairview: L. Henderson

9. Dollymount: P. O'Dalaigh

IRISH CITIZEN ARMY (ICA)

Founded: The concept was suggested in public by James Connolly on 13 November 1913. On 23 November, the Army mustered in Croydon Park under Captain Jack White.

Members in 1916: 340.

Motto: That the entire ownership of Ireland – moral and material – is vested of right in the entire people of Ireland.

CONSTITUTION (ADOPTED MARCH 1914)

1. That the first and last principle of the Irish Citizen Army is the avowal that the ownership of Ireland, moral and material, is vested in the people of Ireland.
2. That its principal objects shall be:
   a. To arm and train all Irishmen capable of bearing arms to enforce and defend its first principle.
   b. To sink all differences of birth, privilege and creed under the common name of the Irish People.
3. That the Citizen Army shall stand for the absolute unity of Irish Nationhood and recognition of the rights and liberties of the World's Democracies.
4. That the Citizen Army shall be open to all who are prepared to accept the principles of equal rights and opportunities for the People of Ireland and to work in harmony with organized Labour towards that end.
5. Every enrolled member must be, if possible, a member of a Trades Union recognised by the Irish Trades Union Congress.

UNIFORM

Captain White gave an order to Messrs. Arnott for fifty uniforms of dark-green serge, and the men eagerly awaited their arrival. For the time being, the rank and file wore on their left arms broad bands of Irish linen of a light blue colour, and the officers a band of crimson on their right arm.[15] Captain Jack White, who had fought in the Second Boer War in the British Army, paid tribute to the Boers by adopting their style of headwear, the Cronje hat, with the left side of the brim turned up and pinned by the Red Hand badge of the Union.

LIST OF ICA OFFICERS, 1916 [16]

Gen. James Connolly, Comdt. Michael Mallin, Staff Capt. Christopher Poole,

Capt. Seán Connolly, Capt. Richard McCormack, Capt. John O'Neill, Lieut. Michael Kelly, Lieut. Thomas Kane, Lieut. Robert De Coeur, Lieut. Thomas Donoghue, Lieut. Peter Jackson[17], Lieut. Countess Markievicz.

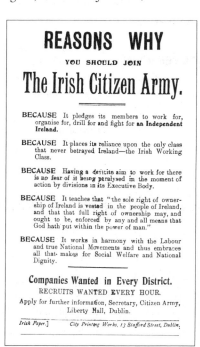

ICA recruitment poster, 1914.

THE RED HAND BADGE

As employers did not deduct union subscriptions from wages, it was up to the individual worker to pay his or her dues at Liberty Hall. To show one was a fully paid-up union member, the ITGWU issued a metal badge for each quarter of the year. The quarters of the year were named after the four provinces of Ireland: Ulster, Munster, Connaught and Leinster.

When the Lockout began in August 1913, the quarter was Ulster, represented by the Red Hand badge. Hence it became the symbol of resistance for the ICA, in memory of the bitter struggle against the Employers' Federation. Curiously the Red Hand symbol was also used by the UVF from 1913 onwards.

ÓGLAIGH NA HÉIREANN OR THE IRISH VOLUNTEERS

Founded: 25 November 1913 in the Rotunda, Dublin.
Members in 1916: Around 12,000.

OBJECTIVE (25 OCTOBER 1914)

1. To secure and maintain the rights and liberties common to all the people of Ireland.
2. To train, discipline and equip for this purpose an Irish Volunteer Force.
3. To unite in the service of Ireland Irishmen of every creed and of every party and class.

EXTRACT FROM GOVERNMENT OF THE IRISH VOLUNTEERS

2. The General Council of the Irish Volunteers will consist of fifty members (50) namely, one delegate direct from each of the thirty-two counties of Ireland (32), one delegate direct from each of the following nine cities: Dublin, Belfast, Cork, Limerick, Derry, Waterford, Galway, Sligo and Kilkenny (9) and nine members other than the delegates direct, resident within ten miles of the City of Dublin. This General Council will meet monthly.

DECLARATION OF POLICY (25 OCTOBER 1914) [18]

1. To maintain the right and duty of the Irish nation henceforward to provide for its own defence by means of a permanent armed and trained Volunteer force.
2. To unite the people of Ireland on the basis of Irish Nationality and a common national interest; to maintain the integrity of the nation and to resist with all our strength any measures tending to bring about or perpetuate disunion or the partition of our country.
3. To resist any attempt to force the men of Ireland into military service

under any Government until a free National Government of Ireland is empowered by the Irish people themselves to deal with it.

4. To secure the abolition of the system of governing Ireland through Dublin Castle and the British military power, and the establishment of a National Government in its place.

Oglaigh na hEireann.

ENROL UNDER THE GREEN FLAG.

Safeguard your rights and liberties (the few left you).

Secure more.

Help your Country to a place among the nations.

Give her a National Army to keep her there.

Get a gun and do your part.

JOIN THE

IRISH VOLUNTEERS

(President: EOIN MAC NEILL).

The local Company drills at_____

_____

Ireland shall no longer remain disarmed and impotent.

Irish Volunteers recruitment poster, 1913.

IRISH VOLUNTEER COMMITTEE

November 1913 to October 1914: The following list classifies who was IRB and who was not. Not all names were on the committee at the same time.

IRB: Patrick Pearse, Joseph Plunkett, Padraig O'Riain, Bulmer Hobson, Seamus O'Connor, Peadar Macken, Seán MacDiarmada, Éamonn Ceannt, Con Colbert, Piaras Béaslaí, Eamon Martin, Liam Mellows, Robert Page, Colum O'Loughlin, Michael Lonergan.

Non-IRB: Eoin MacNeill, Thomas MacDonagh, Tom Kettle, Laurence Kettle, Col. Maurice Moore, Peter White, Liam Gogan, Michael J Judge,

Seán Fitzgibbon, John Gore, J Lenehan, Peter O'Reilly, George P Walsh, The O'Rahilly, Roger Casement.

VOLUNTEER EQUIPMENT

Thomas Fallon of Mary Street in Dublin was one of the suppliers of uniforms and equipment for the Irish Volunteers. Felt-covered water-bottles with a sling were 1 shilling and 9 pence. Leather bandoliers of the approved pattern, made on the premises by members of the Harness Makers' Society, were 5 shillings and 9 pence. Leather waist belts with the harp buckle were two shillings and 6 pence. Putties, blue or khaki, were 1 shilling and 2 pence. Irish Volunteer badges were 6 pence. Irish Volunteer hats, 'Boer Type', could be bought for 2 shillings and 3 pence. Sam Browne belts for officers were 18 shillings and 6 pence. A uniform off the peg could be had for 25 shillings, and for an extra 10 shillings it could be tailor-made.

CAP BADGE

The cap badge had the letters 'FF', which stands for Fianna Fáil ('War-riors of Fál', the name of the mythical warriors of Fionn mac Cumhaill). The Fianna Fáil political party appropriated the name in 1926, and it is often translated as 'Soldiers of Destiny'.

NORMAL DETAILS OF A VOLUNTEER BATTALION

Commandant (1), Vice-Commandant (1), Battalion Adjutant (1), Quar-termaster and Assistant (2), Battalion Engineer Commander (1), Battal-ion Engineer Second (1), Battalion Surgeon and Second (2), Engineer Corps (8), Transport, Supply, Communications (8), Hospital Corps (4). Total = 29. Together with: 4 to 8 Companies of 3 Company Officers (12 to 24) and 100 men (400 to 800).

Total of all ranks in a Battalion = 441 to 853

NORMAL DETAILS OF A VOLUNTEER COMPANY

Commander (1), Half-Company Commanders (2), Company Adjutant (1), Section Commanders (4), Scout Commander (1), 4 Sections of 16 (64), Section of Cycle Scouts (16), Transport and Supply (4), Ambulance (8), Company Signaller (1), Bugler, Piper or Drummer (1)

Total of all ranks in a Company = 103

NORMAL DETAILS OF A VOLUNTEER SECTION

Section Commander (1), Squad Commanders (2), Pioneer (1), Signaller (1), Men (12). Total of all ranks in a Section = 17 (16 men + Commander)

RANK AND SENIORITY (16 DECEMBER 1914)

The following shall be the rank of Volunteer officers:

Members of the Headquarters General Staff

Brigadier-Generals

Vice Brigadier Generals

Commandants

Vice Commandants

Company Commanders (Captains)

Right-Half Company Commanders (1st Lieutenants)

Left-Half Company Commanders (2nd Lieutenants)

Section Commanders

Squad Commanders

Brigade Adjutants shall rank as Commandants, Battalion Adjutants as Captains and Company Adjutants as Section Commanders.

PH Pearse, Director of Organisation[19]

HEADQUARTERS STAFF 1916

Chief of Staff: Eoin MacNeill

Director of Arms: The O'Rahilly

Director of Training: Thomas MacDonagh

Director of Organisation: PH Pearse

Quartermaster General: Bulmer Hobson

Director of Military Operations: Joseph Plunkett

Director of Communications: Éamonn Ceannt

Chief of Inspection: JJ O'Connell

Note: Seán Fitzgibbon was Director of Recruiting but not a member of Headquarters Staff.[20]

CUMANN NA MBAN (THE IRISH WOMEN'S COUNCIL)

Founded: 2 April 1914 in Wynn's Hotel, Dublin.

Provisional Committee: Agnes MacNeill, J Wyse Power, N O'Rahilly, Maureen MacDonagh O'Mahoney, Maire Tuohy, Agnes O'Farrelly, Louise Gavan Duffy, Mary M Colum, M Dobbs.

President in 1916: Countess Markievicz.

Secretary in 1916: Sorcha MacMahon.

MANIFESTO

The Women's Section of the Volunteer Movement

At this time of national crisis we wish to make clear to our country-women the principles for which we stand.

We are the Women's Section of the Irish Volunteers, and have been working side by side with them from the beginning. We are the only women's organisation belonging to the Irish Volunteers, and our activities and aims are solely national. Our work already covers the ground mapped out by suggested societies. At the present juncture we are concerned that the food of Ireland shall be conserved for the people of Ireland, and so prevent a repetition of the Black Famine of '47.

We confidently depend on our Volunteers, men and women, to help us in this vital work. We call on all Irishwomen who realize that our national honour and our national needs must be placed before all other considerations, to join our ranks and give us all the assistance in their power.

GOD SAVE IRELAND

The Provisional Committee

CUMANN NA mBAN

206 Great Brunswick Street, Dublin, August 8th, 1914.

BRANCHES

There were 42 Branches of Cumann na mBan in 1916.[21] These included the Ard Craobh (Central Branch), in Parnell Street, Dublin; Colmcille Branch, Blackhall Place, Dublin; Fairview Branch, Dublin; Inghinidhe na hÉireann, Dublin; Ard Padraic, Limerick; Belfast; Caitlín Ní Houlihan, Cork; three in Co Clare: Carrigaholt, Kildysart and Kilkee; Tipperary; Galway; Laois and Waterford. There was also a Branch in Liverpool, one in London, and the Ann Devlin Branch in Glasgow.[22]

FLAGS AND BANNERS

LIBERTY HALL

With the departure of Jim Larkin for the US in late October 1914, James Connolly was left as Acting General Secretary of the ITGWU. Connolly ordered a banner to be hung across the façade of Liberty Hall: 'We Serve Neither King Nor Kaiser, But Ireland!' It stayed on the building until 19 December, when it was removed by the British Army.[23]

Molly O'Reilly hoisted a green flag with a gold harp up a flagpole on Liberty Hall on Palm Sunday, 16 April 1916, a week before the Rising.[24]

THE GPO

On the roof, the republican tricolour flag of green, white and orange was hoisted at the Henry Street corner. On the Prince's Street side floated a green banner bearing the inscription 'Irish Republic'.[25]

Michael Staines said that he hoisted the tricolour above the GPO. 'I went on to the roof where I hoisted a flag on the corner near to Henry St. on the front. It was a tricolour, probably about 6ft. by 3ft. green next the flag post.'[26]

It has also been suggested that Gearóid O'Sullivan, the youngest officer in the GPO, raised the tricolour.[27] Harry Walpole dismissed this, saying that O'Sullivan was in Cabra that morning.

Walpole said that he and Seán Hegarty hoisted the Prince's Street banner. Kitty O'Doherty said in her witness statement: 'Walpole is the man who claims it; but my own firm belief is that Seán Hegarty was the man who hoisted the flag.'[28]

Eamon Bulfin also claimed that he hoisted up the Prince's Street flag. He remembered Willie Pearse giving it to him: 'I have no recollection as to who put up the other flag, but I think it was a chap whom we afterwards knew as Redmond. He was one of the Liverpool-Irish in the Kimmage Garrison, and I think his real name was Joe Gleeson. I don't remember Gearóid O'Sullivan being there, but I did not know him at the time and he may have been there.'[29] Fintan Murphy stated: 'I believe I saw Eamon Bulfin and Willie Pearse together at the flag-post in Prince's Street.'[30]

THE IMPERIAL HOTEL

On Wednesday of Easter Week, the Starry Plough was hoisted above the Imperial Hotel on Sackville Street by Sean Byrne, Samuel King and Frank Thornton. The field of the flag was green (or blue according to Seán O'Casey[31]) and belonged to the Irish Citizen Army. Its seven gold stars represent the seven brightest stars in the constellation Ursa Major. Stars tend to represent left-wing ideology and are often found on the flags of socialist countries. The plough represents the dignity of physical labour.

The flag was designed by Billy Megahy and woven by the Dun Emer guild.[32] Thornton stated he hoisted the Starry Plough beside the tricolour on Wednesday.[33] Diarmuid Lynch, who researched the flags flown in

1916, said the tricolour was hoisted on Tuesday and the Starry Plough beside it on Wednesday.[34]

THE COLLEGE OF SURGEONS

ICA Sergeant Frank Robbins remembers the flag above the College of Surgeons on Stephen's Green was a tricolour.

FOUR COURTS AREA

Nicolas Laffan recalled that, 'Comdt. Daly got a barrel of sand placed in the centre of the crossing at King St. and Church St., fixed a pole in it and placed a tricolour flag about 6 ft. by 3 ft. in it.'[35] Diarmuid Lynch records Joe McGuinness as hoisting the flag above the Four Courts.[36]

MENDICITY INSTITUTION

The National Museum has a horizontal tricolour, with the green at the bottom and the orange at the top, which was used at the Mendicity Institution.

BOLAND'S MILLS

Andrew McDonnell remembered offering his pike to use as a flagpole to distract the British from bombarding Boland's. 'The flag was hoisted on the water tank [on a malting house] ... Soon after fire was opened by HMS *Helga* from the Liffey, the first shell hit the pike staff in the middle but, in falling, the flag caught on the railing surrounding the water tank and remained there for the week and was later saved.'[37]

Liam Tannam said it was a green flag, three feet by two feet, with a harp.[38] Diarmuid Lynch agreed and added that it was obtained from St. Enda's.[39]

THE SOUTH DUBLIN UNION

Padraig O'Connor remembers trying to join the Volunteers under Ceannt. 'The flag flying on the South Dublin Union was a green flag with a harp, hoisted over the Master's Office facing James's Street.'[40]

Diarmuid Lynch suggested it was a tricolour – but he was not sure. Lynch also states from his research and questioning of Volunteers that there was a green flag with a harp at Marrowbone Lane.[41] The Marrowbone Lane flag is in the National Museum.

CITY HALL

Seán McLoughlin, who traversed Dublin a number of times during the Rising, remembered in his witness statement: 'Round the vicinity of the City Hall like the Post Office there was no one to be seen but a green, white and orange flag was flying over the City Hall and I took it that we were in possession and did not investigate.'[42] Diarmuid Lynch, from his research, was 'uncertain' about which flag flew here.[43]

JACOB'S BISCUIT FACTORY

Diarmuid Lynch said that a tricolour that was made on Thursday was flown at Jacob's. He quoted T Meldon: 'We had forgotten to bring our Tricolour on Easter Monday. On Thursday … with green and white bunting … and some yellow grass cloth … we made a very fine Tricolour and hoisted it.'[44]

BRITISH GOVERNMENT IN 1916

When the Rising broke out in Dublin, the British government was led by Liberal Prime Minister Herbert Henry (H. H.) Asquith in coalition with the Conservatives. The Chief Secretary for Ireland was Augustine Birrell. His Under-Secretary was Sir Matthew Nathan. King George's representative in Ireland, the Lord Lieutenant, was known as Lord Wimborne or Ivor Churchill Guest, 1st Viscount Wimborne.[45]

Section Six:
The 16 Executed
Leaders

James Connolly: Born in Edinburgh on 5 June 1868, Connolly joined the British Army at fourteen and left after seven years. He married a Wicklow native, Lillie Reynolds, in Scotland, where he became involved in socialism. In 1896 he moved to Dublin and founded the Irish Socialist Republican Party and later the *Workers' Republic* newspaper. Connolly spent seven years in New York, where he lectured and organised. Returning to Ireland in 1910, he campaigned for the Socialist Party. Jim Larkin appointed him as Ulster Organiser for the ITGWU in Belfast. Active during the Lockout, Connolly was one of the founders of the Irish Citizen Army. Throughout his life he wrote and published extensively on Irish and socialist issues; his best-known work was *Labour in Irish History*. During the Rising he was appointed Commandant-General of the Dublin Brigade, directing the Army of the Irish Republic from the GPO. Badly wounded in two separate incidents, Connolly was executed strapped to a chair on 12 May 1916.

Thomas James Clarke: Born in Hurst Castle, Hampshire, England, on 11 March 1858. His father was a sergeant in the British Army. When Tom was eight, his family moved to Dungannon, Co. Tyrone. At sixteen he formed a nationalist club that attracted IRB members. Clarke went to America in 1880 and joined Clan na Gael. In 1883 he arrived in England as part of an IRB bombing campaign but was arrested and received a life sentence. He was released after fifteen years and married Kathleen Daly in 1901. He returned to Dublin in 1907 and set about reorganising the IRB with **Seán**  **MacDiarmada**. Instrumental in the foundation of the Irish Volunteers, he was also Treasurer of the IRB and a member of the Supreme Council. In 1915 Clarke organised the funeral of Jeremiah O'Donovan Rossa. As the oldest and most respected member of the Military Council, Clarke signed the Proclamation first. He was executed on 3 May 1916.

Patrick Pearse: Born in Dublin on 10 November 1879, son of the English sculptor James Pearse and his second wife, Margaret, a Dubliner. In 1898 he became a member of the Executive Committee of the Gaelic League. He gained a degree in Arts and was called to the Bar in 1901 but did not pursue law. Pearse's literary output was constant; he published extensively in both Irish and English and became the editor of the language newspaper *An Claidheamh Soluis.* He spent time in Rosmuc and on the Aran Islands; it was there that he first met **Thomas MacDonagh**. He condemned the English educational system in his essay 'The Murder Machine' and established two schools, St. Enda's for boys and St. Ita's for girls. One of the founder members of the Irish Volunteers, and possibly the main author of the Proclamation, Pearse was the President of the Provisional Government of the Irish Republic and Commander-in-Chief in the GPO. He was executed on 3 May 1916.

Thomas MacDonagh: Born on 1 February 1878 in Cloughjordan, Tipperary. He received his primary education from his father; both of his parents were teachers. He went to Rockwell College in Cashel, where he considered becoming a priest but chose to become a teacher instead. Having met **Patrick Pearse** on the Aran Islands, he moved to Dublin to study and joined the teaching staff of St. Enda's. Later, having taken a master's degree in Arts, he lectured in English at UCD. He was an accomplished poet, and his play *When the Dawn Is Come* was produced at the Abbey Theatre. Like his friend **Joseph Plunkett**, he edited *The Irish Review* and was a Director of the Irish Theatre. MacDonagh was appointed Director of Training for the Irish Volunteers in 1914, and later joined the IRB. He was co-opted to the Military Council only weeks before the Rising. He was Commandant of the Second Battalion of Volunteers in Jacob's during Easter week and was executed on 3 May 1916.

Seán MacDiarmada: Born in January 1883 in Kiltyclogher, Leitrim, he moved to Belfast in 1905 and worked on the trams. A member of the Gaelic League, he was very active in the Dungannon Clubs with Bulmer Hobson and Denis McCullough and was sworn into the IRB. As the Dungannon Clubs formed into Sinn Féin, he became an organiser for the party. He later transferred to Dublin, where he developed a close friendship with **Thomas Clarke**. He travelled extensively as a national organiser for the IRB and ran the newspaper *Irish Freedom* in 1910. MacDiarmada was afflicted with polio in 1911, but by 1912 he went to the US as an IRB delegate at the Clan na Gael convention. He was appointed as a member of the

Provisional Committee of the Irish Volunteers from 1913 and was Secretary of the Supreme Council of the IRB. He was stationed in the GPO during the Rising. He was executed on 12 May 1916.

Joseph Plunkett: Born in Dublin on 21 November 1887, the son of a papal count, Plunkett was educated in Dublin and Stonyhurst College, England. He was the co-founder of the Irish Theatre and co-editor of *The Irish Review* with **Thomas MacDonagh**. In 1911 and 1912, Plunkett travelled around the Mediterranean and spent time in Algiers for his ailing health. He joined the Irish Volunteers in 1913 and was sworn into the IRB in 1914. He travelled to Germany to meet **Roger Casement** in 1915 and also went to New York to brief John Devoy, head of Clan na Gael, on the plans for a Rising. Plunkett was appointed Director of Military Operations, with overall responsibility for military strategy. He suffered from ill-health and had an operation for TB only weeks before the Rising. He fought in the GPO, where Michael Collins was his aide-de-camp. Joseph Plunkett was a member of the Military Council of the IRB and the Provisional Government. He married Grace Gifford in Kilmainham Gaol just hours before his execution on 4 May 1916.

Éamonn Ceannt: Born Edward Kent in Ballymoe, Co. Galway, on 21 September 1881. His father brought the family to Dublin when he retired from the RIC in 1892. There, Ceannt became an accomplished uilleann piper and co-founded Cumann na bPíobairí (The Pipers' Club). He began using the Irish version of his name when he joined the Gaelic League. He worked in Dublin Corporation as a clerk. In 1907 he joined the Dublin branch of Sinn Féin. He played the pipes for Pope Pius X during a visit to Rome in September 1908. In

1911 he was on a committee (to protest the proposed visit of George V) that included **Patrick Pearse**, **Seán MacDiarmada** and **Thomas MacDonagh.** Ceannt was an original founder of the Irish Volunteers and was involved in the Howth gunrunning operation of 1914. He was sworn into the IRB by MacDiarmada and later became a member of the Military Council. He commanded the Fourth Battalion in the South Dublin Union during the Rising. He was executed on 8 May 1916.

Roger Casement: Born in Sandycove, Dublin, on 1 September 1864. His father, an army officer, died when Roger was a baby, and his mother died when he was nine. He was raised by his uncle in Antrim. At the age of twenty, he joined a ships company to Africa and travelled widely. From 1884 to 1891 and 1898 to 1903 he lived in the Congo, where he was made British Consul in 1901. As British Consul in the Congo Free State, he investigated and reported on the horrific regime that forced native workers into slavery on the rubber plantations; he later did similar work in South America. He was awarded a knighthood in 1911, left the British consular service in 1913, and was an original founder of the Irish Volunteers. Casement went to America and from there to Germany, ostensibly to raise an Irish Brigade from Irish POWs. He organised the arms for the *Aud* and came to Kerry on board *U-19* in the days before the Rising, where he was arrested. In London, he was tried on charges of high treason under a statute that was 565 years old. On 3 August 1916, he was hanged in Pentonville Prison. His body was returned to Ireland in 1965 and buried in Glasnevin Cemetery.

John MacBride: Born in Westport, Mayo, on 7 May 1868. MacBride attempted to become a medical doctor but gave up his studies and came to Dublin to work in a chemist's. He joined the IRB and was involved in the early days of the GAA. Through the Celtic Literary Society, he became friends with Arthur Griffith. He went to America on behalf of the IRB in 1895, and the following year went to South Africa to work in the goldmines. He fought alongside the Irish Transvaal Brigade against the British in the Second Boer War. The Boer government gave him the rank of Major; the Irish Brigade became commonly known as MacBride's Brigade. **James Connolly**, Arthur Griffith and Maud Gonne were active in campaigning against the Boer War. MacBride's marriage to Gonne in 1903 ended in divorce in 1906. He was not a member of the Irish Volunteers, but during the Rising he was second to **Thomas MacDonagh** in Jacob's Biscuit Factory. He was executed on 5 May 1916.

Thomas Kent: Born on 29 August 1865 in Kilbarry House, Coole, Castlelyons, County Cork, and raised in nearby Bawnard House. His family had a long tradition of fighting against the injustices suffered by small farmers, particularly during the Land War. When Kent was nineteen, he emigrated to Boston, where he worked for a Catholic publisher. He returned

home after his brothers were imprisoned for boycotting a local farmer. He was also arrested and spent two months in prison for agitation. Later Kent joined the Gaelic League and, along with his brothers, the Irish Volunteers in 1914. He rose to the rank of Commandant of the Galtee Battalion. After the Rising, the RIC tried to arrest the Kent brothers in their home in Cork, and a Head Constable, William Rowe, was killed. On 4 May, William and Thomas Kent were court-martialed. William was acquitted, but Thomas was executed in Cork Detention Barracks on 9 May 1916.

Michael Mallin: Born in Dublin on 1 December 1874, his youth was spent in the British Army as a drummer boy. He was stationed in India and was promoted to the rank of non-commissioned officer. After over thirteen years in the service, he returned to Dublin. He became a silk weaver and got involved in organised labour. He was elected Secretary to the Silk Weavers' Union. During the Lockout, Mallin became involved with **James Connolly** and the Irish Citizen Army and eventually became the Chief of Staff. He reorganised the ICA and turned it into a highly efficient force. He commanded the Stephen's Green area with Countess Markievicz as his second. Mallin left a wife, Agnes, and four children behind when he was executed on 8 May 1916. Four months after his death, his wife gave birth to their fifth child.

Michael O'Hanrahan: Born in New Ross, Wexford, on 16 January 1877. When he was a child, the family moved to Carlow, where he received his education in the CBS. He had hoped to join the civil service but would not take the oath. O'Hanrahan was heavily involved in the promotion of the Irish language and founded the first Carlow branch of the Gaelic League. He was a founding member of the Carlow Workman's Club in 1899. He wrote two novels, *A Swordsman of the Brigade* and *When the Norman Came*. He joined Sinn Féin in Dublin and was active with the party for a few years, sitting on its National Council. He joined the Irish Volunteers from their inception and rose to the rank of Quartermaster. During the Rising, he was second in command to **Thomas MacDonagh** at Jacob's Biscuit Factory until Major **John MacBride** took over this position. O'Hanrahan was executed on 4 May 1916.

William Pearse: Born on 15 November 1881, the younger brother of **Patrick Pearse.** After receiving his early education in Westland Row CBS, he decided to pursue an artistic career and studied at the Metropolitan School of Art, Dublin, and also in Paris and London. Willie was every bit as passionate a revolutionary, teacher and language enthusiast as Patrick. He taught at St. Enda's school on a full-time basis from 1913 onwards. When his brother became Director of Organisation in the Volunteers, Willie Pearse and **Thomas MacDonagh** were left in effective charge of the school. Willie was a Captain in the Volunteers during the Rising and acted as Patrick's personal attaché. His guilty plea – which is often perceived as a desire to have the same fate as his brother – was accepted, and he was executed in Kilmainham Gaol on 4 May 1916.

Con Colbert: Born Cornelius Colbert in Monalena, Castlemahon, Newcastlewest, West Limerick, on 19 October 1888, Colbert was raised in Athea in the same county. His family moved to Dublin when he was fifteen. He went to CBS North Richmond Street and later worked as a junior baker. He was a fluent Irish speaker and was passionate about Irish history.

He was present on 16 August 1909 when Na Fianna Éireann were founded at 34 Lower Camden Street. Colbert was Centre of an IRB circle composed of Fianna boys. He was elected to the Executive of the Irish Volunteers and became Captain of F Company, Fourth Battalion. **Patrick Pearse** called him 'the gallant Captain Colbert' and asked him to drill the St. Enda's boys. A dedicated Pioneer, Colbert was known not to drink or smoke and even gave up dancing during Lent. He first commanded Watkins' Brewery, then moved to Jameson's Distillery on Marrowbone Lane. He assumed command of the whole garrison upon their surrender on Sunday, 30 April 1916. He was executed on 8 May 1916.

Seán Heuston: Born John Joseph Heuston in Dublin on 21 February 1891. Like **Con Colbert**, Heuston was educated in CBS North Richmond Street. In 1908 he secured a job with the GSW Railway as a clerk. He worked at the Limerick Goods Depot until 1913, when he was transferred to Kingsbridge, now named in his honour as Heuston Station. During his six years in Limerick, he organised the Fianna, gave history lectures and ran courses in small-arms training, signalling and the Irish language. He was the main source of income for his family in Dublin, as his father was estranged and living in London. D Company of the First Battalion of the Volunteers under Heuston commandeered the Mendicity Institution on the orders of **James Connolly**. Only twenty-five years of age, Heuston was executed in Kilmainham Gaol on 8 May 1916.

Edward Daly: Born in Limerick on 25 February 1891, 'Ned' was the only boy amongst nine sisters. He was educated by the Christian Brothers, who considered him 'not by any means a brilliant pupil'. His

father Edward, who died before he was born, had taken part in the Rising of 1867. His uncle John Daly was imprisoned with **Tom Clarke**, whom Ned's sister Kathleen would later marry. In 1912 Daly moved to Dublin and worked for May Roberts, a chemist wholesalers on Westmoreland Street. He was one of the first to join the Volunteers and helped to organise for the O'Donovan Rossa funeral in 1915. In the weeks leading up to the Rising, at **Seán MacDiarmada**'s request, he worked full-time for the Volunteers. Daly was Commander of the First Battalion, who were based around the Four Courts area of Dublin during the Rising. He was executed on 4 May 1916. At twenty-five years of age, four days younger than **Seán Heuston**, he was the youngest of all sixteen men executed.

TRAIN STATIONS NAMED AFTER EXECUTED LEADERS

On 10 April 1966 fifteen train stations in Ireland were officially dedicated to the sixteen men executed for their roles in the Easter Rising. (The Pearse brothers shared one station.)

Tralee, Kerry (1859). Tralee Casement Station/Stáisiún Mac Easmainn. Roger Casement.

Kingsbridge Station, Dublin (1846). Dublin Heuston/Baile Átha Cliath Stáisiún Heuston. Seán Heuston.[1]

Drogheda, Louth (1853). Drogheda MacBride/Droichead Átha Mac Giolla Bhríde. John MacBride.

Dublin Station (1844), Amiens Street Station (1854), Dublin. Dublin Connolly/Baile Átha Cliath Stáisiún Uí Chonghaile. James Connolly.

Westland Row Station (1834), Dublin. Dublin Pearse/Baile Átha Cliath Staisiún Na bPiarsach. Patrick and Willie Pearse and the Pearse family.

Wexford Station (1874). Wexford O'Hanrahan/Loch Garman Ó hAnnrachain. Michael O'Hanrahan.

Glanmire Road Station (1893), Cork. Cork Kent/Stáisiún Kent. Thomas Kent.

Galway Station (1851). Galway Ceannt/Stáisiún Cheannt. Éamonn Ceannt.

Limerick Station (1858). Limerick Colbert/Stáisiún Colbaird. Con Colbert.

Sligo Station (1862). Sligo MacDiarmada/Stáisiún Sheáin Mhic Dhiarmada. Seán MacDiarmada.

Waterford Station (1864). Waterford Plunkett Station/Phort Láirge Stáisiún Phluincéid. Joseph Plunkett.

Dundalk Junction (1849), Louth. Dundalk Clarke Station/Stáisiún Dún Dealgan Ui Cleirigh. Thomas Clarke.

Kilkenny Station (1848). Kilkenny MacDonagh/Stáisiún Mhic Donncha. Thomas MacDonagh.

Bray Station (1854), Wicklow. Bray Daly/Bré Uí Dhálaigh. Edward Daly.

Kingstown Harbour Station (1837), Kingstown (1861), Dún Laoghaire (1922), Dublin. Dún Laoghaire Mallin/Stáisiún Dhún Laoghaire í Mhealláin. Michael Mallin.

.

Section Seven:
Women and the
Easter Rising

A significant number of women were involved in the Rising. It is worth noting that Lieutenant Constance Markievicz was second-in-command in St. Stephen's Green, and that it was Dr. Kathleen Lynn who surrendered on behalf of the City Hall garrison after Seán Connolly and Seán O'Reilly were killed in action. One notable aspect of the Proclamation was that it was addressed to 'Irishmen and Irishwomen' as equals.

There follows a list of women who had some role in the Rising all over Ireland. There are 276 names here. Where possible, the list includes the areas where they were active; the organisations they were with; whether they were arrested; if they were included in the 1936 Roll of Honour; and whether they were awarded a 1916 medal. 216 women were awarded medals for their roles in the Rising. As with the men, many women did not apply for a pension or a medal. On the other hand, a small number of women were arrested who were not involved in the Rising, per se – they are also included in this list.[1]

Adrien, Mary: GPO. Cumann na mBan. Carried dispatches to Ashbourne. 1936 Roll of Honour. Medal recipient, see Section 14, p188.
Allen, Eilis: Brought message to Coalisland from Dublin with five others (mostly Belfast women) to inform Belfast contingent that the Rising would go ahead on Easter Monday.
Barrett, Annie (later Allum): Agricultural Station at Athenry, Co. Galway.

Cumann na mBan. Medal recipient, see Section 14, p188.

Brady, Bridget (later Murphy): City Hall. ICA. Arrested but released on 8 May 1916. Medal recipient, see Section 14, p212.

Breen, Elizabeth 'Bella' (later Pender): Athenaeum, Enniscorthy and Ferns, Co. Wexford. Cumann na mBan. Medal recipient, see Section 14, p219.

Brennan, Una: Athenaeum, Enniscorthy. Cumann na mBan. Medal recipient, see Section 14, p189.

Broderick, Dolly (later Fleming): Athenry and Moyode, Co. Galway. Cumann na mBan. Medal recipient, see Section 14, p199.

Brooks, Christina (later Stafford): GPO. Cumann na mBan. 1936 Roll of Honour. Brother was Christopher Brady. Medal recipient, see Section 14, p189.

Brown, Kate: Arrested but released on 8 May 1916.

Brown, Martha: Arrested but released on 8 May 1916.

Burke, Lillie (later McGinty): GPO. Cumann na mBan. 1936 Roll of Honour. Medal recipient, see Section 14, p210.

Bushell, Ellen: Watkins' Brewery. Involved with the first Fianna Committee. Usher in Abbey Theatre. Medal recipient, see Section 14, p190.

Byrne, Catherine (later Rooney): GPO. Cumann na mBan. 1936 Roll of Honour. Medal recipient, see Section 14, p221.

Byrne, Eileen: Arrested but released on 8 May 1916.

Byrne, Katie: Arrested but released on 8 May 1916. 1936 Roll of Honour.

Byrne, Lillie Elizabeth: Four Courts and GPO. Cumann na mBan. Medal recipient, see Section 14, p190.

Byrne, Margaret (later Copeland): Four Courts. Cumann na mBan. 1936 Roll of Honour.

Byrne, Margaret (later Crean): Louth/Meath. Cumann na mBan. 1936 Roll of Honour.

Byrne, Mary: Four Courts. Cumann na mBan. Arrested but released on 8 May 1916. 1936 Roll of Honour. Medal recipient, see Section 14, p190.

Byrne, May (later Doyle): Marrowbone Lane. Cumann na mBan. 1936 Roll of Honour. Medal recipient, see Section 14, p196.

Byrne, Stasia (later Toomey): GPO. Cumann na mBan. 1936 Roll of Honour. Medal recipient, see Section 14, p191 (Kimmage).

Byrne, Stasia: Athenaeum, Enniscorthy. Cumann na mBan. Medal recipient, see Section 14, p191 (Harold's Cross).

Byrne, Winifred (later Somerville): Marrowbone Lane. Cumann na mBan.

Medal recipient, see Section 14, p222.

Caffrey-Keeley, Christina: St. Stephen's Green. ICA. 1936 Roll of Honour. Medal recipient, see Section 14, p191.

Cardiff, Annie (later Heneghan): Ferns and Athenaeum, Enniscorthy. Cumann na mBan. Medal recipient, see Section 14, p202.

Carney, Winifred (later MacBride): GPO. Cumann na mBan Captain. Came from Belfast, the first woman to charge the GPO in 1916. Secretary and aide to James Connolly. Jailed in Mountjoy and Aylesbury, released 24 December 1916. 1936 Roll of Honour. Medal recipient, see Section 14, p191.

Carron, Maíre 'May': Four Courts. Cumann na mBan. Arrested but released on 8 May 1916. 1936 Roll of Honour. Medal recipient, see Section 14, p191.

Cavanagh-McDowell, Maeve: GPO. ICA. 1936 Roll of Honour. Medal recipient, see Section 14, p209.

Clarke, Kathleen: Sister of Ned Daly and wife of Tom Clarke, signatory of the Proclamation. Kathleen was not 'out' in the Rising but was a member of the Executive of the Ard Craobh of Cumann na mBan and always maintained she was made 'official confidante' on the Supreme Council of the IRB before the Rising. Medal recipient, see Section 14, p192.

Cleary, Mary Josephine (later O'Beirne/Byrne): Athenry, Moyode and Limepark, Co. Galway. Cumann na mBan. Medal recipient, see Section 14, p214.

Cloonan (later Fahy), Margaret: Oranmore and Agricultural Station, Athenry, Co. Galway. Cumann na mBan. Medal recipient, see Section 14, p198.

Colley, Gertrude (later Murphy): GPO. Cumann na mBan. 1936 Roll of Honour. Medal recipient, see Section 14, p212.

Conlon (Ní Conallain), Peig: Four Courts. Cumann na mBan. 1936 Roll of Honour. Medal recipient, see Section 14, p193.

Connolly, Bridget: GPO. Cumann na mBan. Stationed in Hibernian Bank for a period during Easter Week. 1936 Roll of Honour. Medal recipient, see Section 14, p193.

Connolly, Ina (later Heron): Brought message to Coalisland from Dublin with five others (mostly Belfast women) to inform Belfast contingent that the Rising would go ahead on Easter Monday. Cumann na mBan. James Connolly's daughter. Medal recipient, see Section 14, p193.

Connolly, Kathleen (later Barrett): City Hall. ICA Section Commander. Her brother Seán was killed in action in City Hall. Arrested but released on 8 May 1916. 1936 Roll of Honour. Medal recipient, see Section 14, p188.

Connolly, Nora (later O'Brien): Brought message to Coalisland from Dublin with five others (mostly Belfast women) to inform Belfast contingent that the Rising would go ahead on Easter Monday. Cumann na mBan. James Connolly's daughter. Medal recipient, see Section 14, p193.

Connor, Mary Kate: The Square, Athenry, Co. Galway. Cumann na mBan. Medal recipient, see Section 14, p193.

Conroy, Cecilia (later O'Neill): Jacob's. Hibernian Rifles/Clan na Gael Girl Scouts. 1936 Roll of Honour. Medal recipient, see Section 14, p217.

Conroy, Eileen: St. Stephen's Green. ICA. 1936 Roll of Honour.

Cooney-O'Brien, Annie: Marrowbone Lane. Cumann na mBan. 1936 Roll of Honour. Medal recipient, see Section 14, p215.

Cooney, Eileen (later Harbourne): Marrowbone Lane. Cumann na mBan. Arrested but released on 8 May 1916. 1936 Roll of Honour. Medal recipient, see Section 14, p201.

Cooney, Lily (Elizabeth, later Curran): Marrowbone Lane. Cumann na mBan. Arrested but released on 8 May 1916. 1936 Roll of Honour. Medal recipient, see Section 14, p193.

Corr, Elizabeth: Brought message to Coalisland from Dublin with five others (mostly Belfast women) to inform Belfast contingent that the Rising would go ahead on Easter Monday. Belfast Cumann na mBan. Medal recipient, see Section 14, p194.

Corr, Nell: From Belfast. Brought message to Coalisland from Dublin with five others (mostly Belfast women) to inform Belfast contingent that the Rising would go ahead on Easter Monday.

Cosgrave, Marcella: Marrowbone Lane. Cumann na mBan. Arrested but released on 8 May 1916. Medal recipient, see Section 14, p194.

Cregan, Maureen (later Ryan): Carried dispatches for Seán MacDiarmada to Tralee to Austin Stack. Cumann na mBan. Medal recipient, see Section 14, p221.

Crosby, Gretta: Athenaeum, Enniscorthy. Cumann na mBan. Medal recipient, see Section 14, p194.

Cullen, Elizabeth (later O'Brien): Athenaeum, Enniscorthy, Wexford. Cumann na mBan. Medal recipient, see Section 14, p215.

Cullen, Mary (later Breen): Athenaeum, Enniscorthy. Cumann na mBan. Medal recipient, see Section 14, p189.

Cummins, Delia (later McNamara): Clarinbridge, Oranmore, Agricultural Station at Athenry and Moyode, Co. Galway. Cumann na mBan. Medal recipient, see Section 14, p210.

Daly, Josephine (later Pollard): Jacob's. Cumann na mBan. 1936 Roll of Honour.

Daly, Katie (later Beatty): Four Courts. Cumann na mBan. Medal recipient, see Section 14, p188.

Daly, Laura (later O'Sullivan): GPO. Cumann na mBan, Limerick. 1936 Roll of Honour. Medal recipient, see Section 14, p195.

Daly, Nora (later Dore): GPO. Cumann na mBan, Limerick. 1936 Roll of Honour. Medal recipient, see Section 14, p196.

Davis, Bridget (later O'Duffy): City Hall. ICA. Arrested but released on 8 May 1916. Medal recipient, see Section 14, p216.

de Burca, Aoife (Burke, Eva): GPO. Cumann na mBan. 1936 Roll of Honour. Medal recipient, see Section 14, p195.

de Paor, Nancy (Wyse-Power): On Easter Monday she carried a dispatch from Patrick Pearse to Co. Carlow and on Tuesday, delivered dispatches to Kilkenny before returning to the GPO. Cumann na mBan. Medal recipient, see Section 14, p195.

Deegan, Maire: Jacob's. Cumann na mBan. 1936 Roll of Honour.

Devereux, Mary 'Mollie' (later Allen): St. Stephen's Green. ICA. 1936 Roll of Honour. Medal recipient, see Section 14, p188.

Devlin, Ann Anastasia: Mount Street area, Four Courts, St. Stephen's Green. Cumann na mBan. Courier, medical supplies and food supplies. Medal recipient, see Section 14, p195.

Dibiney, Annie (later Howley): Oranmore, Agricultural Station at Athenry and Moyode, Co. Galway. Cumann na mBan. Medal recipient, see Section 14, p202.

Dixon, Grace: Medal recipient, see Section 14, p195.

Dooley, Ellen: Moyode, Co. Galway. Cumann na mBan. Medal recipient, see Section 14, p196.

Doran, Margaret: Athenaeum, Enniscorthy. Cumann na mBan. Medal recipient, see Section 14, p196.

Downie, Margaret 'Peggy' (later Viant): GPO. Jervis Street and Jacob's. Liverpool Cumann na mBan. Medal recipient, see Section 14, p224.

Doyle, Brigid (later Moore): Athenaeum, Enniscorthy and Ferns, Co. Wexford. Cumann na mBan. Medal recipient, see Section 14, p211.

Doyle, Brigid (later Noctor): Athenaeum, Enniscorthy. Cumann na mBan.

Medal recipient, see Section 14, p214.

Doyle, Christine (Ní Dubhghaill, 'Maire'): St. Stephen's Green. Cumann na mBan. 1936 Roll of Honour. Medal recipient, see Section 14, p196.

Doyle, Mary Ellen: Enniscorthy District. Cumann na mBan. Medal recipient, see Section 14, p196.

Doyle, Mary Kate: Enniscorthy District. Cumann na mBan. Medal recipient, see Section 14, p196.

Elliot, Eilis (later Ní Bhríain): Four Courts. Cumann na mBan. 1936 Roll of Honour.

Elliot, Emily (later Ledwith): Four Courts. Cumann na mBan. 1936 Roll of Honour. Medal recipient, see Section 14, p206.

English, Maire: GPO. Cumann na mBan. 1936 Roll of Honour. Medal recipient, see Section 14, p198.

Ennis, Ellen 'Nellie' (later Costigan): Four Courts. Cumann na mBan. Arrested but released on 8 May 1916. 1936 Roll of Honour. Medal recipient, see Section 14, p194.

Fagan, Margaret (later MacSherry): GPO. Cumann na mBan. 1936 Roll of Honour. Medal recipient, see Section 14, p208.

Fahy, Anna: Four Courts. Cumann na mBan. Also sent to Athenry by Éamonn Ceannt with a message for Laurence Lardner but had to give it to Eamonn Corbett. 1936 Roll of Honour. Medal recipient, see Section 14, p198.

Fahy, Katie (later Nelly): Moyode Castle and Ballyglass, Co. Galway. Cumann na mBan. Medal recipient, see Section 14, p214.

Fee, Brigid (Ua Faoithe): GPO. Cumann na mBan. 1936 Roll of Honour. Medal recipient, see Section 14, p198.

ffrench-Mullen, Madeleine: St. Stephen's Green. ICA. Released from Mountjoy on 4 June 1916. 1936 Roll of Honour.[2]

Fleming, Kathleen: Arrested but released by 8 May 1916.

Fleming, Margaret (later Leonard): Sent from Dublin to Athlone, Westmeath, with dispatch on Easter Monday. Liverpool Cumann na mBan. Medal recipient, see Section 14, p207.

Fleming, Monica (later Lawless): Ashbourne. Cumann na mBan. 1936 Roll of Honour. Medal recipient, see Section 14, p206.

Foley, Bridget (Ní Foghludha, later Breeid Martin): Travelled to Birmingham to assist in the escape to Ireland of Liam Mellows, who had been deported. Travelled to Cork with dispatches from Seán MacDiarmada and Éamonn

Ceannt for Terence MacSwiney and Tomás Mac Curtain. Went there again on Sunday, 23 April, before returning to Dublin on Monday, 24 April, and taking part in the Rising. Cumann na mBan. Arrested on Tuesday, 2 May 1916, she was sent to Mountjoy and then to Aylesbury in England; released in August of that year. Medal recipient, see Section 14, p208.

Foley, Cait (later Murphy): On 23 April 1916, she travelled to Cork with her sister Bridget Foley (Martin) with a dispatch from Seán MacDiarmada for Tomás Mac Curtain. Was also in Hibernian Bank on O'Connell Street. Cumann na mBan. Medal recipient, see Section 14, p212.

Forrestal, Ita (later Larkin): Athenaeum, Enniscorthy, Co. Wexford. Cumann na mBan. Medal recipient, see Section 14, p206.

French, Alicia (later Shortall): Athenaeum, Enniscorthy, Co. Wexford. Cumann na mBan. Medal recipient, see Section 14, p222.

Gahan, Mary 'May' (later O'Carroll): St. Stephen's Green. Cumann na mBan. Arrested but released on 8 May 1916. 1936 Roll of Honour. Medal recipient, see Section 14, p215.

Gavan Duffy, Louise: GPO. Cumann na mBan. 1936 Roll of Honour.

Gethings, Lucie: GPO. Cumann na mBan. 1936 Roll of Honour.

Gibney, Maura 'May' (later O'Neill): GPO. Cumann na mBan. 1936 Roll of Honour. Medal recipient, see Section 14, p218.

Gifford, Helen 'Nellie' (later Donnelly): St. Stephen's Green. ICA. Jailed in Mountjoy, released on 4 June 1916. 1936 Roll of Honour. Medal recipient, see Section 14, p200.

Glynn, Kate (later Armstrong): Killeeneen, Co. Galway. Cumann na mBan. Medal recipient, see Section 14, p188.

Gough (Goff), Bridget: St. Stephen's Green. ICA. Arrested but released on 8 May 1916. 1936 Roll of Honour. Medal recipient, see Section 14, p200.

Gray, Mary: Volunteer HQ (known as 'Antwerp'), Mary Street and Athenaeum, Enniscorthy. Cumann na mBan. Medal recipient, see Section 14, p200.

Grealy, Margaret Rose: Active around Galway, medical, cooking also carried dispatches for Liam Mellows. Cumann na mBan. Medal recipient, see Section 14, p201.

Grennan, Julia: GPO. One of the last three women in the GPO. Arrested but released on 8 May 1916.

Hackett, Rosie: ICA. St. Stephen's Green. Arrested but released on 8 May 1916. A bridge over the River Liffey was dedicated to her on 20 May 2014. 1936

Roll of Honour. Medal recipient, see Section 14, p201.

Hayes, Mary Christina (later O'Gorman): Four Courts. Cumann na mBan. 1936 Roll of Honour. Medal recipient, see Section 14, p216.

Healy, Cathleen: Four Courts. Hibernian Rifles. 1936 Roll of Honour. Medal recipient, see Section 14, p201.

Healy, Teresa (later Byrne): Four Courts. Cumann na mBan. 1936 Roll of Honour. Medal recipient, see Section 14, p191.

Hearne, Mary Ellen 'May': Athenaeum, Enniscorthy, Co. Wexford. Cumann na mBan. Medal recipient, see Section 14, p202.

Hegarty, Bridget (later Harmon): Marrowbone Lane. Cumann na mBan. Arrested but released on 8 May 1916. 1936 Roll of Honour. Medal recipient, see Section 14, p201.

Hegarty, Eileen (later Twomey): Keegan's of Irish Street and the Athenaeum, Enniscorthy. Cumann na mBan. Medal recipient, see Section 14, p224.

Heron, Aine: Four Courts. Cumann na mBan. 1936 Roll of Honour. Medal recipient, see Section 14, p202.

Higgins, May: Moyode, Agricultural Station at Athenry, and Limepark, Co. Galway. Cumann na mBan. Medal recipient, see Section 14, p202.

Hoey, Patricia: GPO. Attached to Irish Volunteers. 1936 Roll of Honour.

Howlin, Margaret (later Tobin): Athenaeum, Enniscorthy, Wexford. Cumann na mBan. Medal recipient, see Section 14, p223.

Humphreys, Ellen: Arrested but released on 8 May 1916.

Hyland, Mary (later Kelly): St. Stephen's Green. ICA. 1936 Roll of Honour. Medal recipient, see Section 14, p204.

Joyce, Maggie: St. Stephen's Green. ICA. Arrested but released on 8 May 1916. 1936 Roll of Honour. Medal recipient, see Section 14, p203.

Kavanagh, Mary: St. Stephen's Green. Cumann na mBan. Medal recipient, see Section 14, p203.

Kavanagh, May (later Duggan): Four Courts. Cumann na mBan. 1936 Roll of Honour. Medal recipient, see Section 14, p197.

Kealy, Sarah: Jacob's. Cumann na mBan. 1936 Roll of Honour. Medal recipient, see Section 14, p204.

Kearns, Linda (later MacWhinney): Set up a Red Cross position on North Great George's Street, where she treated the wounded. Later became a Senator. Medal recipient, see Section 14, p208.

Keegan, Ellen: Keegan's of Irish Street, Enniscorthy, where she was involved in munitions. Treasurer, Enniscorthy Cumann na mBan. Medal recipient, see Section 14, p204.

Keegan, Teresa: Keegan's of Irish Street, Enniscorthy, where she was involved in munitions. Captain, Enniscorthy Cumann na mBan. Medal recipient, see Section 14, p204.

Kehoe, Josephine: Athenaeum, Enniscorthy. Cumann na mBan. Medal recipient, see Section 14, p204.

Kelly, Annie: St. Stephen's Green. ICA. 1936 Roll of Honour. Medal recipient, see Section 14, p204.

Kelly, Josephine (later Greene): Marrowbone Lane. Cumann na mBan. Arrested but released on 8 May 1916. 1936 Roll of Honour. Medal recipient, see Section 14, p201.

Kelly, Katie 'Kitty' (later O'Regan): St. Stephen's Green. Cumann na mBan. Arrested but released on 8 May 1916. 1936 Roll of Honour. Medal recipient, see Section 14, p204.

Kelly, Martha: Arrested but released on 8 May 1916.

Kelly, May (later Chadwick): GPO. Officer Commanding, Clan/Hibernians. 1936 Roll of Honour. Medal recipient, see Section 14, p192.

Kelly, Winifred (later Murphy): Athenaeum, Enniscorthy, Wexford. Cumann na mBan. Medal recipient, see Section 14, p213.

Kempson, Lily (later McAlerney): St. Stephen's Green. ICA. Medal recipient, see Section 14, p208.

Kennedy, Margaret: Marrowbone Lane. Cumann na mBan. Arrested but released on 8 May 1916. 1936 Roll of Honour.

Kenny, Bridy: Arrested but released on 8 May 1916.

Kenny, Kathleen (later Blackburn): Four Courts. Cumann na mBan. 1936 Roll of Honour. Medal recipient, see Section 14, p188.

Kilmartin, Mary (later Stephenson): Four Courts. Cumann na mBan. 1936 Roll of Honour.

King, Elizabeth (later MacCarthy): St. Stephen's Green and GPO. Medal recipient, see Section 14, p207.

King, Margaret: Athenaeum, Enniscorthy and Ferns, Co. Wexford. Cumann na mBan. Medal recipient, see Section 14, p205.

Lambert, Bridget (later Doran): GPO. ICA. 1936 Roll of Honour. Medal recipient, see Section 14, p196.

Lambert, Ellen (later Stynes): GPO. ICA. 1936 Roll of Honour. Medal recipient, see Section 14, p223.

Lane, Bridie: Clarinbridge, Oranmore, Athenry and Castlegar, Co. Galway. Cumann na mBan. Medal recipient, see Section 14, p206.

Lardner, Brigid: Town Hall, Athenry and Moyode, Co. Galway. Cumann na mBan. Medal recipient, see Section 14, p206.

Lawless, Eveleen: Saucerstown House, Swords, Dublin. Finglas, Swords and Ashbourne. Cumann na mBan. Medal recipient, see Section 14, p206.

Lawless, Kathleen (later McAllister): Swords, Ashbourne. Cumann na mBan. Medal recipient, see Section 14, p208.

Lawless, Mary: GPO. 1936 Roll of Honour.

Liston, Catherine: Arrested but released on 8 May 1916.

Liston, Mary: Arrested but released on 8 May 1916.

Lucas, Philomena 'Phyllis' (later Morkan): Four Courts. Cumann na mBan. 1936 Roll of Honour. Medal recipient, see Section 14, p212.

Lynch, Elizabeth 'Bessie' (later Kelly): City Hall. ICA. Arrested but released on 8 May 1916. 1936 Roll of Honour. Medal recipient, see Section 14, p204.

Lynn, Dr. Kathleen: City Hall. Chief Medical Officer, ICA. Surrendered the City Hall Garrison in 1916 as the commander. Jailed in Mountjoy and deported to Bath in England. Returned in August 1916. 1936 Roll of Honour.[3]

Lyons, Brigid (later Thornton): Four Courts. Cumann na mBan. Arrested but released on 10 May 1916. 1936 Roll of Honour. Medal recipient, see Section 14, p207.

Mackey, Maura: Medal recipient, see Section 14, p207.

Magee, Teresa: Jacob's. Cumann na mBan. 1936 Roll of Honour. Medal recipient, see Section 14, p208.

Maher, Kathleen: Arrested but released on 8 May 1916.

Malone, Aine (later Fitzgerald): St. Stephen's Green. Cumann na mBan. Wounded on Easter Monday on her way to Jacob's. Sister to Mick Malone. Medal recipient, see Section 14, p198.

Malone, Bridget: Moyode, Athenry and Craughwell, Co. Galway. Cumann na mBan. Medal recipient, see Section 14, p208.

Maloney, May (later McQuaile): Four Courts. Cumann na mBan. 1936 Roll of Honour.

Mapother, Maire: GPO. Cumann na mBan. 1936 Roll of Honour. Medal recipient, see Section 14, p208.

Markievicz, Countess Constance (Gore-Booth): St. Stephen's Green. Lieutenant, ICA, and Second in Command. Jailed in Mountjoy and then Aylesbury Prison in England. Released in June 1917. Included in 1936 Roll of Honour.[4]

Martin, Kathleen 'Kate': Four Courts. Cumann na mBan. Arrested but released on 8 May 1916. 1936 Roll of Honour. Medal recipient, see Section 14, p208.

Martin, Margaret (later Murnane): Four Courts. Cumann na mBan. 1936 Roll of Honour. Medal recipient, see Section 14, p212.

McCarthy, Kathleen (later Lane): Jacob's. Cumann na mBan. 1936 Roll of Honour. Medal recipient, see Section 14, p209.

McCauley, Julia: Arrested but released on 22 May 1916.

McDonald, Kathleen (later Pollard): Jacob's. Cumann na mBan. 1936 Roll of Honour.

McDonnell, Kathleen Keyes: With Irish Volunteers in Cork. Medal recipient, see Section 14, p209.

McElroy, Mairead: GPO. Cumann na mBan. 1936 Roll of Honour. Medal recipient, see Section 14, p209.

McGowan, Josephine 'Josie': Marrowbone Lane. Cumann na mBan. Arrested but released on 8 May 1916. 1936 Roll of Honour. Medal recipient, see Section 14, p210.

McGuinness, Catherine: Four Courts. Cumann na mBan. 1936 Roll of Honour.

McGuinness, Rose: Four Courts. Cumann na mBan. 1936 Roll of Honour.

McLaughlin, Maggie: Arrested but released on 8 May 1916.

McLoughlin, Caroline 'Carrie' (later Mitchell): GPO and Four Courts. Cumann na mBan. Arrested but released on 9 May 1916. Medal recipient, see Section 14, p210.

McLoughlin, Mary: GPO. Hibernian Rifles. 1936 Roll of Honour. Medal recipient, see Section 14, p210.

McNally, Margaret: Ashbourne. Cumann na mBan. 1936 Roll of Honour.

McNamara, Rose (later Murphy): Marrowbone Lane. Cumann na mBan. Arrested but released on 8 May 1916. 1936 Roll of Honour. Medal recipient, see Section 14, p210.

McNamara, Sarah: First-aid station in Michael Dwyer Club, Skippers Alley (off Merchants Quay), Dublin. Cumann na mBan. Medal recipient, see Section 14, p210.

McNamee, Agnes: Marrowbone Lane. Cumann na mBan. Arrested but released on 8 May 1916. 1936 Roll of Honour. Medal recipient, see Section 14, p210.

Meade, Florence 'Flossie' (later Griffin): Four Courts. Cumann na mBan. Arrested but released on 10 May, 1916. Medal recipient, see Section 14, p201.

Molony, Helena: ICA. City Hall. 1936 Roll of Honour. Jailed in Mountjoy and Aylesbury Prison and released on 24 December 1916. Medal recipient, see Section 14, p211.

Moore, May (later Wisely): St. Stephen's Green. Cumann na mBan. Arrested but released on 8 May 1916. 1936 Roll of Honour. Medal recipient, see Section 14, p225.

Moran, Brigid Christina: Athenaeum, Enniscorthy, Co. Wexford. Cumann na mBan. Medal recipient, see Section 14, p211.

Moran, Kathleen (later Whelan): Athenaeum, Enniscorthy, Co. Wexford. Cumann na mBan. Medal recipient, see Section 14, p225.

Moran, Maire (later Fitzpatrick): Athenaeum, Enniscorthy. Cumann na mBan. Medal recipient, see Section 14, p199.

Moran, Sheila (later Lynch, Sighle Bean Ui Loingsigh): Athenaeum, Enniscorthy. Cumann na mBan. Medal recipient, see Section 14, p207.

Morkan, Mary Pauline (later Keating): Four Courts. Cumann na mBan. Arrested but released on 9 May 1916. 1936 Roll of Honour. Medal recipient, see Section 14, p204.

Morrissey, Bridget (later Ruane): Rockfield, Agricultural Station at Athenry, Moyode and Limepark, Co. Galway. Cumann na mBan Captain. Medal recipient, see Section 14, p221.

Mulhall, Lizzie: Arrested but released on 8 May 1916.

Mullally, Rosanna 'Rose' (later Farrelly): Marrowbone Lane, Cumann na mBan. Arrested but released on 8 May 1916. 1936 Roll of Honour. Medal recipient, see Section 14, p198.

Mulligan, Margaret (later Derham): Four Courts. Cumann na mBan. Medal recipient, see Section 14, p212.

Murnane, Brigid (later McKeon): Four Courts. Cumann na mBan. 1936 Roll of Honour. Medal recipient, see Section 14, p210.

Murnane, Elizabeth 'Lily' (later Coleton): Four Courts. Cumann na mBan. 1936 Roll of Honour. Medal recipient, see Section 14, p192.

Murphy, Kate: Athenaeum, Enniscorthy. Cumann na mBan. Medal recipient, see Section 14, p213.

Murphy, Kathleen (later O'Kelly): Falls Road, Belfast. Brought message to Coalisland from Dublin with five others (mostly Belfast women) to inform Belfast contingent that the Rising would go ahead on Easter Monday.

Murphy, Kathleen (later Patton): GPO. Liverpool Cumann na mBan. 1936 Roll of Honour. Medal recipient, see Section 14, p219.

Murphy, Kathleen: Marrowbone Lane. Cumann na mBan. Arrested but released on 8 May 1916. 1936 Roll of Honour. Medal recipient, see Section 14, p213.

Murphy, Martha (Kelly): GPO. Cumann na mBan. 1936 Roll of Honour. Medal recipient, see Section 14, p213.

Murray, Eileen: GPO. Cumann na mBan. 1936 Roll of Honour. Medal recipient, see Section 14, p213.

Murray, Mary (later Allen): Four Courts. Cumann na mBan. 1936 Roll of Honour. Medal recipient, see Section 14, p213.

Murtagh, Bridget (later O'Daly): St. Stephen's Green. Cumann na mBan. Arrested but released on 8 May 1916. 1936 Roll of Honour.

Neary, Josephine (later Flood): O'Connell Street. Cumann na mBan. Medal recipient, see Section 14, p199.

Ní Áinle, Maire (Hanley): GPO. Cumann na mBan. 1936 Roll of Honour.

Ní Briain, Maire: Ashbourne. 1936 Roll of Honour.

Ní Ceallaigh, Mairead: Church Street. Cumann na mBan. Medal recipient, see Section 14, p214.

Ní Foghludha, Nóra (Foley, later O'Donoghue): GPO. 1936 Roll of Honour.

Ní Riain, Eilis (later O'Connell, Ní Conaill): Four Courts. Cumann na mBan. 1936 Roll of Honour. Medal recipient, see Section 14, p215.

Ní Rian, Áine (Ryan): GPO. Cumann na mBan. 1936 Roll of Honour. Medal recipient, see Section 14, p220.

Nic Alastair, Caitlin: Ashbourne, Cumann na mBan. 1936 Roll of Honour.

Noone, Ellen: GPO. Assisted Cumann na mBan. 1936 Roll of Honour. Medal recipient, see Section 14, p214.

Norgrove, Annie (later Grange): ICA. City Hall. Arrested but released on 8 May 1916. 1936 Roll of Honour. Medal recipient, see Section 14, p200.

Norgrove, Emily (later Hanratty): ICA. City Hall. Arrested but released on 8 May 1916. 1936 Roll of Honour. Medal recipient, see Section 14, p201.

O'Brennan, Lily: Cleaver Hall and Marrowbone Lane. Cumann na mBan. Arrested but released on 8 May 1916. Her sister Áine O'Brennan was married to Éamonn Ceannt. Medal recipient, see Section 14, p214.

O'Brien, Eilis 'Elizabeth': Four Courts. Carried messages for Captain Weafer in Reis & Co. on Sackville Street. Cumann na mBan. Medal recipient, see Section 14, p215.

O'Carroll, Mary (later Lawlor): Four Courts, Cumann na mBan. Medal recipient, see Section 14, p206.

O'Connell, Mary: GPO. 1936 Roll of Honour.

O'Daly, Nora: St. Stephen's Green. Cumann na mBan. Arrested but released on 8 May 1916. 1936 Roll of Honour. Medal recipient (medal on display in Kilmainham Gaol), see Section 14, p216.

O'Farrell, Elizabeth: GPO. Inghinidhe na hÉireann. Delivered dispatch to Galway about the Rising. One of three women in Moore Street on Friday night. On Saturday she delivered Pearse's letter of surrender to General Lowe.[5]

O'Flaherty, Margaret (later Timmons): Marrowbone Lane. Cumann na mBan. Arrested but released on 8 May 1916. 1936 Roll of Honour. Medal recipient, see Section 14, p223.

O'Flanagan, Ellen (later Parker): Four Courts. Cumann na mBan. 1936 Roll of Honour. Medal recipient, see Section 14, p219.

O'Hagan, Annie: Jacob's. Clan na Gael. 1936 Roll of Honour. Medal recipient, see Section 14, p216.

O'Hanlon, Mollie: Marrowbone Lane. Cumann na mBan. 1936 Roll of Honour. Medal recipient, see Section 14, p216.

O'Hanlon, Sheila (later Lynch): Marrowbone Lane. Cumann na mBan. Arrested but released on 8 May 1916. 1936 Roll of Honour. Medal recipient, see Section 14, p206.

O'Hanrahan, Eily (later O'Reilly): Delivered dispatch to Seamus Doyle in Enniscorthy. Jacob's. Cumann na mBan. 1936 Roll of Honour. Medal recipient, see Section 14, p218.

O'Hanrahan, Mary: GPO. Cumann na mBan. 1936 Roll of Honour. Medal recipient, see Section 14, p217.

O'Higgins (Higgins), Annie: GPO. Stationed in Hibernian Bank for a period in Easter Week. Arrested and jailed but released on 4 June 1916. 1936 Roll of Honour. Medal recipient, see Section 14, p202.

O'Keefe, Annie (later O'Carroll): Four Courts. Cumann na mBan. 1936 Roll of Honour. Medal recipient, see Section 14, p215.

O'Keeffe, Emily (later Hendley): Marrowbone Lane, Cumann na mBan. Arrested but released on 8 May 1916. 1936 Roll of Honour. Medal recipient, see Section 14, p202.

O'Keeffe, Josephine (later McNamara): Jameson's Distillery, Marrowbone Lane. Cumann na mBan. Arrested but released on 8 May 1916. Medal recipient, see Section 14, p210.

O'Kelly-Barber, Kathleen: GPO. 1936 Roll of Honour.

O'Neill, Annie: Athenaeum, Enniscorthy, Co. Wexford. Cumann na mBan. Medal recipient, see Section 14, p217.

O'Reilly, Aileen Mary (later O'Connor): GPO and North Co. Dublin. Cumann na mBan. Medal recipient, see Section 14, p216.

O'Reilly, Annie: Medal recipient, see Section 14, p218.

O'Reilly, Cathleen: GPO. 1936 Roll of Honour.

O'Reilly, Molly (later Corcoran): City Hall. ICA. Signed for GPO and City Hall for 1936 Roll of Honour. Medal recipient, see Section 14, p194.[6]

O'Reilly, Nora (later Sister Lourdes): GPO. Cumann na mBan. Medal recipient, see Section 14, p218.

O'Sullivan, Dorothy 'Dolly': Medal recipient, see Section 14, p219.

O'Sullivan, Grace: Teacher in London, smuggled a wireless to Dublin. Came over for Rising and smuggled arms and ammunition on the boat from Holyhead.

O'Sullivan, Louisa (later Pollard): Four Courts. Cumann na mBan. Arrested but released on 10 May 1916. 1936 Roll of Honour. Medal recipient, see Section 14, p219.

O'Sullivan, Mary (later O'Carroll): Four Courts. Cumann na mBan. 1936 Roll of Honour. Medal recipient, see Section 14, p215.

Partridge, Mary: Arrested at home but released on 8 May 1916. Wife of William Partridge.

Perolz, Marie (later Mary Flanagan): ICA. She brought a message to Cork to Tomás Mac Curtain (delivered to his wife) to warn the Rising was on, then went on to Tralee. Arrested later and sent to Mountjoy and later to Lewes Prison; released July 1916. Medal recipient, see Section 14, p199.

Price, Leslie (later de Barra/Barry): GPO. Cumann na mBan. Stationed in Hibernian Bank for a period during Easter Week. Married IRA leader Tom Barry. 1936 Roll of Honour. Medal recipient, see Section 14, p188.

Quigley, Maria (later Clince): Marrowbone Lane. Cumann na mBan. Arrested but released on 8 May 1916. 1936 Roll of Honour. Medal recipient, see Section 14, p192.

Quigley, Priscilla (later Kavanagh): Marrowbone Lane. Cumann na mBan. Arrested but released on 8 May 1916. 1936 Roll of Honour. Medal recipient, see Section 14, p203.

Quinn, Margaret: GPO. Cumann na mBan. 1936 Roll of Honour. Medal recipient, see Section 14, p220.

Rabbitt, Mary: Clarinbridge, Oranmore and Moyode, Co. Galway. Cumann na mBan. Medal recipient, see Section 14, p220.

Redmond, Annie: GPO. 1936 Roll of Honour. Medal recipient, see Section 14, p220.

Retz, Barbara: Arrested but released on 8 May 1916.

Reynolds, Mary 'Mollie' Catherine: GPO. Cumann na mBan. 1936 Roll of Honour. Medal recipient, see Section 14, p220.

Richards, Bridie: GPO. Cumann na mBan. 1936 Roll of Honour. Medal recipient, see Section 14, p220.

Roche, Elizabeth 'Lily' (later Ennis): RIC Barracks, Ferns, Co. Wexford. Cumann na mBan. Medal recipient, see Section 14, p198.

Roche, Julia: Clarinbridge and Moyode, Co. Galway. Cumann na mBan. Medal recipient, see Section 14, p221.

Rogers, Sarah (later Sorcha Bhean Mhic Ruáidhrí/MacMathghamhna): GPO. Cumann na mBan. 1936 Roll of Honour. Medal recipient, see Section 14, p221.

Rooney, Mary (later McNamara): Agricultural Station at Athenry and Moyode, Co. Galway. Cumann na mBan. Medal recipient, see Section 14, p210.

Ryan, Ellen 'Nell': Did not take part in Rising but was imprisoned in Lewes and Aylesbury. Released 17 October 1916.[7]

Ryan, Margaret (later Dunne): ICA, St. Stephen's Green. 1936 Roll of Honour. Medal recipient, see Section 14, p197.

Ryan, Mary Kate 'Kit': Did not take part in Rising but was imprisoned. Sister to Ellen, Min and Phyllis.

Ryan, Mary Josephine 'Min' (later Mulcahy): GPO. Cumann na mBan. 1936 Roll of Honour. Medal recipient, see Section 14, p212.

Ryan, Phillis (later O'Kelly): GPO. Cumann na mBan. 1936 Roll of Honour. Seán T O'Kelly's second wife. Medal recipient, see Section 14, p217.

Seery, Kathleen (later Redmond): St. Stephen's Green. ICA. Arrested but released on 9 May 1916. 1936 Roll of Honour. Medal recipient, see Section 14, p220.

Shanahan, Jane 'Jennie': City Hall. ICA. Arrested but released on 8 May 1916. 1936 Roll of Honour. Medal recipient, see Section 14, p222.

Simpson, Tilley (Matilda): GPO. Cumann na mBan. Stationed in Hibernian Bank for some period during Rising. 1936 Roll of Honour. Medal recipient, see Section 14, p222.

Skinnider, Margaret (Maighréad Proinnsias Ní Scineadóra): St. Stephen's Green. ICA Captain. Three gunshot wounds during Rising. 1936 Roll of Honour. Medal recipient, see Section 14, p222.

Smyth, Lucy Agnes (later Byrne): GPO. Cumann na mBan. Married 'Boer' Tom Byrne. 1936 Roll of Honour. Medal recipient, see Section 14, p190.

Spicer, Josephine: Marrowbone Lane. Cumann na mBan. Arrested but released on 8 May 1916. 1936 Roll of Honour.

Stapleton, MJ (later Slevin): GPO. Clan na Gael. 1936 Roll of Honour.

Thornton, Nora: On 23 April 1916, Nora Thornton carried dispatches from Dublin for delivery to officers of the Irish Volunteers in Co. Kerry. Cumann na mBan. Sister to Hugh and Frank Thornton. Medal recipient, see Section 14, p223.

Tierney, Sadie: Town Hall, Athenry and Moyode Castle, Co. Galway. Cumann na mBan. Medal recipient, see Section 14, p223.

Tobin, Annie (later Soalfield): GPO. Cumann na mBan. 1936 Roll of Honour.

Treston, Catherine 'Cathleen': GPO. Cumann na mBan. Arrested but released on 8 May 1916. 1936 Roll of Honour. Medal recipient, see Section 14, p223.

Uí Glasian, Veronica (later Ní Riain/Ryan): GPO. Cumann na mBan. 1936 Roll of Honour. Medal recipient, see Section 14, p220.

Walker (Nic Shiubhlaigh), Máire (later Price): Jacob's. Cumann na mBan. 1936 Roll of Honour. Also an actor in the Abbey Theatre. Medal recipient, see Section 14, p219.

Walsh, Bridie (later Slater): GPO. Cumann na mBan. 1936 Roll of Honour. Medal recipient, see Section 14, p222.

Walsh, Eileen (later Murphy): Four Courts. Cumann na mBan. 1936 Roll of Honour. Medal recipient, see Section 14, p212.

Walsh, Gretta (later Mullins): Clarinbridge, Oranmore, Agricultural Station, Athenry, Moyode, and Limepark, Co. Galway. Cumann na mBan. Medal recipient, see Section 14, p212.

Walsh, Helena: GPO. Cumann na mBan. Medal recipient, see Section 14, p224.

Walsh, Margaret (later Jenkinson): GPO. Cumann na mBan. 1936 Roll of Honour. Medal recipient, see Section 14, p203.

Walsh, Mary Josephine (later Rafferty): GPO. Cumann na mBan. 1936 Roll of Honour. Medal recipient, see Section 14, p220.

Walsh, Sara (later Jordan): Athenaeum, Enniscorthy, Co. Wexford. Cumann na mBan. Medal recipient, see Section 14, p203.

Ward, Christina: Athenaeum, Enniscorthy, Co. Wexford. Cumann na mBan. Medal recipient, see Section 14, p224.

Weston, Julia Mary: Ashbourne. Cumann na mBan. 1936 Roll of Honour. Medal recipient, see Section 14, p224.

Weston, Thomasina (later Lynders): Ashbourne. Cumann na mBan. 1936 Roll of Honour. Medal recipient, see Section 14, p207.

White, Mary: Athenaeum, Enniscorthy, Co. Wexford. Cumann na mBan. Medal recipient, see Section 14, p225.

Wisely, Esther (later O'Moore): GPO. Cumann na mBan. 1936 Roll of Honour. Medal recipient, see Section 14, p217.

Woods, Annie: Medal recipient, see Section 14, p225.

POLITICAL WOMEN NOT ACTIVE IN THE RISING

Hanna Sheehy-Skeffington (1877–1946): Johanna Mary Sheehy was born in Kanturk, Co. Cork. She gained a first-class honours MA in 1902 and married Francis Skeffington the following year. Her husband was a strong supporter of feminism, and they both took each other's surnames. Hanna, Francis and Margaret Cousins founded the Irish Women's Franchise League in 1908 to campaign for votes for women (eventually introduced to an extent in 1918).

Hanna was a close associate of James Connolly's and was active in Liberty Hall during the Lockout. She was imprisoned in 1913 for her direct action in support of votes for women. During the Rising her husband Francis was shot by firing squad on the orders of Captain J.C. Bowen-Colthurst. Hanna refused compensation and demanded an inquiry. Bowen-Colthurst was found guilty but insane; he spent a year in Broadmoor Asylum and the rest of his life in Canada. Hanna was a strong nationalist and was anti-Treaty during the Civil War and after.

Maud Gonne (1866–1953): Edith Maud Gonne was born in Surrey, England. As a young woman she campaigned for the release of Fenian prisoners, and in the late 1890s was a close associate of James Connolly's. While living in Paris, she ran a French newspaper with a pro-nationalist stance, *L'Irlande Libre*. She was a founding member of Inghinidhe na hÉireann in Dublin and also a renowned actress.

W.B. Yeats asked her to marry him at least four times, and he wrote the plays *The Countess Cathleen* and *Cathleen Ní Houlihan* for her. She had a son, Georges, and a daughter, Iseult, with her lover Lucien Millevoye; Georges died in infancy. Maud converted to Catholicism and married Major John MacBride not long after he returned from fighting the British in the Second Boer War. They had a son, Seán MacBride, but the marriage was a failure. Maud was in Paris during the Rising, but she returned to Dublin after MacBride was executed.

Margaret Keogh (1871–1916): Born in Carlow, Margaret worked in the South Dublin Union as a nurse.[8] She was killed by the British military during the Rising. For a long time Margaret Keogh was considered to have been a 'Red Cross nurse' who fought alongside the Volunteers in the SDU, but this is simply not true.

PHOTOGRAPH OF WOMEN FROM THE RISING

This photograph of sixty women who were involved in the Rising was taken sometime after August 1916, when Dr. Kathleen Lynn had her deportation order lifted and Bridget Foley had been released from Aylesbury. Bridget Murtagh is holding a copy of the *Irish War News*, which was distributed in the GPO during the Rising.[9]

Back Row, standing, L–R: May Kelly, Bridget Brady, Jane Shanahan, Kathleen Barrett, Rosie Hackett, Margaret Ryan, Bridget Davis, Chris Caffrey, Patricia Hoey.

Fifth Row, standing, L–R from girl scout: Annie Tobin, Aoife Taafe, Marcella Cosgrave, Kathleen Murphy, Lucy Agnes Smyth, Miss Foley, Nóra Ní Foghludha, Mary Pauline Morkan, Dorothy O'Sullivan, Emily Elliot, Mollie O'Sullivan, Tilley Simpson, Catherine Treston, Martha Kelly, Máire Walker, Lily O'Brennan, Elizabeth O'Farrell, Nora O'Daly (girl scout), Mary Murray.

Fourth Row, sitting, L–R: Nora Thornton, Rosanna Mullally, Sheila O'Hanlon, Maria Quigley, Margaret O'Flaherty, Josephine McGowan, Lily Cooney, Josephine O'Keeffe.

Third Row, sitting, L–R: May Moore, Kathleen McCarthy, Sarah Kealy, Gertrude Colley, Mary O'Hanrahan, Esther Wisely, Bridget Murtagh, Priscilla Quigley, Julia Grennan, Stasia Byrne (Twomey), Bridie Walsh.

Second Row, sitting, L–R: Rose McNamara, Kathleen Kenny, Mary Josephine Walsh, Unidentified, Monica Fleming, Jenny Milner, Eileen Walsh, Margaret Kennedy, May Byrne, Annie Cooney-O'Brien.

Front Row, sitting, L–R: Madeline ffrench-Mullen, Bridget Foley, Dr. Kathleen Lynn.

Section Eight: Positions Occupied & Garrison Strengths

HEADQUARTERS

The General Post Office, Sackville Street. The GPO was occupied in 1916 as the HQ for the Army of the Irish Republic. As communication was integral to the administration of Ireland and the British Empire, it made perfect sense to occupy the centre of communication in Dublin city. The GPO is still used as a post office. Five of the seven members of the Provisional Government were here during the Rising: Patrick Pearse, James Connolly, Tom Clarke, Seán MacDiarmada and Joseph Plunkett.

Muster Point: Liberty Hall

Number in the GPO at any stage during the Rising: 617 [1]

FIRST BATTALION

HQ: Initially the North Brunswick Street area, then Father Mathew Hall on Church Street. Edward Daly decided the Four Courts would be more suitable as a HQ towards the end of the Rising on Friday. The four courts that give the building its name were Exchequer, Chancery, King's Bench and Common Pleas.

Muster Point: Blackhall Place

Commandant: Edward Daly

Vice-Commandant: Piaras Béaslaí

Number with the First Battalion: 451

The North Dublin Union at the top of Church Street was also occupied by the Volunteers of the First Battalion, who set fire to the Linen Hall Army Pay Corps Barracks. Reilly's Pub at the corner of North King Street and Church Street was also occupied by the First. It was called Reilly's Fort for many years after, and is now The Tap pub.

The **Mendicity Institution** was commanded by Captain Seán Heuston of D Company, First Battalion, Irish Volunteers. The purpose of this position was to provide cover for their main troops across the Liffey. Their position could also command the Quays, especially on the southside, and they could harass British troops from the Royal Barracks.

Muster Point: Liberty Hall (they were under the direct command of James Connolly)[2]

Commandant: Captain Seán Heuston

SECOND BATTALION

HQ: W&R Jacob's Biscuit Factory, situated between Bishop Street and Peter Street. The factory had a good command over the Aungier Street area and hindered British movements from Portobello Barracks into the city.

Muster Point: St. Stephen's Green

Commandant: Thomas MacDonagh, Commander Dublin Brigade, Irish Volunteers

Vice-Commandant: Michael O'Hanrahan, replaced by John MacBride

Number with the Second Battalion: 247

THIRD BATTALION

HQ: Boland's Mills, Grand Canal Street

Muster Point: St. Andrew's Catholic Club (Company HQ), 144 Great Brunswick Street (now Pearse Street)

Commandant: Éamon de Valera, Adjutant, Dublin Brigade, Irish Volunteers

Vice-Commandant: Joseph O'Connor.[3] The VC of the Third Battalion was Seán Fitzgibbon, but he was not a member of the IRB and was sent to Limerick some time before the Rising. He was replaced by P. Begley for the Rising, but Begley was reported missing on Thursday and was replaced by O'Connor.

Number with the Third Battalion: 222

Clanwilliam House and 25 Northumberland Road were also occupied and saw some of the fiercest fighting in what became known as the Battle of Mount Street Bridge.

Muster Point: Earlsfort Terrace

Irish Volunteers parading before the Rising.

FOURTH BATTALION

HQ: The South Dublin Union, now St. James's Hospital

Muster Point: Emerald Square

Commandant: Éamonn Ceannt

Vice-Commandant: Cathal Brugha

Number with the Fourth Battalion: 280

Roe's Distillery at Mount Brown was occupied by Captain Thomas McCarthy but abandoned. Watkins' Brewery on Ardee Street was occupied by Captain Con Colbert, who then joined with the larger forces at Jameson's.[4] Jameson's Distillery on Marrowbone Lane was occupied by Captain Seamus Murphy.[5]

FIFTH BATTALION

HQ: Ashbourne in Co. Meath, where the Fifth engaged the RIC Barracks
Muster point: Knocksedan, near Swords, North County Dublin
Commandant: Thomas Ashe
Number with the Fifth Battalion: 94

IRISH CITIZEN ARMY

HQ: St. Stephen's Green and on Tuesday of Easter week, the College of Surgeons
Muster Point: Liberty Hall
Commandant: Michael Mallin, Chief of Staff of the ICA
Vice-Commandant: Lieutenant Constance Markievicz of the ICA
Number in Stephen's Green and College of Surgeons: 169

A detachment of the Irish Citizen Army, led by Seán Connolly, occupied City Hall beside Dublin Castle.
Muster Point: Liberty Hall
Commandant: Seán Connolly, ICA (killed in action)
Vice-Commandant: Seán O'Reilly, ICA (killed in action)
After Connolly and O'Reilly were killed, command was assumed by Dr. Kathleen Lynn, ICA.
Number in City Hall: 59

Total number with the Dublin Brigade: 2,139

Three British soldiers at a barricade on Holles Street during Easter week.

BRITISH ARMY IN DUBLIN, 1916

INITIALLY:

6th Reserve Cavalry Regiment: 35 officers, 851 other ranks.

3rd Royal Irish Regiment: 18 officers, 385 other ranks.

10th Royal Dublin Fusiliers: 37 officers, 430 other ranks.

3rd Royal Irish Rifles: 21 officers, 650 other ranks.

At 12:30pm on Easter Monday, the General Officer Commanding, William Lowe, was asked to mobilise troops in the Curragh; they arrived by train at 4.45pm. They were the 3rd Reserve Cavalry Brigade and consisted of 1,600 officers and men.

THE FOLLOWING WERE THEN ORDERED TO DUBLIN:

(a) A battery of four 18-pounders from the Reserve Artillery Brigade at Athlone.

(b) The 4th Dublin Fusiliers from Templemore.

(c) A composite battalion from Belfast.

(d) An additional 1,000 men from the Curragh.

The defence of the docks at North Wall was undertaken by Major HF

Somerville with a detachment from the School of Musketry, Dolly-mount, reinforced by 330 officers and men of the 9th Reserve Cavalry Regiment. Two Infantry brigades of the 59th Division were dispatched from England.

TUESDAY, 25 APRIL 1916

Brigadier-General William Lowe, commanding the Reserve Cavalry Brigade at the Curragh, arrived at Kingsbridge (now Heuston) Station at 3.45am with troops from the 25th (Irish) Reserve Infantry Brigade and assumed command of the forces in the Dublin area. These encompassed roughly 2,300 men of the Dublin garrison, the Curragh Mobile Column of 1,500 dismounted cavalrymen, and 840 men of the 25th Irish Reserve Infantry Brigade.

During the day the 4th Dublin Fusiliers from Templemore, the composite battalion from Belfast, and the battery of four 18-pounders arrived.

Towards evening the 178th Infantry Brigade began to arrive at Kingstown (Dun Laoghaire). The left column, consisting of the 5th and 6th Battalions Sherwood Foresters, came to Dublin via the Stillorgan-Donnybrook Road, then onto the South Circular Road to the Royal Hospital in Kilmainham, without opposition.

The right column, consisting of the 7th and 8th Battalions Sherwood Foresters, came via the Ballsbridge route.

Four officers were killed, 14 wounded, and of other ranks 216 were killed and wounded at the Battle of Mount Street Bridge.

WEDNESDAY, 26 APRIL 1916

Throughout the day further troops of the 176th Brigade arrived in the Dublin area.

THURSDAY, 27 APRIL 1916

By nightfall the 177th Infantry Brigade arrived in Kingstown, where it remained for the night.

A detachment was sent by sea from Kingstown to Arklow to reinforce the garrison at Kynoch's Explosive Works.

FRIDAY, 28 APRIL 1916

A battalion of the Sherwood Foresters was dispatched by rail to Athlone to protect the military store and command the River Shannon.

SATURDAY, 30 APRIL 1916

Brigadier-General Stafford, the Garrison Commander at Queenstown (Cobh, Co. Cork), was directed to use his discretion in the employment of troops under his command. On 30 April he was reinforced from England by one battalion of the 179th Brigade, 60th Division; a battalion of the Royal Marines; and later by the remainder of the 179th Brigade.

POSITIONS HELD BY THE SEVEN SIGNATORIES
OF THE PROCLAMATION

Patrick Pearse: Commandant-General and Commander-in-Chief of the Army of the Irish Republic. President of the Provisional Government of the Irish Republic. Member of the Military Council and also the Supreme Council of the Irish Republican Brotherhood (IRB).

James Connolly: Commandant-General of the Dublin Division of the Army of the Irish Republic. Member of the Military Council of the IRB.

Thomas Clarke: Treasurer of the Supreme Council and member of the Military Council of the IRB. Member of the Provisional Government, but Clarke held no military rank as such.

Joseph Plunkett: Commandant-General. Member of the Provisional Government and member of the Military Council of the IRB.

Seán MacDiarmada: Secretary of the Supreme Council of the IRB, member of the Military Council and member of the Provisional Government.

Éamonn Ceannt: Member of the Military Council of the IRB. Member of the Provisional Government of the Irish Republic and Commandant of the Fourth Battalion of the Irish Volunteers.

Thomas MacDonagh: Commander, Dublin Brigade, Irish Volunteers. Member of the Military Council of the IRB and member of the Provisional Government.

THE MILITARY COMMITTEE OR COUNCIL?

Patrick Pearse, Joseph Plunkett and Éamonn Ceannt made up the Military Committee of the IRB, appointed in May 1915. With the addition of Thomas Clarke and Seán MacDiarmada (not long after his release from prison) in October 1915, it became known as the Military Council. James Connolly was added to the Council in January 1916.[6] The seventh member, Thomas MacDonagh, was co-opted in the first week of April 1916.[7]

NOTABLE FACTS

The Steps of the GPO: It is often said that Patrick Pearse read the Proclamation from the steps of the GPO. There were no steps into the GPO, but many historians repeat it. Diarmuid Lynch has pointed out that there 'was but one low step'. This 'one step' was obviously the doorstep, which is now most definitely gone.

Reader of the Proclamation: Patrick Pearse read the Proclamation, in the company of James Connolly, at 12.45pm on 24 April 1916 outside the GPO.

O'Rahilly's Car: The O'Rahilly did not drive his own car around Ireland with MacNeill's instructions to cancel the Rising. Rather, he hired a taxi to drive to Limerick with the countermanding order. He also went to his native Kerry (he was from Ballylongford), West Cork and Tipperary. The taxi ride cost over £20, which Nancy O'Rahilly paid after the Rising to the A & B Taxi Co. in Portobello.[8]

He did drive from his home in Herbert Park to Liberty Hall on Easter Monday morning in his own car, a De Dion-Bouton, the burnt-out shell of which was found after the Rising on Prince's Street.

Shells from the 18-Pounders: The British did not have incendiary shells in the 18-pounders. The only rounds available in Dublin were fixed-shrapnel 'anti-personnel shells' that were made up of balls of lead-antimony. (See Section Three, Weapons.)

The Germans Arrived Too Early: The Germans expected to land the weapons from the *Aud* between Thursday, 20 April, and Saturday, 23 April 1916; the IRB Military Council expected the weapons to arrive on Sunday, 24 April, just as the Rising broke out. As far as the Germans were aware, they had landed right on time. It was a communication breakdown rather than a mistake. (See Section Four, Subsection II.)

Route Taken by the GPO Garrison: The last group to leave Liberty Hall on Easter Monday was the GPO Garrison. They marched up Lower Abbey Street, turned right onto Sackville Street and halted outside the GPO. Connolly shouted either 'Left Wheel. Charge!'[9] or 'Left turn, the GPO – Charge!'[10]

The 'Attempt' to Blow up Nelson's Pillar: Diarmuid Lynch wrote in 1957, 'Tuesday 25 April, 7.30am: Commandant Connolly ordered barbed wire erected across O'Connell Street from each end of the

GPO to keep curious or interested citizens from venturing too near this increasingly dangerous zone. Sufficient wire not being available for an effective barrier it was decided to secure the overhead tram wires by blowing down the iron standards. The wires came down; the poles withstood the explosions.'

In the 1950s, the fractured bases were 'reminders of the myth which arose from this incident, viz. that the insurgents attempted to blow down the Nelson Pillar. Though the IRA would indeed have wished to see this memento of England's naval victories removed from Ireland's capital, our meagre military stores were meant and required for a more immediate purpose.' [11]

The *Helga* and the GPO: The HMS *Helga* did not fire at the GPO in 1916. She fired at Liberty Hall, Boland's Mills, and the Malting Tower near the Mills.

Sackville Street or O'Connell Street: Drogheda Street was renamed Sackville Street in the late 1700s, after Lionel Cranfield Sackville, 1st Duke of Dorset and Lord Lieutenant of Ireland from 1731–1737 and 1751–1755. In 1884, Dublin Corporation attempted to rename it O'Connell Street; the residents of the street took legal action and were successful in blocking the change, but the name was popularised. It was officially renamed O'Connell Street in 1924. [12]

Section Nine:
Casualties & Destruction

Over 500 people were killed and 2,600 wounded during and after the 1916 Rising. The financial cost was reckoned to be over £2.5 million, with over 200 buildings in Dublin destroyed.

There were 63 insurgents killed in action. A further 16 were executed, and three men drowned in Ballykissane. Fourteen men died from their wounds or ill-treatment in prison. This gives a total of 96 insurgents who died, including four children.

Most of those who died were civilians: a total of 276. This includes 35 civilian children.

Eighteen policemen were killed and 126 British soldiers, including five members of the Georgius Rex Brigade and one Canadian, Neville Fryday, who was 16 years of age.

THREE MEN DROWNED IN BALLYKISSANE

Before any shots were fired during the Rising, Con Keating, Daniel Sheehan and Charlie Monaghan drowned in the River Laune at Ballykissane. These three Volunteers were on a mission with two others, Colm O'Lochlainn and Denis Daly. All five travelled by train from Dublin to Kerry, where they were picked up by two cars and driven towards Cahirciveen. Their job was to dismantle a wireless transmitter, reassemble it in Tralee, and broadcast to the *Aud*. As it transpired, the *Aud* did not have a radio on board.

It was getting dark when the two cars were separated on the road.

The second car stopped for directions, which were misinterpreted and resulted in Tom McInerney driving off Ballykissane Pier into the River Laune where it meets the sea on 21 April 1916. Of the four men in the car, only the driver, McInerney, survived the crash.

Keating, Cornelius 'Con'. From Caherciveen, Kerry. Drowned, Ballykissane 21 April 1916. Buried Killovanogue, Caherciveen.
Sheehan, Daniel (Donal). From Ballintubrid, Newcastle West, Limerick. Drowned, Ballykissane, 21 April. Buried Dromavalla, Killorglin, Kerry.
Monaghan, Charles. From Belfast, drowned, Ballykissane, 21 April. Buried Dromavalla, Killorglin, Kerry.

63 ARMY OF THE IRISH REPUBLIC KILLED IN ACTION

Adams, John F. ICA, killed St. Stephen's Green, 25 April. Glasnevin Cemetery.[1]
Allen, Thomas. Irish Volunteers, killed Four Courts, 29 April. Reinterred Co. Meath.
Burke, William Francis. Irish Volunteers, shot by sniper, South Dublin Union, 25 April. Golden Bridge Cemetery.
Byrne, Andrew Joseph. Irish Volunteers, killed Boland's Mills, 27 April. 1916 Plot, Deansgrange.
Byrne, Louis. ICA, killed City Hall, 24 April. 1916 Plot, St. Paul's.
Byrne, Séamus. Irish Volunteers, killed Jacob's area, 27 April. St. Paul's.
Carrigan, Charles. From Glasgow, Kimmage Garrison. Irish Volunteers, fought in GPO, killed in Moore Street charge. St. Paul's.
Cavanagh, Ernest. Killed on steps of Liberty Hall. Cartoonist for *The Irish Worker*. St. Paul's. Technically a non-combatant but may have wanted to find the ICA and join the Rising.
Clarke, Philip. From Slane, Co. Meath. ICA, killed St. Stephen's Green, 25 April. Glasnevin.
Connolly, Seán. ICA Captain, killed by sniper, City Hall, 24 April. Glasnevin.
Corcoran, James. From Cranford, Gorey, Co. Wexford. ICA, killed St. Stephen's Green, 25 April. Family plot, Glasnevin.
Costello, Edward Joseph. Irish Volunteer, wounded Church Street, died Jervis Street Hospital, 25 April. 1916 Plot, Glasnevin.
Costello, Seán. From Athlone. Irish Volunteer, wounded Grand Canal

Street, died 26 April, Sir Patrick Dun's Hospital. 1916 Plot, Deansgrange Cemetery.

Coyle, Harry. Irish Volunteer, GPO. Killed Henry Place, 28 April. Glasnevin.

Crenigan, John. From Roganstown, Swords. Irish Volunteer, killed Ashbourne, 28 April. Killossory, Kilsallaghan, Dublin.

Cromien, John. Irish Volunteer, killed Prussia Street, 24 April. Glasnevin.

Cunningham, Andrew. Irish Volunteer, shot Ringsend Road, died 1 May. Deansgrange.

Darcy, Charlie. Aged 15. ICA, killed by sniper, 24 April. 1916 Plot, St. Paul's.

Derrick, Patrick. Irish Volunteer, shot in his home on 28 April by the British. Glasnevin.

Donelan, Brendan. From Loughrea, Galway. Na Fianna. Killed South Dublin Union. Glasnevin.

Doyle, Patrick. Irish Volunteer, killed Clanwilliam House, Mount Street Bridge, 27 April. Remains never found.

Dwan, John. Irish Volunteer, killed Church Street area, 24 April. Glasnevin.

Ennis, Edward. Irish Volunteer, killed Boland's area, 27 April. 1916 Plot, St. Paul's.

Farrell, Patrick. Irish Volunteer, killed Church Street, 28 April. 1916 Plot, St. Paul's.

Fox, James. Aged 16. Born in Meath. Fianna, fought with ICA, killed St. Stephen's Green, 25 April. Knockmark Cemetery, Co. Meath.

Geoghan, George. From Kildare. ICA, killed City Hall, 26 April. 1916 Plot, St. Paul's.

Healy, Seán. Aged 14. Fianna, shot Phibsboro, died 27 April. Glasnevin.

Howard, Seán Bernard. Na Fianna, wounded Church Street, died 29 April, Richmond Hospital. Family plot, Glasnevin.

Hurley, Seán. Irish Volunteer, killed Church Street, 28 April. 1916 Plot, St. Paul's.

Keely, John. Irish Volunteer, killed entering the GPO, 25 April. Deansgrange.

Kelly, James J. Aged 15. Na Fianna, died of wounds, 25 April. Glasnevin.

Kent, Richard. Irish Volunteer, brother of Thomas Kent (executed), wounded at home, Bawnard House, died Fermoy Hospital, 4 May. Buried Castlelyons, Cork.

Keogh, Gerald. Fianna, shot dead passing Trinity College, 27 April. 1916 Plot, St. Paul's.

Macken, Francis. Irish Volunteer, GPO, killed in Moore Street charge. St.

Paul's, Glasnevin.

Macken, Peadar. Irish Volunteer, Alderman and Labour activist. Shot by one of his comrades at Boland's Bakery, 27 April. Glasnevin.

Malone, Michael. Irish Volunteer, killed 25 Northumberland Road, 26 April. Glasnevin.

Manning, Peter Paul. Irish Volunteer, killed North Brunswick Street, 28 April. Glasnevin.

McCormack, James. From Julianstown, Meath. ICA, killed near Liberty Hall, 28 April. 1916 Plot, St. Paul's.

McDowell, William. Irish Volunteer, killed South Dublin Union. Reinterred Glasnevin.

Mulvihill, Michael. From Ardoughter, Ballyduff, Kerry. Irish Volunteer, killed Moore Lane after evacuation of the GPO, 28 April. St. Paul's.

Murphy, Richard. Irish Volunteer, killed Clanwilliam House, Mount Street Bridge, 27 April. Remains never found.

Murray, Daniel Joseph. Irish Volunteer, wounded 25 April, College of Surgeons, died St Vincent's Hospital, 13 May. Glasnevin.

O'Carroll, Richard. Irish Volunteer, shot by Captain Bowen-Colthurst, 26 April, Camden Street, died Portobello Hospital, 5 May. St. Paul's.

O'Connor, Patrick. From Rathmore, Kerry. Irish Volunteer joined in with GPO Garrison, killed in action 28 April. St. Paul's.

O'Flanagan, Patrick Joseph. Irish Volunteer, killed Reilly's Fort, North King Street, 29 April. 1916 Plot, St. Paul's.

O'Grady, John James. Irish Volunteer, shot York Street whilst on a mission from Jacob's, 29 April. St. James's Churchyard.

O'Rahilly, Michael Joseph (The). From Ballylongford, Kerry. Director of Arms for Irish Volunteers. Shot leading charge on Moore Street, 28 April. Glasnevin.

O'Reilly, John (Seán). ICA, second in command, City Hall, killed 24 April. Glasnevin.

O'Reilly, Richard. Irish Volunteer, killed South Dublin Union, 24 April. Glasnevin.

O'Reilly, Thomas. ICA, killed in action, 27 April, GPO. Glasnevin.

Owens, John. Irish Volunteer, killed South Dublin Union, 24 April. Buried Dr. Steevens' Hospital Grounds.

Quinn, James. Irish Volunteer, killed South Dublin Union, 24 April. St. Paul's.

Rafferty, Thomas. From Lusk. Irish Volunteer, killed Ashbourne, 28 April. Lusk Churchyard.

Reynolds, George. Irish Volunteer, killed Clanwilliam House, Mount Street Bridge, 27 April. Remains never found.

Ryan, Fred. Age 17. ICA, St. Stephen's Green, killed Harcourt Street, 27 April. 1916 Plot, St. Paul's.

Shortis, Patrick. Born Ballybunion, Kerry. Irish Volunteer, killed Moore Street charge, 28 April. St. Paul's.

Traynor, John Joseph. Irish Volunteer, killed South Dublin Union, 24 April. Glasnevin.

Walsh, Edward. Hibernian Rifles, killed Parliament Street, 24 April. 1916 Plot, St. Paul's.

Walsh, Philip. Irish Volunteer, killed Church Street, 29 April. Glasnevin.

Weafer, Thomas Joseph. From Enniscorthy. Irish Volunteer, killed corner of Abbey Street and O'Connell Street, 27 April. Remains never found.

Weekes, Arthur. From Norwich, possibly Jewish. ICA, killed Moore Lane, 28 April.

Whelan, Patrick. Irish Volunteer, killed Boland's area, 27 April. Glasnevin.

Wilson, Peter. From Swords, Dublin. Irish Volunteer, killed Mendicity Institution, 26 April. Buried Dr. Steevens' Hospital Grounds.

14 DIED AS A RESULT OF IMPRISONMENT OR WOUNDS AFTER THE RISING:

Brady, Christopher. Imprisoned Frongoch POW Camp, Wales. Died from pneumonia, 28 January 1917.[2]

Byrne, Joseph. Irish Volunteer, Jacob's. Jailed in Frongoch, released July 1916. Died 17 March 1917.[3]

Courtney, Bernard. Died as a result of imprisonment in Frongoch, 20 March 1917. Glasnevin.

Cullen, John. Irish Volunteer Lieutenant, fought in Mendicity Institution, sentenced to death but imprisoned in Portland and Lewes, where his health suffered. Died 29 May 1918, aged 21.[4]

Halpin, John. Irish Volunteer, jailed in Frongoch. Suffered from depression, died in Grangegorman Asylum in 1917.[5]

MacCormack, Bernard. Irish Volunteer, wounded near GPO, continued fighting in St. Stephen's Green. Commenced hunger strike in Frongoch, released

Christmas 1916. Died 2 April 1918, aged 26.

MacMackin, Bernard. Irish Volunteers. Imprisoned in Richmond, Stafford and Wandsworth. Died 29 May 1917, age 21.[6]

O'Doherty, Michael. ICA, shot multiple times, College of Surgeons. Died 22 December 1919. [7]

O'Brien, William P. Died Sir Patrick Dun's Hospital, 28 November 1916. Buried Galbally, Limerick.

Sheridan, Frank. Irish Volunteer. Died from ill-treatment in prison, 20 November 1916. Glasnevin.

Staines, Liam. Irish Volunteer, Mendicity Institution, seriously wounded by grenade. Imprisoned in Frongoch, released under amnesty. Died 2 November 1918.[8]

Stokes, Thomas. Imprisoned in Frongoch, released at Christmas. Died 29 September 1917, aged 24.

Wallace, John W. Died in Frongoch, 14 March 1917.

Ward, Bernard MacCartan. Died Wandsworth Prison, London, 8 May 1917. Latlurcan Cemetery, Monaghan.

CONFIDENTIAL DOCUMENT ON THE EXECUTIONS

CONFIDENTIAL.

In the event of any of the Sinn Fein prisoners being condemned to death today, they will be segregated (as far as circumstances permit) and asked whether they want to see relatives or friends or chaplains; and these persons will be sent for as required by the prisoners.

A number of motor cars will be stationed at Richmond Barracks for this purpose, and more may be asked for from H.Q., Irish Command, as necessary.

The whole of the visitors and friends are to be taken back to their homes before 3:30 a.m. the next day, at which time the first firing party will parade.

The first man to be shot will be brought out at 3:45 a.m. facing the firing party of one officer, and 12 men at 10 paces distant.

The rifles of the firing party will be loaded by other men behind their backs, 1 rifle with a blank cartridge, and eleven with ball, and the Firing Party will be told that this is the arrangement, and no man is to know which rifle is loaded with blank. There will be 4 Firing Parties, who will fire in turn.

After each prisoner has been shot, a Medical Officer will certify that he is dead, and his body will be immediately removed to an ambulance, with a label pinned on his breast giving his name.

When the ambulance is full, it will be sent to Arbour Hill Detention Barracks, entering by the gate at the Garrison Chapel.

A party there will put the bodies close along side one another in the grave (now being dug), cover them thickly with quicklime (ordered) and commence filling in the grave. One of the officers with this party is to keep a note of the position of each body in the grave taking the name from the label. A Priest will attend for the funeral Service.

16 MEN EXECUTED [9]

Clarke, Thomas J. Executed Kilmainham, 3 May.

Pearse, Patrick H. Executed Kilmainham, 3 May.

MacDonagh, Thomas. Executed Kilmainham, 3 May.

Plunkett, Joseph. Executed Kilmainham, 4 May.

Pearse, Willie. Executed Kilmainham, 4 May.

O'Hanrahan, Michael. Executed Kilmainham, 4 May.

Daly, Edward. Executed Kilmainham, 5 May.

MacBride, John. Executed Kilmainham, 5 May.

Ceannt, Éamonn. Executed Kilmainham, 8 May.

Heuston, Seán. Executed Kilmainham, 8 May.

Colbert, Con. Executed Kilmainham, 8 May.

Mallin, Michael. Executed Kilmainham, 8 May.

Kent, Thomas. Executed Cork Detention Barracks, 9 May. [10]

MacDiarmada, Seán. Executed Kilmainham 12 May.

Connolly, James. Executed Kilmainham, 12 May.

Casement, Roger. Hanged, Pentonville Prison London, 3 August. [11]

35 CIVILIAN CHILDREN KILLED [12]

Allen, Bridget (16), 27 April

Andrews, Christopher (14), 26 April

Brunswick, Mary Anne (15), 28 April

Caffrey, Christina (2), 25 April

Cathcart, Christopher (10), 24 April

Doyle, Moses (9), 24 April

Fetherstone, Patrick (12), 24 April

Foster, John Francis (2), 24 April

Fox, William (13), 25 April

Gibney, James (5), 2 May

Hickey, Christopher (16), 29 April

Ivers, Patrick (14), 27 April

Kavanagh, Charles (15), 28 April

Kelly, Mary (12), 30 April

Kelly, Patrick (12), 28 April

Kirwan, John (15), 24 April

Lynch, Eugene (8), 28 April

McKane, Bridget (15), 28 April

McNamara, John (12), 28 April

Mullen, William (9), 28 April

Murray, Joseph (14), 28 April

O'Neill, William (16), 29 April

O'Toole, Unidentified (14), 24
    April

Redmond, Mary (16), 27 April

Ryan, Patrick (13), 26 April

Sainsbury, George Percy (9), 27 April

Scott, Walter Eric (8), 5 July

Stewart, Bridget (11), 28 April

Sweny, William Lionel, 26 April

Unidentified Boy

Unidentified Infant [13]

Veale, Margaret Mary (13), 30 April

Walsh, Philip (11)

Warbrook, Eleanor (15), 24 April

Whelan, Christopher (15), 28 April

240 ADULT CIVILIANS KILLED

Armstrong, John Herbert, 24 April

Ballantyne, John, 1 May

Bambrick, Alice, 25 April

Barry, Bridget, 29 April

Barter, William, 26 April

Bealin, Patrick, 29 April

Beirnes, John, 29 April

Blayney, James, 26 April

Bond, Henry, 25 April

Brady, James, 29 April

Brennan, John, 28 April

Brennan, Malachy, 28 April

Brown, George, 27 April

Brunell, Julia, 2 May

Buckley, Lucy, 1 May

Butler, Richard, 25 April

Byrne, Edward, 26 April

Byrne, John, 25 April

Byrne, Patrick, 26 April

Cahill, George William

Caldwell, Anne Jane, 28 April

Carrick, William

Carroll, James Joseph, 28 April

Casey, Joseph, 25 April

Casey, Thomas

Cashman, James, 28 April

Clarke, Joseph, 26 April

Clarke, Richard, 29 April

Coade, James, 25 April

Coghlan, Thomas

Cole, Mary Ann, 29 April

Condron, Julia, 28 April

Connolly, Mary, 14 May

Connolly, Peter, 29 April

Connolly, William, 26 April

Connor, Christopher, 1 May

Cooke, John, 30 April

Corbin, Unidentified

Corrigan, Mary Anne, 29 April

Cosgrave, Edward, 25 April

Costello, Jane, 27 April

Costello, John, 26 April

Coughlan, Thomas, 28 April

Courtney, Clement, 26 April

Cowley, Thomas, 28 April

Coy, Unidentified

Crawford, Julia, 28 April

Creevan, John

Cunningham, James, 26 April

Cunningham, Mary, 1 May

Curley, Francis, 29 April

Daly, Margaret, 28 April

Davis, Catherine, 2 May

Dawson, John, 28 April

Dickson, Thomas, 26 April

Dignam, Patrick, 29 April

Dillon, Robert, 29 April

Dockeray, Cecil Eustace, 29 April

Donnelly, John, 25 April

Donnelly, Thomas, 28 April

Donohoe, Dominick Thomas, 27 April

Donohoe, Joseph, 27 April

Dorgan, Denis, 27 April

Doyle, Daniel, 2 June

Doyle, John, 28 April

Doyle, John, 26 April

Doyle, John, 1 May

Doyle, Stephen Patrick, 29 April

Doyle, Thomas, 30 April

Dunlea, Richard, 28 April

Dunne, Edward, 29 April

Dunne, Moses, 25 April

Dunphy, J, 28 May

Dwyer, Mary, 25 April

Ennis, George, 29 April

Fahey, Peter, 25 April

Farrell, Jeremiah, 27 April

Farrelly, John, 30 May

Feeney, Paul, 28 April

Fennell, John Joseph, 28 April

Fennell, Patrick, 30 April

Ferris, Arthur, 28 April

Finlay, Francis, 9 May

Finnegan, James, 29 April

Finnegan, William, 1 May

Flynn, John

Flynn, Michael

Foran, Thomas, 30 April

Frazer, James, 26 April

Friel, Patrick, 28 May

Geraghty, Joseph, 28 April

Geraghty, Patrick Joseph, 27 April

Glennon, Daniel, 29 April

Glynn, Michael, 27 April

Goulding, Andrew, 19 May

Green, Patrick, 27 April

Gregg, William, 29 April

Hall, Robert Cantebury, 27 April

Halliday, William James, 27 April

Hanratty, Elizabeth, 28 April

Harris, Abraham, 24 April

Harris, Patrick, 25 April

Hayes, Morgan, 28 April

Hayter, Charles, 28 April

Healy, James Patrick, 29 April

Heavey, William Joseph, 29 April

Heeney, Robert, 26 April

Hickey, Thomas, 29 April

Higgins, Christopher, 2 May

Hoey, John, 5 May

Hoey, Patrick, 29 April

Hogan, James, 30 April

Hogan, Jeremiah, 28 April

Hughes, Michael, 29 April

Hyland, Charles Hachette, 27 April

Jessop, James, 26 April

John Meagher, 28 April

Johnston, Robert

Jordan, Christopher, 29 April

Jozé, Thomas Moran, 28 April

Kane, Jane, 27 April

Kavanagh, Michael, 17 May

Keane, Alexander, 24 April

Kearns, Johanna, 25 April

Keegan, Francis, 6 May

Keep, Albert, 5 May

Kehoe, Margaret, 24 April

Kelly, Denis, 26 April

Kelly, Lawrence, 24 April

Kenny, Mary, 27 April

Kenyon, Thomas, 28 April

Keogh, Michael

Knowles, Henry, 26 April

Lawless, Peter Joseph, 29 April

Lawlor, Christopher, 9 May

Leahy, Michael, 28 April

Lennon, Kate, 14 May

Lennon, Mary, 27 April

Long, Samuel, 4 May

Loughlin, John

MacKenzie, Robert, 27 April

Maguire, Joseph

Maguire, William, 25 April

Mallen, William

Mallon, John, 27 April

Martin, Patrick, 26 April

McCabe, Harriet, 27 April

McCabe, Michael, 27 April

McCarthy, John, 23 May

McCartney, James, 29 April

McCormack, James, 27 April

McDonnell, Andrew, 26 April

McDonnell, William

McElvery, John, 27 April

McGaley, Edward, 26 April

McGuinness, Margaret, 3 May

McIntyre, Patrick James, 26 April

McKillop, Michael, 27 April

McLoughlin, James, 27 April

McLoughlin, Raphael, 30 April

McManus, Patrick, 29 April

Meegan, John, 27 April

Meleady, Thomas, 29 April

Meron, Julia Frances, 28 April

Moore, James, 29 April

Moore, William, 26 April

Moran, Elizabeth, 29 April

Morris, Mary, 29 April

Mulligan, Laurence, 1 May

Murphy, Catherine, 7 May

Murphy, Edward, 25 April

Murphy, Georgina, 29 April

Murphy, John, 29 April

Murray, John, 24 April

Myers, Annie, 27 April

Naylor, Margaret, 29 April

Neal, John

Nealon, Patrick, 18 June

Neil, James Crawford, 10 May

Neill, Mary, 30 April

Nolan, Margaret, 25 April

Nunan, Michael, 29 April

O'Beirne, Robert F, 28 April

O'Callaghan, John

O'Connor, Ellen, 7 June

O'Connor, John

O'Connor, Michael, 26 April

O'Donoghue, Dominic

O'Donoghue, John, 1 May

O'Duffy, John, 30 April

O'Flaherty, Joseph, 25 April

O'Flaherty, Richard

O'Grady, Edward, 2 May

O'Grady, Patrick, 24 April

O'Leary, Martin, 27 April

O'Reilly, John, 24 April

Pentony, Thomas, 29 April

Pierce, George, 29 April

Playfair, George Alexander, 25 April

Power, James, 30 April

Purcell, Christina, 10 June

Quirke, Elizabeth, 27 April

Redmond, Christopher, 1 May

Reilly, John, 28 April

Reilly, Thomas, 28 April

Reilly, Unidentified, 24 April

Reynolds, Patrick, 4 August

Rice, William John, 29 April

Salmon, Francis

Scherzinger, Abalone, 26 April

Shargine, Joseph

Sheehy-Skeffington, Francis, 26 April

Shiels, Florence, 24 April

Simpson, Vincent Paul, 26 April

Smyth, Elizabeth, 30 April

Spellman, Timothy, 4 May

Stephenson, Patrick, 29 April

Stillman, John, 27 April

Stodart, Holden, 26 April

Sweeney, Frederick William

Swords, David

Synnot, George, 30 April

Taaffe, Rosanna, 30 April

Tierney, Paul

Timmons, Mary, 29 April

Trevor, Patrick

Vantreen, Prudence, 25 April

Varnals, Edward, 29 April

Walsh, James Joseph, 11 May

Walsh, John, 29 April

Walsh, Kate

Waters, Richard, 25 April

Watson, William, 26 April

Watters, Felix Joseph, 8 May

West, William, 28 April

Whelan, Daniel, 29 April

Whelan, Sarah, 1 May

White, Myles

Wilkinson, Elizabeth, 2 May

Woodcock, Richard

18 POLICE KILLED

Cleary, James. RIC, Constable, Ashbourne, 28 April

Frith, William. DMP, Constable, Dublin, 27 April

Gormley, James. RIC, Constable, Ashbourne, 28 April

Gray, Alexander. RIC, County Inspector, Ashbourne, 10 May

Hetherton, James. DMP, Constable,

Dublin, Suicide, 7 May [14]

Hickey, James. Constable, RIC, Ashbourne, 28 April

Hurley, James. RIC, Constable, Tipperary, 26 April

Lahiff, Michael. DMP, Constable, Dublin, 24 April

McGee, Charles. RIC, Constable, Castlebellingham, Louth

McHale, Richard. Constable, RIC, Ashbourne, 28 April

Miller, Christopher. RIC, Constable, Dublin, 27 April

O'Brien, James. DMP, Constable, Dublin, 24 April

Rourke, Thomas F. RIC, Sergeant, Tipperary, 24 April

Rowe, William Nelson. RIC, Head Constable, Cork, 2 May

Shanagher, John. RIC, Sergeant, Ashbourne, 28 April

Smyth, Harry. RIC, District Inspector, Ashbourne, 28 April

Whelan, Patrick. RIC, Constable, Galway, 26 April

Young, John. RIC, Sergeant, Ashbourne, 28 April

126 BRITISH ARMY KILLED

Acheson, Percival Havelock, 24 April

Allatt, Henry Thomas, 8 May

Banks, Arthur, 29 April

Banting, Frederick Charles, 29 April

Barks, George, 26 April

Barnett, George William, 27 April

Barratt, Harold, 27 April

Barratt, John, 29 April

Bentley, Oscar, 24 April

Blissett, John Samuel, 26 April

Blundell, James, 2 May

Bourne, Harold, 29 April

Bowcott, John Reginald, 29 April

Bradford, James Horace, 5 May

Brennan, Francis, 24 April

Brennan, John, 24 April

Brindley, Harold, 28 April

Brosnan, Patrick, 25 April

Browne, Montague Bernard, 30 April

Browning, Francis (Georgius Rex), 26 April

Burke, Frederick William, 28 April

Byrne, James, 1 May

Calvert, James Howard, 24 April

Carr, Michael, 24 April

Cavanagh, James, 26 April

Chapman, Thomas, 27 April

Chick, James, 29 April

Clery, Reginald (Georgius Rex), 24 April

Cobbold, Arthur Elias, 29 April

Collins, Thomas Albert, 29 April

Cordwell, John Herbert, 24 April

Cornwell, James Hamlet, 2 May

Coxon, Richard, 26 April

Coyle, John, 30 April

Crockett, Charles Love, 28 April

Cullen, Joseph, 25 April

Daffen, Harold, 26 April

Davenport, Ernest, 28 May

Dickinson, Harry, 12 May

Dietrichsen, Frederick, 25 April

Dixey, Henry Charles, 27 April

Dixon, Charlie Thomas,

Dooley, James, 08 May

Duffy, James, 24 April

Duggan, Cornelius, 29 April

Elliott, Alfred Goddard, 26 April

Ellis, Alfred, 1 May

Ennis, Peter, 25 April

Farnsworth, Ernest, 26 April

Fletcher, John Henry, 27 April

Forth, John Robert, 27 April

Fox, Ernest, 29 April

Fryday, Neville Nicholas (16), 30 April

Gamble, Robert, 26 April

Gibbs, John Henry (Georgius Rex), 24 April

Glaister, Robert, 28 April

Goss, Joseph, 26 April

Gray, George, 28 April

Hanna, John, 28 April

Harborne, Thomas (Georgius Rex), 24 April

Hare, Henry, 26 April

Harrison, Thomas, 29 April

Hawken, William Victor, 26 April

Headland, James David, 24 April

Hewitt, Henry Meyrick, 27 April

Holbrook, Arthur, 26 April

Holland, Luke, 26 April

Hosford, Joseph (Georgius Rex), 26 April

Hoyle, Charles, 26 April

Hughes, Frederick John, 24 April

Humphreys, John William, 25 April

Humphries, William Henry, 29 April

Hunter, Godfrey Jackson, 26 April

James, William Edgar, 24 April

Jeffs, Percival, 26 April

Jobber, Francis, 29 April

Kitchen, Albert James, 26 April

Knox, Francis William, 27 April

Lang, William, 26 April

Leen, Patrick, 1 May

Llewellyn, Wilfred, 29 April

Lucas, Algernon, 29 April

Lucas, Francis, 26 April

McClelland, Alexander, 27 April

McCullough, James, 2 May

Miller, Thomas Henry, 26 April

Moore, Christopher, 26 April

Morton, Nathaniel, 29 April

Mulhern, John, 24 April

Mulraney, William, 26 April

Mulvey, James Arthur, 24 April

Neilan, Gerard Aloysius, 24 April

Newland, Albert, 2 May

Nolan, James, 24 April

O'Gorman, Charles, 24 April

Osborne, Clarence, 27 April

Perry, Percy Vivian, 26 April

Phillips, Harry, 25 April

Pinfield, Guy Vickery, 24 April

Purser, Philip Addison, 30 April

Ramsay, Alan Livingston, 24 April

Rodgers, Harold, 27 April

Saunders, Charles, 28 April

Scarlett, Arthur James, 24 April

Shepherd, H., 24 April

Sherwood, John Henry, 5 May

Sibley, Alfred, 26 April

Smith, Arthur Charles, 29 April

Speed, Bert, 29 April

Tempest, David Percival, 29 April

Thompson, John, 24 April

Treacy, Thomas, 24 April

Tunnicliffe, Walter, 26 April

Tyler, Alfred, 27 April

Walker, William, 27 April

Walton, Austin Joseph, 27 April

Warmington, Alfred, 24 April

Warner, Arthur, 27 April

Watchorn, Abraham, 26 April

Whelan, John, 21 May

Wilson, David, 24 April

Wood, Albert Edward, 17 May

Worsley-Worswick, Basil Henry, 29 April

Wright, William Thomas, 28 April

Wyld, George, 26 April

Young, Sidney Leonard, 25 April

BULLET HOLES & MARKS FROM THE RISING

THE GPO

Both the north-end and south-end columns in the portico of the GPO have several holes that are about one inch in diameter. Besides the occasional small hole from a .303, the majority are from the half-inch balls of shrapnel (called bullets) that were fired from the British 18-pounders. The small holes between the columns, in a line, are drill holes for banners.

In the façade of the GPO, there is a row of holes about two feet from ground level – these are from a railing that used to adorn the building. There are a few other chips in the stonework that are most likely from the Rising, but the end columns provide the observer with the best example of the damage from 1916.

THE O'CONNELL MONUMENT

There are about twenty bullet holes in the O'Connell Monument at the lower end of O'Connell Street, including about a half-dozen in the Liberator's torso. There is one directly above his middle finger, on the Red Hand crest. The Maid of Erin has one in her ankle, another in the harp she is holding, and one in her bicep muscle. As you face the statue, the winged figure on your right, Fidelity, has a bullet hole between the wolf-hound and her gown. On your left, Patriotism has holes in her right clavicle and under the fold of her gown. In her right elbow, there is an entry and a partial exit hole – the bullet failed to completely exit. Eloquence also has an elbow wound and a bullet mark in her right wing. Perhaps the most well-known bullet hole in Dublin is on the winged Victory of Courage, in her right breast. The damage under her left wing is from the UVF bomb of 27 December 1969.

THE COLLEGE OF SURGEONS

There are many bullet holes in the façade and the columns of the College of Surgeons on St. Stephen's Green. Note that they are in clusters of twos and threes, which is indicative of machine-gun fire from the Shelbourne. There is a deep bullet hole from 1916 in a brass plate on an inside door in the college boardroom on the first floor. This room was occupied by the Irish Citizen Army during the Rising.

FUSILIERS' ARCH

The arched entrance into St. Stephen's Green at the top of Grafton Street was built in 1907 and dedicated to the Royal Dublin Fusiliers who died in the Second Boer War of 1899–1902. The arch was known to Dubliners as 'Traitors' Gate' for most of the 20th Century. With Grafton Street at your back, look up at the left side of the granite arch – between eight and ten feet from the ground, it is easy to spot the bullet holes from British weapons during the Rising.

ELVERY'S CRICKET BAT

The National Museum of Ireland houses a cricket bat with a bullet from the Rising firmly lodged into the timber. The bat was on display in the window of John W Elvery and Co., 46 and 47 Lower Sackville Street. Five men initially occupied the block from Kelly's Gun Powder Office (on the corner of O'Connell Street and Bachelors Walk) to Elvery's. They were reinforced but came under intense fire and were ordered to withdraw back to the GPO on Wednesday.[15] Someone, presumably from Elvery's, inscribed the words 'Easter Week, 1916, Front Window' just beside the bullet.

THE MALT HOUSE

On Grand Canal Quay there is a building known as the Malt House. It has numerous bullet holes in its side, which were unearthed after the building was restored around 1999. During the Rising, a green flag with a harp was erected on the roof to draw fire from the *Helga* and from British snipers away from nearby Boland's Mills.

MARSH'S LIBRARY

The British Army, who were firing a machine gun towards Jacob's during the Rising, inadvertently raked a few shots into Marsh's Library, next to St. Patrick's Cathedral. There are still bullet holes in some of the books there today.

THE CAR IN ENGLAND

There is a car in the National Motor Museum in Beaulieu, England, that has some damage to the steering wheel said to be from the Rising. It is a Hispano-Suiza and the model is an Alfonso XIII, named after the King of Spain. The car was owned by Alfred Gaynor of Gaynor & Son Cork Merchants, 75 Middle Abbey Street. This building is listed as destroyed during the Rising, so if the car was in the area, it is conceivable that it was damaged. A gouge in the steering wheel, which was never repaired, is said to be a bullet hole. Whether it is a bullet hole or just damage will never be proven; however, it is interesting to think that damage from the Rising in Dublin is visible today in England.[16]

Section Ten: The 1936 Roll of Honour

Garrison	Total	Women	Men
GPO	416	56	360
Jacob's	188	10	178
City Hall	46	10	36
Boland's Mills	177	0	177
Four Courts	306	34	272
St Stephen's Green	142	19	123
South Dublin Union	62	0	62
Marrowbone Lane	138	21	117
Mendicity Institution	24	0	24
Ashbourne	59	6	53
Magazine Fort	12	0	12
Cabra Bridge	8	0	8
Louth and Meath	59	1	58
Roe's Distillery (1948)[1]	18	0	18
Total	**1,655**	**157**	**1,498**

In 1936, signatures were collected for a Roll of Honour. The Roll is now housed in the National Museum of Ireland, Collins Barracks. The inclusion of a named individual on the Roll of Honour is proof of his or her participation in the Rising – but exclusion does not mean that the person did not participate.

There are a number of reasons for this. The Roll includes only Dublin and a handful of other locations, thereby excluding Galway, Laois, Wexford, etc. Some people did not want to sign the Roll. Some other people may simply have been forgotten. Similarly, the List of Medal Recipients (see Section 14) excludes some obvious names such as Countess Markievicz, Cathal Brugha, George Plunkett and Jack Plunkett.

It is hoped that by including the Roll of Honour here, the Prisoner Lists in Section 11, and the Medal Recipients in Section 14, anyone who had a role in the Rising will appear at least once.

GPO GARRISON

Adrien, Mary
Agnew, Arthur P.
Behan, Michael
Bermingham, Andrew J.
Bermingham, John
Billings, Joseph P.
Bird, Patrick
Boland, Edmund
Boland, Harry
Boland, Michael
Bracken, Peadar
Brady, Michael
Breen, Liam
Brophy, Daniel
Bulfin, Eamonn
Burke, Frank
Burke, Nicholas
Byrne, Catherine
Byrne, Christopher C.
Byrne, Edward
Byrne, James
Byrne, John C.
Byrne, Louis, Junior
Byrne, Patrick Joseph
Byrne, Peter S.

Byrne, Thomas, F.
Caddell, Patrick
Caffrey, Matthew
Caldwell, Patrick
Callan, Joseph
Canny, Daniel
Carmichael, Bernard
Carney, Winifred
Carpenter, Peter
Carpenter, Walter P.
Carrigan, James
Cassells, James
Cassidy, James P.
Cavanagh MacDowell, Maeve
Clarke, Thomas J.
Clinch, Patrick J.
Coade, John
Cole, Seán
Colley, Harry
Collins, Michael
Connaughton, Patrick
Connolly, James
Conroy, Andrew
Conway, Sean S.
Corbally, Lawrence

Corbally, Richard
Corbally, Thomas
Corrigan, Charles
Courtney, Daniel
Cowley, Michael
Coyle, Harry
Cripps, Joseph A.
Croch, Tomas (T Croke)
Crofts, Gerard
Croke, Michael
Cullen, William F.
Cummins, Tom
Dalton, Patrick
Daly, Denis
Daly, Laura (later O'Sullivan)
Daly, Liam
Daly, Nora (later Dore)
Daly, Seamus
de Barra, Leslie (Mrs Tom Barry)
de Burca, Aoife
de Staineas, Miceal
Dennany, Francis
Derham, Joseph

Devereux, Patrick

Devine, Francis

Devine, Thomas, W.

Devoy, Seamus

Donnelly, Charles

Donnolly, Patrick

Dore, Eamon T.

Dowling, Michael

Doyle, J.J.

Doyle, John

Doyle, John

Doyle, John J.

Doyle, Peter

Duffy, Edward

Duffy, Joseph

Dunne, Francis

Dunne, John

Dunne, Joseph

Dunne, Thomas

Dwyer, Michael

Dyas, Albert

Early, John

English, Maire

English, Patrick

Ennis, Tom

Finegan, Michael

Fitzgerald, Desmond

Fitzharris, John J.

Fitzpatrick, Andrew
    Joseph

Flanagan, Matthew

Flanagan, Rev John,
    CC

Flynn, Ignatius

Fogarty, Thomas

Fox, Michael

Friel, Bernard

Furlong, Andrew

Gahan, Joe

Gallagher, Patrick

Galligan, Paul

Gannon, Henry

Garland, Patrick

Gavan, John James

Gethings, Lucie

Gibson, Richard

Giffney, Michael

Gleeson, Joe

Gleeson, Martin

Gogan, Richard P.

Good, Alfred Joseph

Harris, Thomas

Hayes, James Joseph

Healy, Richard

Heffernan, Michael

Hegarty, Seán

Higgins, Frederick P.

Higgins, Peter

Hoey, Patricia

Hughes, Patrick

Hughes, T.

Hutchinson, Joseph

Hynes, John F.

Inglis, Frainnc (Frank
    English)

Jackson, P.

Jenkinson, Margaret
    (née Walsh)

Jones, Thomas

Joyce, Brian

Kavanagh, Seamus

Kealy, John

Kearney, Thomas

Kearns, Hubert

Keating, Con

Keeley, Joseph W.

Keeling, Christopher

Kelly, Edward

Kelly, Frank

Kelly, John

Kelly, Joseph

Kelly, May (later
    Chadwick)

Kennan, Austin

Kennedy, Luke

Kenny, Henry Vincent

Kenny, James

Kenny, John

Kenny, Michael

Keogh, Bernard P.

Keogh, Michael

Kerr, Sean

Killeen, Robert

Kilmartin, P.

King, George

King, John

King, Patrick

King, Samuel

Kirwan, P.

Knightly, Michael

Lambert, Bridget

Lawless, Edward

Lawless, Mary

Leahy, Thomas

Ledwith, Joseph

Lee, Hugh

Lee, Joseph

Lemass, Noel

Lemass, Sean F.
Lynch, Diarmuid
Lynch, John
Lynch, Martin
Lynch, Patrick Leo
Mac Fionnlaic,
    Conchobhar (C.
    McGinley)
Mac Siubhlaigh, M.S.
    (Walker)
MacCrábháin, Tomás
    (T Craven)
MacCraich, Miceal
MacDermott, Rory
MacDiarmada, Seán
MacDonnell, John
MacFounraic,
    Prionsíos (Frank
    Henderson)
Macken, Frank
Mackey, Laurence
Mackey, Michael
MacLaughlin, D., Dr.
MacMahon, Patrick
MacMullen, Brian
MacNeive, Liam
MacSherry, Margaret
    (née Fagan)
Madden, Sean
Maguire, J.
Maguire, Matthew
Mahon, Patrick
Mahon, Patrick
    Joseph
Mahon, Thomas
Malone, J.J.

Manning, Henry
Mapotar, Máire
Marie, Louis
Mason, Thomas
McAuliffe, Gearoid
McCabe, Kevin J.
McCleane, William, J.
McCrea, Patrick
McDonagh, Joseph
McElligott, J.J.
McElroy, Mairead
McEntagart, John
McEntee, Sean
McEvoy, Thomas
McGallogly, James
McGallogly, John
McGarry, Sean
McGinley, Liam
McGinley, Patrick
McGinn, Conway
McGinty, L., Mrs
    (née Burke)
McGrane, Christo-
    pher
McGrath, Patrick J., Jr
McGrath, Patrick J., Sr
McGrath, Thomas
McLoughlin, Mary
McMahon, Daniel
McMahon, Seán
McManus, Patrick
McNally, John
McPartland, Frank
McPartlin, Peter C.
Meagher, Patrick
Mhic Ruáidhrí,

Sorcha Bhean (S.
    Rodgers)
Milroy, Sean
Mooney, Patrick
Moore, Edward J.
Mulcahy, Mary J.
    (née Ryan)
Mulvey, Dominick
Mulvey, W.P.
Mulvihill, Michael
Murphy, Charles
Murphy, Fintan
Murphy, Gertrude
    (Gertie Colley)
Murphy, Kathleen
Murphy, Martha
Murphy, Michael
Murphy, Robert J.
Murphy, Stephen
Murray, Eileen
Murray, Patrick
    Joseph
Murray, Thomas
Murtagh, Francis D.
Ni Ainle, Maire
Ni Conghaile, Brigid
    (B. Connolly)
Ni Dubhthaig, Luise
    Ghabhanach
Ní Foghludha, Nóra
Ni Riain, Veronica
    (Bean Uí Glásáin)
Ní Rían, Áine
Noonan, Seán
Noone, Ellen
Norton, James

Nugent, Michael

Nugent, Patrick

O'Braonain, Seamus

O'Briain, Eoghan

O'Briain, Tomas

O'Brien, John

O'Brien, Matthew

O'Brien, Michael

O'Byrne, James

O'Byrne, James

O'Cáoimh, Padraig

O'Carroll, Kevin

O'Ceallaigh, Eamonn

O'Ceallaigh, Sean T.
(O'Kelly)

Ó'Cearbhaill, Peadar

O'Colgain, Padraic

O'Connell, Mary

O'Connor, James

O'Connor, Johnny
'Blimey'

O'Connor, Patrick

O'Connor, Peter

O'Donnchadha,
Tomas

O'Gorman, Liam

O'Hanrahan, Mary

O'Higgins, Annie

O'Kelly Barber,
Kathleen

O'Kelly, Fergus F.

O'Mahony, Eamon J.

O'Mahony, Mathew

O'Mangain, Tomas
(T. Mangan)

O'Moore, Donough

O'Mordha, Padraig

O'Murchada, Peadar

O'Murchú, Miceal

O'Neill, James

O'Neill, John

O'Neill, John

O'Neill, Maire (May,
née Gibney)

O'Neill, Seamus

O'Raghallaig, M.L.
(O'Reilly)

O'Rahilly, The
(Michael Joseph
O'Rahilly)

O'Raogáin, Liam

O'Reilly, Cathleen

O'Reilly, J. K.

O'Reilly, Joe

O'Reilly, John

O'Reilly, Joseph

O'Reilly, Mary (Mrs.
Corcoran)

O'Reilly, Thomas

O'Riain, Seamus (Dr.
Jim Ryan)

O'Rinn, Liam

O'Sullivan, Gearoid

O'Sullivan, James

O'Toole, William

Oman, George

Parnell, Matthew

Pearse, P.H.

Pearse, William

Pedlar, Liam

Plunkett, Joseph

Price, Sean

Purcell, C.

Quinn, Margaret

Rafferty, M.J. (née
Walsh)

Rankin, Patrick

Rath, Thomas

Redmond, Andy

Redmond, Annie

Reid, John

Reilly, Matthew

Reynolds, John R.

Reynolds, Mollie

Reynolds, Peter J.

Richards, Bridie

Ridgeway, Harry

Ring, Christopher

Ring, Joseph

Ring, Patrick

Robinson, Seamus

Roche, Thomas J.

Roche, William

Rossiter, C.

Ryan, Oliver

Ryan, Phyllis

Ryan, Thomas

Saurin, Charlie

Scollan, John J.

Scullin, Francis

Scullin, Patrick

Seville, James

Sexton, James

Sheridan, Frank

Sheridan, James

Shields, Arthur

Shortis, Patrick

Simpson, Tilley

Slater, Mrs. B. (née
    Walsh)
Slattery, Peadar
Slevin, M.J., Mrs.
    (née Stapleton)
Smith, Charles
Smith, Lucy (Mrs.
    Tom Byrne)
Stafford Brooks,
    Christina
Stanley, Joseph
Steinmayer, Charles
    Joseph
Stephenson, Patrick J.
Stritch, Jim
Stynes, Ellen (née
    Lambert)
Supple, Padraig
Swan, Andrew
Sweeney, James
Sweeney, Joseph
Sweeney, Patrick
Tallon, Christopher
Tallon, James
Tannam, Liam
Thornton, Frank
Thornton, Hugh
Thornton, Patrick
Tobin, Annie (Mrs.
    Soalfield)
Toomey, Joseph
Toomey, Stasia (Mrs.
    Byrne)
Traynor, Oscar
Treston, Cathleen
Trimble, Joseph

Tuohy, J.J., Dr.
Tuohy, Patrick
Turner, Cormac
Turner, Francis
Turner, Joseph
Twamley, John J.
Tyrrell, Timothy
Ua Buachalla,
    Domhnall
Ua Faoithe, Bean
    Brigid
Wade, Michael
Walker, Charles
Walpole, R.Harry
Walsh, Christopher
Walsh, Edward
Walsh, James Joseph
Walsh, Mark
Wardach, James
Weafer, Patrick
Weafer, Thomas
Wheatley, Thomas
Whelan, Joseph
White, John, J.
White, Michael
Willis, Henry
Wisely, Esther (Mrs.
    O'Moore)
Wren, James

JACOB'S GARRISON

Aodha, Seoirse
Barrett, James
Barrett, William
Barry, William

Begley, Joseph
Bermingham, John
Blake, William J.
Brady, Francis
Brady, Patrick
Brennan, Laurence
Breslin, Patrick
Brien, John
Buckley, William J.
Burke, Thomas
Byrne, Joseph
Byrne, Vincent
Byrne, William
Carberry, James
Carney, Francis
    Joseph
Cassells, James
Chambers, Daniel F.
Christie, Peter
Colbert, Sean
Comerford, Andrew
Cotter, Joseph A.
Cotter, Richard
Cotter, Thomas
Cullen, Peter
Cunningham, James
Darcy, Patrick Leo
de Bruin, Seorais
Deegan, Máire
Dolan, Peter
Doogan, Sean
Doyle, Patrick
Doyle, Thomas
Drumm, Thomas
Ellis, Samuel
Ennis, Christopher

Ennis, Michael

Farrell, James

Farrelly, Christopher

Fitzpatrick, Michael

Furlong, John

Furlong, Mathew

Gahan, Tadgh

Gleeson, D.P.

Goulding, Charles

Goulding, James

Grattan, Richard

Gregory, John

Hannon, James

Hunter, Thomas

Joyce, John

Joyce, Joseph James

Kavanagh, Daniel

Kealy, Sara

Kearns, Frank

Kearns, John

Kearns, Joseph

Kearns, Tom

Kelly, Henry

Kelly, John E.

Kenny, James J.

Keogh, Thomas

King, Sean

Lane, Edward

Lane, Kathleen (née McCarthy)

Lane, Michael

Lanigan, Patrick

Lawlor, M.

Long, Patrick

Losty, Thomas

Lynch, Sean

Lynch, William

Lyons, Edward

Mac Daibhís, Risteard

MacBride, John

MacDonagh, John

MacDonagh, Thomas

MacMahon, Bernard J.

Magee, Teresa

Maher, William

Manning, Patrick

McDermott, Owen

McDonnell, Matthew

McDonnell, Patrick

McDonnell, Patrick

McEvoy, Patrick

McGlure, John

McGrane, Thomas

McGrath, Daniel

McKee, Richard

McParland, James

Meade, Michael

Meade, Owen

Meldon, John

Meldon, Thomas J.

Molloy, Richard

Moran, Patrick

Mullen, Martin

Murphy, John J.

Nic Shiubhlaigh, Maire (later Price)

Nolan, Patrick

O'Beoláin, Gearoid

O'Byrne, Patrick

O'Cahill, Art

O'Carroll, James

O'Carroll, James Joseph

O'Carroll, Richard

O'Cathasaigh, Seamus

O'Ceallacháin, Sean

O'Ceallaigh, Pádraig

O'Cearnaigh, Peadar

O'Connell, Patrick

O'Corgain, Mícheál

O'Donnell, Christopher

O'Donnell, James

O'Grady, John

O'Hagan, Annie

O'Hagan, Hugh

O'Hanrahan, Edward

O'Hanrahan, Eily (later O'Reilly)

O'Hanrahan, Henry

O'Hanrahan, Joseph

O'Hanrahan, Michael

O'hAodha, Micheal

O'hAodha, Séamus

O'Malley, Christopher R.

O'Murain, Séamus

O'Neill, Cecilia (née Conroy)

O'Reilly, Patrick

O'Reilly, Thomas

O'Reynolds, John

O'Ríordáin,

Domhnall

O'Rourke, Frederick

O'Rourke, John

O'Rourke, Michael

O'Ruairc, Seán

O'Ruairc, Tomás

O'Shea, Dermot

O'Shea, James

O'Toúma, Seosaimh

Phelan, Michael J.

Pollard, Josephine
(later Daly)

Pollard, Kathleen
(later McDonald)

Pounch, James

Price, Eamon

Pugh, Thomas W.

Redmond, Patrick

Redmond, William J.

Roche, Sean

Roe, Richard

Rooney, Patrick

Ryder, John

Ryder, William

Schweppe, Frederick

Shanahan, Philip

Sheils, James

Shelly, Denis

Shelly, Thomas

Sheppard, Michael S.

Simpson, Terence

Slater, Michael

Slater, Thomas

Slater, William

Slattery, James J.

Smyth, Michael

Somers, Daniel
Charles

Stapleton, William
James

Stokes, Dick

Sweeney, P. Emmet

Turner, John

Tyrell, Andrew

Ua Cathalain, Padraig

Ua Ceallaigh, Seórais

Ua Dálaigh, Liam

Ua Maoilfinn,
Séamus

Walker, J.

Walker, Michael

Walsh, John

Walsh, Patrick

Ward, George

Ward, Nicholas

Watson Lake, John

Whelehan, Christo-
pher

Williams, Henry J.

Williams, Peter

CITY HALL GARRISON

Barrett, Kathleen

Brady, Brigid

Brady, Christopher

Byrne, John

Byrne, John

Byrne, Louis

Byrne, Patrick

Connolly, Mattie

Connolly, Sean

Coyle, Thomas

D'Arcy, Charles

Daly, Thomas

Elmes, Ellett

Farrell, Denis

Finlay, John

Geoghegan, George

Halpin, William

Halpin, William

Hanratty, Emily (née
Norgrove)

Kain, Thomas

Kelly, Bessie

King, Arthur

King, George

King, Samuel

Lambert, James

Lynn, Kathleen F.

McDonnell, James

Molony, Helena

Mullally, Michael

Nelson, Thomas

Nolan, John

Norgrove, Annie

O'Duffy, Brigid (née
Davis)

O'Dwyer, James

O'Keeffe, John C.

O'Leary, Philip

O'Reilly, John

O'Reilly, John

Oman, William

Poole, John

Seery, James

Sexton, Michael

Shanahan, Jennie

Walsh, Thomas
Williams, Patrick
  Joseph
Winstanley, Henry

BOLAND'S MILLS
GARRISON

Banks, Henry
Banks, Seán
Bermingham, John
Boylan, Stephan
Bracken, John
Bracken, John, Jr.
Brady, William
Breen, Sean
Brennan, Patrick
Brennan, Patrick
Breslin, Toby
Browne, James
Browne, William
Burton, Frederick
Byrne, C.
Byrne, D.
Byrne, Henry
Byrne, John
Byrne, Joseph
Byrne, Michael
Byrne, Michael
Byrne, Michael
Byrne, Patrick
Byrne, Patrick
Byrne, Peter
Byrne, Thomas
Carroll, Dudley
Casey, Leo
Cassidy, Thomas

Coates, Peter
Colgan, Daniel
Conroy, William
Cooper, Robert
Cosgrave, John
Coyne, Thomas
Cullen, Michael
Cullen, Sean
Daly, James
de Valera, Eamon
Donnelly, Simon
Donovan, Michael
Doyle, James
Doyle, James H.
Doyle, Patrick
Doyle, Patrick
Doyle, Seamus
Dunne, John
Ennis, Edward
Fallon, Thomas
Finn, Timothy
Fitzgerald, James
Fitzgerald, Leo
Fitzgerald, Thomas
Fitzgerald, William
Flanagan, Patrick
Flemming, Michael
Flynn, John A.
Gill, James J.
Gordon, Edward
Grace, James Joseph
Griffin, Martin
Guilfoyle, Joseph
Henry, James
Hickey, Michael
Humphreys, Richard

Jackson, Francis
Jackson, Joseph
Kavanagh, James
Kavanagh, Liam
Kavanagh, Peadar
Kavanagh, Peter Paul
Kelly, Patrick
Kelly, Thomas
Kelly, Thomas
Kenny, Charles
Kinsella, John
Kirwan, Edward
Lalor, Eamon
Leonard, Edward
Liffiroi, Leo
Lyons, George A.
Mac an Bhaird,
  Padraic
Mac Dowell, Cathal
Mac Giolla Bhríde,
  Padraic
Mac Giollaphol, Sean
  (Guilfoyle)
Mac Uinseann, Sean
Macken, Peadar
MacMahon, Sean
Maguire, James
Mallon, James
Malloy, Joseph
Malone, Michael
Malone, Robert
Martin, Joe
McArdle, Owen
McBride, Patrick
McCabe, Patrick
McCabe, Patrick

(signed twice)

McCabe, William
(Liam)

McCarthy, Bernard

McCarthy, Michael

McCurran, Joseph

McDermott, Joseph

McDonnell, Andrew

McDowell, Patrick

McDubhghaill,
Padraig

McGrath, Sean

Meagher, Michael

Meagher, Patrick

Merriman, Michael

Mullen, Murtagh
Patrick

Murphy, Christo-
pher J.

Murphy, John J.

Murphy, Liam

Murphy, Richard

Murray, Frank

Murray, Michael

Murray, Seamus

Nolan, P.

Nolan, Patrick

Nugent, John

Nugent, Joseph

O hAodha, Aghuistín

O'Brien, William

O'Broin, Liam

O'Byrne, Joseph

O'Byrne, Tom

O'Caomhanaigh,
Micheal

O'Connor, Joe

O'Connor, Joseph

O'Cuirbre, Cristoir
(Carbury)

O'Donoghue, Denis

O'Duinn, Sean

O'Grady, Anthony

O'Greagain, Seumas

O'Hanlon, John

O'Keeffe, Sean

O'Leannain, Micheal

O'Meadra, Peadar

O'Neill, Andrew

O'Reilly, Christopher

O'Reilly, Patrick

O'Rourke, Thomas

O'Scolaige, T.

O'Shea, Sean

Parfield, James

Pearle, Richard

Peate, Thomas

Peelo, Denis

Pender, James

Porter, Eugene
(Owen)

Power, Patrick

Quin, Sean

Quin, Thomas

Raftis, Liam

Redican, James

Reid, John J.

Reid, Patrick

Reynolds, George

Roe, Patrick

Roe, William C.

Rownan, William

Ryan, Cornelius

Stanley, Liam

Stokes, John J.

Tannam, Miceal

Thompson, Alex-
ander

Traynor, Thomas

Ua Broin, Sean

Walker, John

Walsh, James

Walsh, Thomas

Waters, James

Whelan, Patrick

Williams, Patrick

Woodrock, William

FOUR COURTS GARRISON

Allen, Mary (née
Murray)

Allen, Thomas

Anderson, Thomas

Archer, Liam

Augustine, Father,
O.M.C.

Béaslaí, Piaras

Beggs, Robert

Begley, Daniel J.

Bent, John

Bevan, Charles S.

Bevan, James

Bevan, Joseph

Bevan, Thomas J.

Bibby, Albert, Father,
O.M.C.

Bird, James

137

Blackburn, Kathleen
(née Kenny)
Blanchfield, Peter
Brabazon, Joseph
Breslin, James
Breslin, Peadar
Breslin, Thomas
Bridgeman, Edward
Burns, James
Butler, George
Byrne, Ambrose
Byrne, Charles
Byrne, John
Byrne, Laurence
Byrne, Mary
Byrne, Patrick
Byrne, Seamus
Byrne, Seán
Byrne, Teresa (née
Healy)
Byrne, William (Billy)
Cahill, James
Callender, Ignatius
Campbell, M.J.
Carron, Máire
Cassidy, Thomas
Catlin, John Patrick
Clancy, Peadar
Clarke, James
Cody, Seán
Coffey, Joseph
Coghlan, Francis
Xavier
Coleton, Elizabeth
(née Murnane)
Collins, Maurice

Condron, Luke
Conroy, James
(Senior)
Copeland, Margaret
(née Byrne)
Cosgrove, Michael
Costigan, Nellie (née
Ennis)
Cox, Redmond
Coyle, William
Cullen, Joseph
Cullen, Thomas
Daly, Edward
Darker, William
Delemere, Edward
Dempsey, James
Derham, Michael
Derrington, Liam
Doggett, Christopher
Domican, John
Donohoe, Sylvester
Dowling, Andrew
Dowling, John
Dowling, Thomas
Doyle, John
Doyle, Thomas J.
Duffy, Christopher
Duggan, E.J.
Duggan, May (née
Kavanagh)
Dunne, Thomas
Dwan, John
Edwards, Michael
Ellis, Seán
Fagan, John
Fagan, Michael

Fahy, Anna
Fahy, Frank
Farrell, John
Farrell, Patrick
Farrell, Thomas
Farrelly, Christopher
(Junior)
Farrelly, Seán
Farren, Stephen
Feeney, Gerald
Fitzpatrick, Denis
Flood, Seán
Fogarty, John
Fogarty, Patrick
Forde, Seán
Foy, Frederick
Frawley, Denis
Gahan, Mathew
Gaynor, Arthur
Geraghty, Sean
Gilsenan, Patrick
Graham, James
Green, Patrick
Griffith, William
Grimley, Michael
Halpin, John
Halpin, Peadar
Hamill, Thomas
Harding, Frank
Harnett, Alf
Healy, Cathleen
Healy, Peadar
Hendrick, Edward
Hendrick, James
Joseph
Heron, Aine

Hogan, P.J.

Hogan, William
Conor

Howard, Con

Howard, Seán

Howlett, Michael

Hurley, Seán

Hyland, Thomas

Hynes, Sean

Kavanagh, James

Kavanagh, James

Kearns, Patrick

Keating, Pauline (née
Morkan)

Kelly, Joseph

Kelly, Michael

Kelly, Patrick

Kennedy, James J.

Kennedy, John

Kennedy, Sean

Kenny, John

Kenny, John

Laffan, Nicholas

Lawlor, Frank

Lawlor, Larry

Lawlor, Mary (née
O'Carroll)

Lawlor, Sean

Ledwith, Emily (née
Elliot)

Ledwith, Peter

Leggett, Robert

Lennon, Nicholas

Lowe, Arnold

Lynch, Gilbert

Lyons, Charles

Lyons, Edward

Lyons, John E.

Mac an Bháird,
Gilbert

Mac Cearbhaill,
Peadar

MacDonagh, Joseph

Macken, Patrick

MacMeachtaigh,
Motoin

Mac Meánmain,
Maighneas

MacNamara, Patrick

Magee, Michael

Maguire, Thomas

Manning, Peadar

Martin, Kathleen

Mason, Frank

Mason, G.

McCabe, Frank

McCann, Thomas
Joseph

McCormack, Chris-
topher J.

McCormack, John

McDonnell, Thomas

McEvatt, Louis

McGill, Joseph

McGuinness, Cath-
erine

McGuinness, Joseph

McGuinness, Rose

McKeon, Brigid (née
Murnane)

McKeon, Owen

McKeon, William

McLoughlin, Peter

McMenarigh, Joseph

McNally, Francis

McNamara, James

McNestry, Patrick

McNulty, Micheal

McNulty, Peadar

McQuaile, May (née
Moloney)

Meade, Henry

Meade, Walter

Meade, William

Merrigan, Thomas

Mooney, Patrick

Morkan, Eamon

Morkan, Phyllis

Mulkearns, James J.

Mullen, Peter

Munroe, Thomas G.

Murnane, Liam

Murnane, Margaret
(née Martin)

Murphy, Eileen (née
Walsh)

Murphy, Francis
Charles Stuart

Murphy, Hubert J.

Murphy, Martin

Murphy, Michael

Murphy, Michael

Murphy, William

Murray, Joseph M.

Murtagh, Laurence
Joseph

Murtagh, Patrick

Musgrave, Denis J.

Neary, Denis

Neilan, Arthur

Nevin, Patrick

Ní Bhríain, Eilis (née Elliot)

Ní Conaill, Eilis (née Ní Riain)

Ní Conallain, Peig

O'Banáin, Tomás

O'Braonain, Eamonn

O'Briain, Sean

O'Brien, John

O'Brien, Michael

O'Brien, Patrick

O'Brien, Patrick

O'Carroll, Annie (née O'Keeffe)

O'Carroll, Mary (née O'Sullivan)

O'Carroll, Michael

O'Carroll, Robert

O'Carroll, Sean

O'Conaill, Mort

O'Conallain, Mairtín

O'Connor, John

O'Connor, John S.

O'Connor, Patrick J.

O'Dea, Michael

O'Doherty, Fionan

O'Doherty, Liam

O'Donnabháin, Conn

O'Duffy, Sean M.

O'Flanagan, Francis

O'Flanagan, George

O'Flanagan, Maurice

O'Flanagan, Michael

O'Flanagan, Patrick

O'Foghludha, Micheál

O'Gorman, Liam

O'Gorman, Mary Christina (née Hayes)

O'Hanlon, Bernard

O'Hanlon, Patrick

O'hEigheartaigh, Diarmuid

O'Kelly, Michael

O'Leary, Patrick Joseph

O'Loinsaigh, Fionan

O'Loinsaigh, Micheál

O'Moore, Sean

O'Murchadha, Christóir

O'Murchadha, Micheál

O'Neill, Joseph

O'Neill, Michael

O'Neill, Patrick Francis

O'Neill, William

O'Nualláin, Tomás

O'Reardon, Michael

O'Reilly, Luke

O'Reilly, Peter

O'Reilly, Thomas

O'Riain, Liam S.

O'Scargaidh, Einroí

O'Scollaighe, Miceal

O'Sullivan, James

Oman, Robert

Parker, Ellen (née O'Flanagan)

Pollard, Frank D.

Pollard, Louisa (née O'Sullivan)

Pollard, Stephen

Prendergast, Sean

Rawley, Albert Sylvester

Regan, Laurence

Reid, Seán

Richmond, John

Roache, Joseph

Roche, Michael Joseph

Ryan, William

Sanders, Michael

Savage, Martin

Scully, William

Sheehy, Charles

Sheerin, Thomas P.

Sheridan, James

Sheridan, John

Shouldice, Frank

Shouldice, Jack

Simptéal, Liam

Smart, Thomas

Stephenson, Mary (née Kilmartin)

Swan, Patrick

Sweeney, Joseph

Thornton, Brigid (née Lyons)

Tierney, Michael

Tobin, Liam

Tobin, Michael
Travers, Edward
Ua Briain, Tomas
Ua Ceallacháin,
    Donncadh
Ua Cearbhaill, Liam
Ua Murchadha,
    Brian
Walsh, James
Walsh, Philip
Ward, George
Ward, Sean
Whelan, George
Williams, John J.
Wilson, Mark

ST. STEPHEN'S GREEN GARRISON

Adams, John
Alexander, Nicholas
Bermingham, Peter
Bradley, Patrick
Branghain, James
Burke, Edward
Buttner, Paddy
Byrne, Christopher
Byrne, Denis
Byrne, James
Byrne, Joseph
Byrne, Joseph
Caffrey Keeley,
    Chriss
Carton, Owen
Chaney, Patrick
Charleton, Michael
Clarke, Philip

Clifford, Tom
Coates, Peter
Conroy, Eileen
Conroy, Sean
Corcoran, James
Courtney, Bernard
Craven, Barney
Crothers, Christopher
Cullen, Patrick
Daniels, Harry
de Coeur, Robert
Devereux, Mollie
    (later Allen)
Donnelly, James
Donnelly, Michael
Doyle, Denis
Doyle, Joseph
Duffy, Joseph
Duffy, Patrick
Dwyer, James
Dwyer, Michael
Dynan, Christopher
ffrench-Mullen,
    Madeleine
Fitzmaurice, Gerald
Fox, James
Fox, James
Fox, Patrick J.
Foy, Martin
Fullerton, George
Gahan, Mary
Geragthy, Eugene
Gifford, Helen (later
    Donnelly)
Goff, Gough Bridget
Gough, James

Hackett, Rosie
Halpin, William
Hampton, James
Hand, Matthew
Hendrick, John J.
Henry, Francis
Henry, Fred
Holden, Patrick J.
Humphreys, Robert J.
Hyland, James
Hyland, Mary
Jackson, Peter
Jennings, Thomas
Jennings, Thomas
Joyce, Edward
Joyce, James
Joyce, Maggie, Mrs.
Kavanagh, John
Kavanagh, Patrick
Kavanagh, Seamus T.
Keenan, Thomas
Kelly, Annie
Kelly, Francis
Kelly, Hugh
Kelly, James
Kelly, James
Kelly, Joseph
Kelly, Katie
Kelly, first name
    unknown
Kelly, William
Keogh, Edward
Keogh, James
King, Martin
Lacey, Phillip
Lambert, J.

Lawless, Michael J.

Lawlor, Patrick J.

Leddy, Peter

Little, James

MacGrath, Peter P.

MacMahon, J.

Maguire, James

Mahon, John

Mallin, Michael

Mannering, Edward

Markievicz, Madam

McArt, Daniel

McCormick, Richard

McDonald, John

McDonnell, William

Meagher, John W.

Monks, Andrew

Moore, May (née Wisely)

Murphy, Fred

Murray, Daniel

Murtagh, Bernard

Nelson, James

Ní Dubhgaill, Christine Maire

Nicholls, Harry

O'Briain, Liam

O'Briain, Liam

O'Brien, Frank

O'Daly, Bridget (née Murtagh)

O'Daly, Nora

O'Doherty, Michael

O'Donnchadha, Tomas

O'Donoghue,

Henry V.

O'Kelly, Michael

O'Leary, David

O'Neill, Jim

O'Neill, John

O'Reilly, Joseph

O'Reilly, Patrick

O'Rógáin, Sean

O'Shea, James J.

O'Shea, Robert

Partridge, William

Reardon, Laurence

Reynolds, Percy

Robbins, Frank

Ryan, Frederick

Ryan, Margaret

Scott, William

Seery, Cathleen

Seery, John

Seery, Patrick

Shannon, Martin

Sheils, Thomas

Skinnider, Margaret

Tuke, Edward

Ua Conchubhair, Sean

Whelan, John

SOUTH DUBLIN UNION GARRISON

Arnold, James

Boylan, Thomas J.

Brugha, Cathal

Burke, Frank

Burke, James

Byrne, Joseph P.

Byrne, Liam

Carroll, Leo Bartholomew

Ceannt, Éamonn

Coady, William

Condron, William

Cosgrave, W.T.

Cullen, Thomas

Donnellan, Brendan

Downey, John

Doyle, Gerald

Doyle, Peadar S.

Evans, Robert J.

Farrell, Michael

ffrench-Mullen, Douglas

Foran, James

Gibson, Edward

Gibson, Michael

Glynn, James

Irvine, George

Joyce, John

Keegan, Edward

Kelly, Joseph F.

Kenny, James

Kerr, Michael

MacCarthy, Dan

Maguire, James

McDowell, William

McGlynn, Sean

McKenna, John

McMahon, Daniel J.

Moloney, Patrick

Morrissey, James

Morrissey, Patrick S.

Murphy, John

O'Brien, Denis
O'Brien, James
O'Brien, Stephen L.
Ó'Broin, Cathal
O'Corrigan, William
  Patrick
O'Doherty, John J.
O'Flaherty, Liam
O'Flaherty, Séamus
O'Loughlin, Patrick
O'Reilly, Patrick
O'Reilly, Richard
O'Shaughnessy, Seán
Owens, Sean
Quinn, James
Rigney, Paddy
Russell, James
Sears, David
Sweeney, Michael
Tracey, Seán
Traynor, Sean
Ward, Peter
Whelan, Richard

MARROWBONE LANE GARRISON

Adams, John
Bailey, Patrick J.
Bowman, Joseph
Breathnach, Séamus
Burke, Matthew
Butler, Con
Butler, James
Byrne, Alphonsus
Byrne, Christopher
Byrne, Frank

Byrne, James
Byrne, Kate
Byrne, Michael
Byrne, Michael
Byrne, Patrick
Byrne, Patrick
Carty, Thomas
Clarke, Joseph
Clinch, Maria
Colbert, Con
Cooney-O'Brien,
  Annie
Cooney, Eileen (later
  Harbourne)
Cooney, Lillie
Corcoran, Joseph (Bro.
  Louis O.F.M.)
Corrigan, James
Cosgrave, Philip
Cullen, John
Darcy, John
Dempsey, William
Dempsey, William
Downey, Joseph
Doyle, Christopher
Doyle, May (née
  Byrne)
Doyle, Thomas
Doyle, Thomas J.
Dunne, Denis K.
Dunne, Patrick J.
Dwyer, Michael
Edwards, John
Farrelly, Rose (née
  Mullally)
Fitzpatrick, James

Greene, Josephine
  (née Kelly)
Grehan, James
Harbourne, Patrick
Harbourne, Seán
Harman, Patrick
Harmon, Brigid (née
  Hegarty)
Hendley, Emily (née
  O'Keeffe)
Holland, Daniel
Holland, Robert
Holland, Walter
Judge, John Patrick
Kavanagh, James
Kavanagh, Martin J.
Kavanagh, Priscilla
  (née Quigley)
Kelly, William
Kennedy, Joseph P.
Kennedy, Margaret
Kenny, James
Kenny, Kieran
Keogh, John
Kerrigan, Owen
Keys, John
Lamb, Patrick
Liston, Michael
Lynch, Sighle (née
  O'Hanlon)
MacLughaidh, Diar-
  muid
MacNéill, Diarmuid
Mason, Patrick
McCabe, Edward
McCabe, Michael B.

McCabe, Peter
McCabe, William
McCarthy, Patrick
McEvoy, Christopher
McGowan, Josephine
McGrath, Joseph
McGrath, Patrick
McGrath, Patrick
McGrath, Sean
McKenna, Bernard
McNamara, Rose
McNamee, Agnes
McVeigh, James
Merriman, Edward
Morgan, John
Mullen, Martin
Mullen, Patrick
Murphy, Francis
Murphy, Kathleen
Murphy, Séamus
Murphy, Thomas
Murray, Gabriel B.
Murray, Henry
Nolan, George
O'Brennan, Lily M.
O'Briain, Donncada
O'Brien, Laurence
O'Brien, Patrick
O'Brien, Peadar
O'Broin, Pádg
O'Byrne, Hugh
O'Byrne, Seán
O'Caomhánaighe, Tomas
O'Carroll, Joseph
O'Connell, James

O'Duinn, Peadar
O'Gorman, John
O'Gorman, Joseph
O'Hagan, James
O'Hanlon, Mollie
O'Neill, Edward
O'Neill, Joseph
O'Neill, Michael
O'Riordan, Michael
O'Rourke, Patrick
O'Toole, John
Páircéir, Seosamh
Pender, Henry
Power, Arthur
Power, Joseph
Power, Liam
Roche, William
Saul, John
Spicer, Josephine
Teehan, James
Timmons, Margaret
(née O'Flaherty)
Troy, Daniel
Troy, Patrick
Venables, Thomas
Walsh, James
Walsh, Patrick
White, Michael
Young, E.C.
Young, Patrick J.
Young, Robert
Young, Thomas

MENDICITY INSTI-
TUTION GARRISON

Balfe, Richard C.

Brennan, James J.
Brooks, Fred J.
Clarke, John
Coleman, Richard
Crenigan, James
Cullen, John Francis
de Roiste, Eamonn
Derrington, John
Heuston, Sean
Levins, George
Marks, James
Meehan, William
Norton, Joseph
O'Ceallaigh, Pádraig
O'Dea, William
Peppard, T.
Staines, Liam
Stephenson, P.J.
Ua Broin S. S.
Wilson, James
Wilson, Peter
Wilson, Peter
Wilson, William

ASHBOURNE
GARRISON

Ashe, Thomas
Aungier, Richard
Belton, Patrick
Birney, Patrick
Brogan, Patrick
Ceallaigh, Peadar
Connor, James
Crenigan, Jack
Dempsey, William
Derham, Matthias

Volunteers and ICA in the GPO, 1916.

Devine, John
Doyle, Patrick
Doyle, Thomas
Doyle, William
Early, Patrick J.
Golden, Jerry
Gough, James
Kelly, Joseph
Kelly, Matthew
Kelly, Richard
Kelly, Thomas
Lawless, Colm
Lawless, Frank
Lawless, Joseph L.
Lawless, Monica (née Fleming)
Leaver, Thomas
Lynders, Thomasina (née Weston)
MacDomhnaill,

Séamus
Masterson, James
Maxwell, Thomas
McAllister, Bennie
McAllister, John
McArdle, Thomas
McCann, John
McGowan, John
McNally, Margaret
Moran, Christopher
Moran, Peter
Murphy, Eamon
Ni Briain, Maire
Nic Alastair, Caitlin
Norton, William
Nugent, Christopher
O'Ceallaig, Seamus
Rafferty, John
Rafferty, Thomas
Reilly, Thomas

Rickard, James
Ryan, Patrick Joseph
Sherlock, John
Stafford, Edward
Taylor, Christopher
Taylor, Joseph
Taylor, Thomas
Ua Droighneáin, Seoirse
Weston, Bartle
Weston, Charles
Weston, Julia
Weston, Thomas

MAGAZINE FORT

Boland, Patrick
Dempsey, James
Gilligan, Bob
Holahan, Patrick Hugh

Marié, Louis
Martin, Christopher
Martin, Eamon
Murphy, John
O'Briain, Seán
Parker, Bernard
Roche, Timothy
Ua hUallacháin,
    Gearóid

CABRA BRIDGE

Blanchfield, Thomas
    Patrick
Brennan, Maurice
Dempsey, James
Dunne, Patrick
Faulkiner, John
McArdle, John
O'Higgins, James
O'Reilly, Samuel P.

LOUTH AND MEATH AREAS

Bailey, Edward
Boylan, Peter
Butterly, Nicholas
Butterly, Sean H.
Butterly, Thomas
Byrne, Peter
Casey, Patrick
Clifford, Owen
Clifford, Peter
Coburn, Francis
Conlon, Gerard
Crean, Aidan
Crean, Margaret

(née Byrne)
Donnelly, Michael
Dunne, James
Finegan, John
Finn, Patrick
Garvey, Patrick
Greene, Arthur
Hall, Samuel R.
Hamill, Thomas
Hearty, Thomas
Hughes, James
Hughes, Patrick
Jameson, Richard
Kearney, Hugh
Keating, James
Keating, Peter
Kelly, James
Kelly, Thomas
Kieran, John
Kiernan, Edward
King, Owen
Larrissey, Joseph
Leahy, Denis
Litchfield, Henry
Lowndes, Francis
Lynam, Christopher
Madden, Daniel
Maguire, James
Martin, Frank
McCrave, Thomas
McGuill, James
McHugh, Patrick
Mulholland, Patrick
Mulholland, Thomas
Mullally, James
Mullally, Patrick

O'Broín, Gearoid
O'Broin, Giolla
    Criost
O'Broin, Liam
O'Ceallaigh, Seamus
O'Dowd, Richard
O'Dubhda, Eoghan
O'Hannigan, Donal
O'Neill, Felix A.
Quinn, Hugh Patrick
Reilly, James
Tuite, Daniel

ROE'S DISTILLERY (NAMES COLLECTED 1948)

Bowles, William P.
Byrne, George
Cunningham,
    Michael
Dowling, Seán
Egan, Patrick
Fagan, William
Gaskin, Henry
Gaskin, Thomas
Gogan, John Gerard
Horan, Daniel
Keogh, Martin
Kiely, Seán
Nugent, John
O'Grady, Charles
Quinn, George J.
Ward, Bernard
Ward, Patrick
Ward, Patrick J.

Section Eleven: Prisoner Lists

In the immediate aftermath of the Rising, hundreds of men and women were arrested. The following were mostly held in Richmond Barracks before being deported to prisons in England and Scotland. The majority were then housed in Frongoch Prisoner-of-War Camp in north-west Wales.

200 TO KNUTSFORD ON 1 MAY 1916 [1]

The following prisoners were removed from Richmond Barracks, Dublin, on 30 April and lodged in Knutsford Detention Barracks, England, on 1 May. This list was issued on Wednesday, 10 May:

Alexander, N; Begley, D; Begley, J; Bermingham, J; Berry, W; Billings, J; Blanchfield, M; Bradley, P; Brophy D; Buckingham, J; Burke, B; Burns, J; Byrne, C; Byrne, J; Byrne, J; Byrne, P; Byrne, T; Byrne, T; Caffrey, M; Callan, J; Campbell, G; Canny, D; Carmichael, B; Carpenter, P; Carraty, T; Carrol, P; Cassells, J; Cathan, J; Charlton, M; Clarke, J; Coleman, P; Condron, L; Conroy, H; Conway, J; Courtney, D; Cox, R; Craven, T; Croke, T; Daniel, H; Decceur, E; Delaney, H; Doherty, J; Donnelly, C; Donnelly, M; Donohoe, W; Doyle, E; Doyle, J; Doyle, T; Dreeland, W; Duffy, P; Dunn, A; Ellis J; Ellis, S; Farren, S; Flanagan, J; Fogarty, T; Foley, N; Foran, J; Foy, M; Frawley, D; Friel, B; Gannon, H; Gaynor, A; Gleeson, W; Good, J; Halpin, P; Harnett, J; Haughton, G; Healy, R; Hegarty J; Hickey, R; Holohan, H; Howlett, M; Hughes, P; Humphreys, R; Hunter, J; Hyland, T; Hynes, J; Jackman, N; Kavanagh, J; Kavanagh, P; Kelly, F; Kelly, J; Kelly, M; Kelly, W; Kennealy, J; Kennedy, J; Kenny, A; Kenny, H; Kenny, J; Keogh, C; Keogh, E; Keogh, J; Lafferty, J; Lawler, L; Lawless, E; Lee, J; Lee, T; MacGuire, T; Mahon, P; Maloney, J; McAulliffe, G; McCormack, B; McCormack,

R; McDermott, R; McDonald, W; McGill, J; McGinley W; McGrath, PB; McGrath, T; McLaughlin, J; McManus, P; McNally, F; McNally, J; McNamara, J; McNamara, P; McNieve, W; McQuade, T; Monahan, J; Mooney, J; Mooney, P; Moran, P; Morkan, M; Mulkearns, J; Mulligan, A; Mulvey, D; Mulvey, W; Murphy, E; Murphy, F; Murphy, M; Murphy, William; Neary, D; Neilan, A; Nelson, P; Neville, P; Nicholls, H; Nolan, P; Norton, J; Nugent, P; O'Brien, J; O'Carroll, J; O'Neill, P; O'Neill, W; O'Reilly, H; O'Shea, J; O'Shea, R; O'Brien Ml; O'Brien, W; O'Brien; O'Brien; O'Cahill, J; O'Callaghan, D; O'Carroll, P; O'Carroll, W; O'Connor, P; O'Donoghue, T; O'Neill, J; O'Reilly, L; O'Reilly, SP; O'Ryan, O; O'Shea, M; Power, W; Prendergast, J; Purcell, C; Redmond, J; Regan, M; Reid, J; Reilly, M; Reilly, P; Ridgeway, A; Robbins, F; Rocarter, O; Roche, M; Rooney, J; Russell, J; Saurin, C; Savage, M; Sexton, J; Shannon, M; Sheppard, M; Sheridan, J; Shields, A; Simpson, T; Stephenson, P; Stynes, J; Sweeney, J; Tallon, C; Toomey, J; Toomey, T; Traynor, C; Trell, P; Tuke, E; Tully; Ward, G; Warham, T; Whelan, M; Whitley, T; Williams, P.

289 TO STAFFORD ON 1 MAY 1916

The following prisoners were removed from Richmond Barracks, Dublin, on 30 April and lodged in Stafford Detention Barracks, England, on 1 May. This list was issued on Thursday, 11 May:

Agnew, A; Bagley, T; Bird, J; Boland; Bolger, J; Brennan, E; Breslin, J; Breslin, P; Breslin, T; Bridgeman, E; Broughman, EJ; Bryan, T; Burke, E; Burke, F; Byrne, A; Byrne, C; Byrne, C; Byrne, J; Byrne, J; Byrne, J; Byrne, J; Byrne, L; Callaghan, J; Carroll, R; Carroll, M; Carton, O; Casey, H; Cassidy, J; Cassidy, T; Chaney, P; Chaney, W; Clifford, D; Clinch, P; Coates, P; Cody, J; Coffey, J; Cole, P; Collin, P; Collins, M; Connaughton, P; Conroy, J; Corbally, R; Corbally, T; Cosgrove, M; Coughlan, F; Coughlan, J; Cowley, M; Cowling, J; Coyle, W; Craven, B; Cremen, M; Croke, M; Cullen, J; Dalamere, E; Daly, D; Darcy, W; Darritt, D; Dennany, P; Dervin, P; Doggett, C; Donegan, J; Donnelly, P; Donohoe, R; Donohoe, S; Dore, E; Dowling, A; Dowling, J; Doyle, J; Doyle, J; Doyle, J; Duffy, C; Duffy, J; Duffy, J; Dunne, J; Dunne, P; Dunne, T; Dwyer, J; Early, J; Edwards, M; English, P; Ennis, T; Farrell, M; Farrelly, J; Feeney, G; Fitzharris, J; Fitzmaurice, G; Fitzsimons, M; Flanagan, F; Flanagan, G; Flanagan, M; Flanagan, M; Flood, J; Foran, J; Ford, J; Fox, J; Fox, M; Foy, F; Fullam, T; Gahan, M; Gallagher, P; Garland, P; Garvey, M; Gavan, J; Geoghegan, JJ; Geraghty, C; Gleeson, T; Gough, J; Halpin,

P; Hammill, T; Hands, N; Harper, J; Hayden, J; Hayes J; Hayes, J; Healy, J;
Healy, P; Heery, J; Henderick, E; Henderson, F; Henderson, M; Henderson,
T; Henry, F; Henry, F; Hughes, T; Jackson, P; Joyce, B; Joyce, E; Kavanagh,
J; Kavanagh, P; Kavanagh, P; Kearney, T; Kearns, P; Keating, C; Kelly, FM;
Kelly, J; Kelly, P; Kelly, P; Kenny, J; Keogh, J; Kerr, J; Kerwin, P; Kilgallon, J;
King, G; King, G; King, M; King, P; Lawlor, L; Ledwith, P; Little, J; Lowe, A;
Lundy, J; Lynch, M; Lynch, P; Lyons, J; MacGinley, E; Madden, J; Magee, R;
Maghar, J; Mahon, J; Marie, L; Mason, F; Mason, Frank; McArdle, J; McArdle,
P; McCormack, J; McDonough, J; McElligott, M; McEntee, JF; McEr-
ratt, L; McGrath, M; McGuire, FJ; McGuire, R; McGuirk, P; McKeon, O;
McMahon, D; McNulty, M; McNulty, P; McPartlin, P; Meade, H; Meade, W;
Meagher, P; Meekin, G; Monks, A; Mooney, J; Mooney, P; Moore, J; Munroe,
T; Murnane, W; Murphy F; Murphy F; Murphy, C; Murphy, H; Murphy,
J; Murphy, P; Murray, T; Murtagh, FD; Murtagh, L; Musgrave, L; Nolan,
M; Nolan, T; Noonan, C; Noonan, E; Noonan, J; O'Borke, J; O'Brien, J;
O'Brien, M; O'Brien, O; O'Brien, T; O'Brien, W; O'Brien, P; O'Byrne,
J; O'Byrne, J; O'Connell, M; O'Connor, J; O'Connor, J; O'Connor, J;
O'Connor, J; O'Connor, T; O'Doherty, W; O'Gorman, W; O'Hanlon, P;
O'Higgins, B; O'Kelly, M; O'Neal, M; O'Neill, J; O'Neill, J; O'Neill, T;
O'Neill, W; O'Reilly, D; O'Reilly, J; O'Reilly, J; O'Reilly, J; O'Reilly, P;
O'Reilly, T; O'Reilly, W; O'Reilly; Oman, R; Perry, W; Pollard, F; Poole,
C; Poole, P; Price, J; Rankin, P; Rat, T; Redmond, A; Richmond, J; Ring,
C; Ring, J; Ring, W; Ross, W; Ryan, J; Ryan, L; Ryan, D; Seery, J; Shelly, C;
Sheridan, J; Shortall, W; Shouldice, F; Skeils, T; Smith, J; Steinmayer, C; Sul-
livan, J; Sullivan, J; Summers, J; Swan, P; Sweeney, J; Sweeney, J; Sweeney, P;
Thornton, H; Toban, M; Tobin, M; Tuohy, S; Turmley, J; Turner, H; Tyrrall, T;
Vize, J; Walpole, H; Walsh, J; Walsh, J; Ward, G; Ward, T; Water, P; Whelan, G;
Whelan, J; Whelan, J; Whelan, W; White, J.

308 TO KNUTSFORD ON 3 MAY 1916

The following prisoners who removed from Richmond Barracks, Dublin,
on 2 May and lodged in Knutsford Detention Barracks, England, on 3 May.
This list was issued on Friday, 12 May:
Archibold, William; Betler, Christopher; Blanchfield, Peter; Boland, Gerald;
Bowman, Joseph; Boylan, Thomas; Bracken, Thomas; Brady, James; Breslin,
Patrick; Brian, Patrick; Brogan (Drogan), Patrick; Buckley, Daniel; Buckley,

Republican prisoners being transported to British jails.

William, J; Burke, M; Burne, James; Byrne, Charles; Byrne, Christopher; Byrne, Frank; Byrne, Hugh; Byrne, John; Byrne, Joseph; Byrne, Joseph; Byrne, Joseph; Byrne, Lawrence; Byrne, M; Byrne, Michael; Byrne, Patrick; Byrne, Patrick; Byrne, Patrick; Byrne, Thomas; Byrne, William; Byrne, William; Caffrey, F; Caffrey, Leo; Cahill, Arthur; Callan, P; Carlton, TG; Carroll, Bartholomew; Carroll, James; Carroll, Peter; Carty, Thomas; Casey, James; Cassidy, H; Caulfield, John; Cavanagh, Martin; Cavanagh, Thomas; Christie, Peter; Clarke, Joseph; Collins, John; Comerford, Andrew; Corcoran, Joseph; Cordy (Coady), William; Corrigan, James; Corrigan, William; Cotter, Joseph; Cotter, Joseph; Cotter, Richard; Coughlan, James; Cullen, John; Cunningham, James; Curran, W; Daly, Philip; Delaney, M; Dempsey, William; Devine, John; Doherty, John; Donoghue, Thomas; Doolan, Joseph; Dowling, Edward; Doyle, Christopher; Doyle, Joseph; Doyle, Patrick; Doyle, Peter; Doyle, Thomas; Doyle, Thomas; Doyle, William; Drumm, Thomas; Dunne, John Joseph; Dunne, Denis; Dunne, P; Durham, Matthias; Edwards, John; Egan, Patrick; Ennis, Christopher; Ennis, Michael; Farrell, James; Farrell, M; Farrell, William; Fitzpatrick, Andrew; Fitzpatrick, James; Fitzpatrick, John; Fitzsimons, John; Fleming, M; Fogarty, James; Foran, James; Fullerton, George; Furlong, Joseph; Furlong, Matthew; Gahan (Galvin) Timothy; Goulding, Charles; Goulding, James; Graham, James; Graham, Thomas; Grant, Patrick; Gregory, John; Griffen, John; Gunning, J; Hagan,

James; Hanney, Francis John; Hannon, James; Harney, John; Harvey, Robert; Harvey, Thomas; Heron, James; Holland, Daniel; Holland, Robert; Hutchinson, Joseph; Jordan, Michael; Joyce, J; Judge, J; Kavanagh, James; Kavanagh, P; Kearns, Frank; Kearns, John; Kearns, Joseph; Kearns, Thomas; Keating, James; Kelley, Thomas; Kelly, Henry; Kelly, Isaac; Kelly, J; Kelly, Joseph; Kelly, Joseph; Kelly, Matthew; Kelly, P; Kelly, Kelly, Thomas; Kelly, William; Kennedy, Joseph; Kenny, J; Kenny, James; Kenny, K; Keogh, James; Kerr (Carr) Neill; Kerr, Michael; Kerr, Thomas; Kerrigan, Owen; Killeen, Robert; King, John; Laughlin, Patrick; Lawless, James; Lawless, James; Liston, M; Losty, Thomas; Lynch, John; Lynch, Michael; Lynch, William; Lyons, E; MacKay, Lawrence; Mackey, Michael; Makanaltis, Antli; Malone, William; Maloney, J; Malony, Henry; Martin, Peter; Masterson, James; Maxwell, Thomas; McAllister, Bernard; McCabe, Edward; McCabe, Kevin; McCabe, P; McCabe, William; McCann, John; McCormack, John; McDonagh, John; McDonald, J; McDonald, John; McDonald, Michael; McDonnell (McDonald), Patrick; McDonnell, Seamus (James); McDonnell, John; McDonnell, Matthew; McEvoy, James; McGinley, Patrick; McGloughlin, M; McGlynn, John; McGrath, John; McGrath, Patrick; McGuire, James; McKeag, David; McKee, Richard; McKenna, Bernard; McLoughlin, Peter; McMahon, Peter; McQuaid, John; McVeigh, James; Meade, Dnl; Meldon, John; Meldon, Thomas; Molloy, Charles; Molloy, Michael; Molloy, Richard; Moore, John; Moore, William; Moran, Patrick; Morgan, John; Mulcahy, Richard; Mullen, Martin; Mullen, Martin; Mullen, Patrick; Murphy, F; Murphy, J; Murphy, James; Murphy, John; Murphy, Joseph; Murphy, M; Murphy, Patrick; Murray, G; Murray, Ger; Murray, Henry; Murray, Nicholas; Murtagh, Bernard; Neary, Joseph; Nolan, Thomas; O'Brien, Denis; O'Brien, Lorcan; O'Brien, Peter; O'Brien, William; O'Byrne, John; O'Byrne, Joseph; O'Callaghan, J; O'Callaghan, Michael; O'Connell, J; O'Connor, Thomas; O'Donnell, James; O'Dwyer, Michael; O'Flaherty, Liam; O'Flaherty, Martin; O'Gorman, John; O'Halloran, C; O'Neill, E; O'Neill, Frank; O'Neill, Joseph; O'Neill, Michael; O'Rafferty, John; O'Reilly, Patrick; O'Rourke, Michael; O'Rourke, P; O'Shea, Dermott; Perry, George; Perry, James; Phelan, Michael; Phillips, John; Power, Arthur; Power, Joseph; Power, Thomas; Power, Thomas; Power, William; Price, Edward; Pugh, Thomas; Quigley, John; Reardon, Michael; Redmond, Patrick; Reynolds, Charles; Roche, Thomas Q; Roche, William; Rooney, Edward; Rooney, James; Rungien, Richard; Russell, J; Saul, John; Schweppe,

Fred; Server, Thomas; Shanahan, Philip; Shelley, Denis; Shelley, Thomas; Shiels, Jas; Shortall, P; Sieman, Charles; Slattery, James; Smith, Michael; Smith, Thomas; Stafford, Edward; Stapleton, William; Stokes, Richard; Swanzy, Patrick; Tobin, Michael; Toole, John; Tracy, John; Troy, Daniel; Troy, Patrick; Venables, Thomas; Walsh, Patrick J; Walsh, Patrick; Ward, Patrick W; Weston, Bartle; Weston, Charles; Whelan, M; Whelan, Richard; Whiteham, Chris; Whitmore, William; Williams, W; Young, Robert; Young, Thomas.

376 TO WAKEFIELD ON 6 MAY 1916

The following prisoners were arrested by the military authorities and received at Wakefield Detention Barracks, England, on 6 May. This list was issued on Saturday, 13 May:

From Ballsbridge: Allwell, Joseph; Banks, Henry; Banks, Henry; Birmingham, Patrick; Boland, Michael; Bracken, John Jnr; Bracken, John Snr; Bradley, Richard; Breen, John; Brennan, Patrick; Brennin; Breslin, TF; Burton, Frederick; Byrne, John; Byrne, Chris; Byrne, Edward; Byrne, Henry; Byrne, J; Byrne, Lawrence; Byrne, Michael; Byrne, Patrick; Byrne, Peter; Cahill, Patrick; Campbell, Michael; Carberry, Chris; Carroll, Dudley; Carroll, Nick; Carroll, Thomas; Carter, Richard; Casey, Leo; Cassidy, Thomas; Christian, William; Clarke, Joseph; Coffey, William; Colgan, Daniel; Cooper, Robert; Cosgrove, John; Cranwell, Edward; Cregg, Laughlin; Cuff, James; Cuffe, Patrick; Cullen, John; Cullen, Michael; Delaney, Joseph; Dempsey, Charles; Donnelly, Simon; Dowling, Charles; Dowling, Lewis; Dowling, Stephen; Dowling, Thomas F; Doyle, James; Doyle, James; Doyle, Patrick; Ducia, Patrick; Duff, Henry; Duffy, Thomas; Dunne, Andrew; Dunne, James; Dunne, James; Dunne, John; Dunne, Joseph; Dunne, Timothy; Dunphy, John; Fay, James; Finn, Luke; Finn, Timothy; Flannigan, Patrick; Fleming, Michael; Fulham, Thomas; Gaffikin, Edward Digby; Gaskin, Frank; Gibbons, Patrick; Gill, James; Gillies, Thomas; Goulding, John; Grace, James; Griffen, M; Guilfoyle, John; Guilfoyle, Joseph; Hannon, James; Hardy, Joseph; Hardy, Octavius; Harvey, Joseph C; Harvey, Patrick; Hayes, Augustine; Henry, James; Hickey, Michael; Hill, Sam H; Hynes, John; Irwin, Samuel; Jackson, Francis; Jackson, Joseph; Jennings, M O'S; Johnston, Edward; Jones, Peter; Joyce, John; Joyce, John; Judge, Richard; Kavanagh, James; Kavanagh, Michael; Kavanagh, Patrick; Kavanagh, Patrick; Kavanagh, Peter; Kavanagh, William; Kelly, Michael; Kelly, Patrick; Kelly, Richard; Kelly, Thomas; Kenny, Charles; Kenny, James;

Kerford, Patrick; Kiernan, Edward; Kinsella, John; Knightly, Michael; Lamgare, Patrick; Lang, Francis; Largan, Michael; Lawlor, Ed; Layden, Mathew; Leonard, Joseph; Leonard, Michael; Lindsay, John; Lynch, Daniel; Lynch, John; Lyng, Thomas; Lyons, George; Mahon, James; Mahon, John; Mallen, James; Malone, Robert; Mannering, Ed; Martin, Joseph; McBride, Patrick; McCabe, Patrick; McCabe, William; McCarthy, Bernard; McCarthy, Michael; McCline, Hubert; McDermott, Joseph; McDermott, Owen; McDowell, Cecil; McGinn, Michael C; McGrath, John; McKenna, Joseph; McLoughlin, Patrick; McMahon, John; McMahon, John; McNamara, John; Meagher, Michael; Meagher, Patrick; Miller, George; Molloy, Joseph; Moriarty, Denis; Mullally, Joseph; Murphy, Charles; Murphy, James; Murphy, John; Murphy, Peter; Murphy, William; Murray, Chris; Murray, Frank; Murray, James; Murray, Joseph; Navin, Michael R; Nolan, Patrick; Nolan, Peter; O'Byrne, William; O'Connor, Joseph; O'Malley, Chris; O'Brien, Patrick; O'Brien, Peter; O'Brien, Tim; O'Byrne, Thomas; O'Connor, Alf; O'Connor, Joseph; O'Connor, Thomas; O'Donaghue, Thomas; O'Duffy, James P; O'Grady, Anthony; O'Hanlon, John; O'Leary, Arthur; O'Mara, Peter; O'Moore, Patrick; O'Neill, Andrew; O'Reilly, Chris; O'Reilly, Patrick; Parle, Richard; Peate, Thomas; Pender, James; Pender, William; Phelan, Patrick; Porter, Owen; Power, Patrick; Purcell, Phillip; Quinn, John; Quinn, Thomas; Rafferty, Thomas; Reilly, James; Reilly, Robert; Ribton, Thomas; Robinson, Thomas; Rowley, William; Ryan, John; Ryan, Cornelius; Ryan, John; Scully, Thomas; Shelly, John; Slack, Patrick; Smith, Albert; Tannan, Michael A; Tevercuse; Patrick; Thackaberry, William; Timbrenan, Tobias; Tobin, Martin; Tobin, Patrick; Trayner, Thomas; Treacy, James; Tully, George; Tully, William; Turner, Frank; Turner, Joseph; Tyrell, James; Walker, John; Wall, Michael F; Wall, William; Walpole, Leo; Walsh, Colman; Walsh, Richard; Walters, James; Ward, Patrick; Welch, James; Williams Patrick; Woodcock, William.

From Kilmainham: Allen, George; Arnold, James; Barry, Joseph; Breen, Patrick; Buckle, J; Burke, Michael; Byrne, James; Byrne, Joseph; Carter, John; Clarke, James; Condron, William; Coney, Patrick; Cooney, William; Cooper, John; Cullen, Michael; Cullen, Thomas; Cullen, William; Cunningham, John; Cunningham, Patrick; Darby, Charles; Darcy, John; Darney, John E; Dowling, Michael; Doyle, Thomas; Doyle, William; Duffy, James; Duggan, Edward; Dunne, Frank; Farrell, Joseph; Farrelly, James; Farrington, Leo; Filey, Matthew; Fitzpatrick, Martin; Fitzpatrick, Thomas; Gibson,

Edward; Giffney, Michael; Goga (Gogan), John; Halpin, James Francis; Halpin, Joseph; Humphries, Richard; Kelly, Daniel; Kelly, Michael Joseph; Kelly, Patrick Bealan; Kelly, Thomas; Kenny, Joseph; King, Leo; Lambert, Thomas; Larkin, John; Leeson, John; Lennon, Michael John; Lynch, James; Lyndon, Patrick; Macken, Aloysius; Magee, George; Maguire, John; Manning, Michael; McGill, Edmund; McMahon, Dan Joseph; Moore, Patrick; Moore, Peter; Morgan, Henry; Moroney, Thomas; Murphy, Joseph; Murphy, Thomas; Newman, John; Nolan, John; Norries, David Henry; Nugent, Michael; O'Brien, Stephen; O'Connell, Edward; O'Connor, Patrick; O'Kelly, Frank; O'Kelly, John; O'Neill, George; O'Reilly, John; O'Toole, William; Parker, George; Phelan, Thomas; Quinn, Hugh; Rowman, William; Saul, James; Staines, Michael; Stritch, James; Sweeney, Michael; Tallon, Joseph; Wall, Thomas; Whelan, John; Whelan, Patrick.

From Arbour Hill: Beggs, Joseph; Bent, John; Cadden, Matthew J; Corcoran, Patrick; Cusack, John; Daly, James; Derham, Robert; Du Bourdien, Arthur; Dunne, Patrick; Farrell, John; Fitzgerald, James; Fitzgerald, Leo; Fitzgerald, Thomas; Ganley, William; Gibbons, Pete; Gibson, Denis; Gibson, James; Griffiths, Nicholas; Griffiths, Patrick; Griffiths, William; Hand, Thomas; Jenkinson, William; Jordan, Patrick; Keane, Peter; Keogh, Patrick; Kilmartin, Patrick; Lacey, Michael; Leggett, Robert; Lynch, James; Maguire, Denis; Maguire, Philip; McCarthy, D; McCormack, Peter; McDermott, Patrick; McDonald, Joseph; McGuinness, Joseph; McHugh, Edward; McHugh, Miles; McHugh, Patrick; McHugh, William; Moore, J William; Moran, John; Munster, Thomas; O'Reilly, John; O'Reilly, Thomas; O'Toole, John; Oglesby, Joseph; Reynolds, Henry; Ryan, Michael; Shanley, Michael; Sheridan, John; Sherlock, John; Shiels, Joseph; Tallon, James; Tarpey, Patrick; Whelan, Daniel.

203 TO STAFFORD ON 8 MAY 1916

The following list of 203 prisoners were removed from Richmond Barracks, Dublin, on 8 May 1916 and lodged in Stafford Detention Barracks, England, on 9 May 1916. This list was issued on 14 May 1916:

Alexander W; Allen, A; Barnes, J; Barrett, J; Black, E; Boland, C; Boyne, W; Brandon, J; Bulfin, E; Byrne, J; Byrne, J; Byrne, P; Byrne, W; Cahill, M; Carney, FJ; Carolan, M; Carroll, J; Carty, M; Casey, P; Chapman T; Chapman, P; Clear, T; Coady, J; Coady, J; Coady, P; Colgan, P; Conlon, J; Connolly, M; Connor, M; Connors, P; Conway, J; Corish, R; Courtney, C; Courtney,

J; Courtney, W; Cullen, J; Cullen, M; Cullen, T; Cummins, M; Darcy, P;
Darcy, P; Davis, M; Derham, M; Devereux, P; Devitt, E; Doherty, J; Don-
nelly, N; Donoghue, J; Doody, P; Doolan, J; Dorin, D; Doyle, A, Jnr; Doyle,
A; Doyle, PJ; Doyle, R; Doyle, T; Doyle, T; Du Bourdien, J; Dwyer, J; Ellett,
E; Ennis, M; Ennis, M; Farnon, L; Farrell, H; Fielding, T; Finn, E; Fitzharris, J;
Fitzpatrick, M; Fitzpatrick, P; Fortune, R; Fortune, W; Fox, B; Fox, T; Frank-
lin, J; Franklin, M; Furlong, J; Gahin, W; Garrett, J; Gascoigne, J; Goodall, J;
Gorman, W; Halpin, P; Hayes, J; Hayes, T; Hayes, TJ; Heffernan, M; Hegarty,
J; Hendrick, W; Hickey, B; Holbroke, M; Holmes, D; Horan, M; Hutchin, W;
Hyland, J; Irwin, CJ; Jordan, J; Kane, C; Kavanagh, J; Kavanagh, M; Kavanagh,
P; Keeffe, P; Keegan, P; Kehoe J; Kehoe, P; Kehoe, P; Kehoe, P; Kelly, M;
Kelly, P; Keogh, P; Kingarroff, T; Lacey, J; Lacey, J; Maguire, J; Maguire, M;
Maher, D; Maher, J; Maher, T; Mahon, P; Mangan, T; Mardley, F; Mardock,
W; McCarthy, T; McGowan, J; McMacken, B; Moran, J; Moran, J; Moran, M;
Moran, P; Moran, T; Murphy, J; Murphy, J; Murphy, J; Murphy, P; Murphy,
P; Murphy, P; Murphy, W; Murray, B; Nash, P; Neill, J; Nolan, M; O'Brien,
D; O'Brien, J; O'Brien, M; O'Connell R; O'Connor, D; O'Donoghue,
H; O'Driscoll, R; O'Hara, P; O'Kane, J; O'Keegan, T; O'Leary, P; O'Neill,
J; O'Neill, M; O'Reilly, J; O'Reilly, J; O'Shea, J; Osborne, H; Parker, T;
Reddin, GM; Reddin, K; Reddin, T; Redmond, E; Reinhardt, WJ; Reynolds,
P; Rigley, P; Ring, P; Robinson, J; Rogers, M; Rossiter, J; Royce, W; Ruth,
W; Ryan, P; Sharkey, T; Sheehan, P; Sherwin, P; Shiel, M; Sinnott, J; Sin-
nott, TD; Smyth, P; Stafford, J; Stafford, T; Stafford, W; Stokes, T; Synnott, J;
Thorpe, W; Thorpe, W; Treanor, T; Tumbleton, P; Tyrell, P; Walker, J; Walker,
M; Walsh, J; Walter, JJ; Welsh, P; Whelan, J; Whelan, J; White, M; Williams, H;
Wilson, J; Wilson, M; Wilson, R.

197 TO WANDSWORTH ON 9 MAY 1916

The following list of 197 prisoners were removed from Richmond Barracks,
Dublin, on 8 May and lodged in Wandsworth Detention Barracks, London,
on 9 May. This list was issued on 15 May:

Amos, George; Armstrong, James; Barnes, Michael; Barnes, Thomas; Bevan,
Joseph; Boland, William; Boylan, Edward; Boylan, Peter; Bracken, Joseph;
Brady, Joseph; Breen, Christopher; Breen, Miles; Brennan, Matthew; Breslin,
James Francis; Brown, Arthur; Burke, John; Burke, John; Burke, Thomas;
Burke, William; Burke, William; Byrne, John; Byrne, John; Byrne, William;

Carberry, Charles; Carr, Joseph; Carter, James; Cassidy, Patrick; Coghlan, William; Collins, Maurice; Collins, Michael; Condon, Thomas; Connelly, Joseph; Connors, John; Conroy, Edward; Cooley, Patrick; Cornese, PJ; Cullen Alexander; Cummins, Joseph; Cunningham, John; Daly, James; Derham, Joseph; Donoghue, Daniel; Doyle, Henry; Doyle, James; Doyle, Michael; Doyle, Patrick; Duff, Thomas; Duke, Richard; Duke, Thomas; Dunbar, Martin; Dunleary, Christopher; Earley, PJ; Evans, Robert; Fahy, Patrick J; Farrell, Denis; Farrelly, James; Finnegan, Joseph; Flannigan, Thomas; Flynn, Frank; Flynn, John; Fox, Peter; Fuge, Joseph; Fuller, John; Gahan, Joseph; Galvin, James; Gaskin, Thomas; Gaynor, Patrick; Geoghegan, E; Gleeson, Martin; Glynn, John; Golding, Francis; Golding, James; Golding, Thomas; Grogan, James; Halpin, Thomas; Hampton, James; Hanbury, P; Hanlon, Michael; Hannigan, Thomas; Hardiman, Francis; Hart, Henry; Haskin, Michael; Hastings, John; Hogan, Patrick; Hogan, Patrick; Hogan, William; Howley, Peter; Hughes, William; Humphreys, James; Hynch, John; Hynes, Thomas; Kain, Thomas; Kavanagh, JJ; Kavanagh, John Michael; Kavanagh, William; Keenan, Michael; Kelly, Thomas; Kelly, Alderman JJ; Kelly, Joseph; Kelly, Peter; Kenny, Moses; Kent, Matthew; Keogh, Michael; Kilkelly, Michael; Kilkelly, Patrick; Kinsella, Robert; Kirwin, Patrick; Leech, Stephen; Logue, Edward; Lynch, John; Lyons, Charles; Lysham, Christopher; Mannion, John; Mathews, John; Mathews, Thomas; McAlduff, James; McCann, Andrew; McDonagh, J; McDonald, Edward; McElvogue, James; McElvogue, John; McGill, William; McGrane, Thomas; McGuire, James; McGuirk, Patrick; McManus, William; McTaggart, Thomas; Molloy, John; Moran, Christopher; Moroney, John; Mullally, Michael; Murphy, James; Murphy, Matthew; Murphy, Patrick; Murphy, Patrick; Murray, Patrick; Nelson, Thomas; Nicholls, George; Norgrove, Alfred; Nugent, Christopher; O'Brien, James; O'Brien, William; O'Brien, William; O'Byrne, John; O'Connor, Thomas; O'Dwyer, James; O'Grady, Standish; O'Hehir, Michael; O'Leary, Cornelius; O'Leary, Philip; O'Maille, Patrick; O'Neill, John; O'Neill, Peter; O'Reilly, John N; O'Reilly, Kevin; O'Rourke, Michael; Parnell, Matthew; Pedlar, William; Poole, John; Quigley, James; Quinn, James; Quinn, William; Redmond, Joseph; Redmond, Owen; Riley, Thomas; Roche, Thomas; Ronan, Patrick; Ronayne, Michael; Ryan, James; Scallon, Thomas; Sears, William; Sexton, Michael; Sheehan, Patrick; Sherrin, Thomas; Smith, John; Smullen, Patrick; Steinberger, Val; Sweetman, John; Taylor, Christopher; Taylor, Joseph; Taylor, Thomas; Thornton, Michael; Waldron, Richard; Ward, Bernard; Ward, Patrick; Welsh, Thomas; Whelan, James; Whelan, John; Whelan, Patrick; Whelan, Thomas; White, Patrick.

54 TO WANDSWORTH ON 13 MAY 1916

The following prisoners were removed from Richmond Barracks, Dublin, on 12 May and lodged in Wandsworth Detention Barracks, London, on 13 May. This list was issued on 16 May:

Bermingham, Thomas; Burke, Patrick; Cryan, Barty; Cryan, Thomas; Crystal, Hugh; Conway, Andrew; Curtis O'Leary, W; Cole, DL; Derry, Thomas; Duffy, Michael; Daly, Michael; Daly, Patrick; Foley, Thomas; Fagan, Hugh; Fagan, John; Fagan, James; Griffith, Arthur; Gammon, Edward; Gavin, Charles; Gilmartin, Charles; Gilmartin, John; Gilmartin, John; Gilmartin, William; Gardiner, George; Geraghty, Martin; Gavin, John; Gunnigle, Lawrence; Gunnigle, Robert; Hughes, Owen; Heraty, Hubert; Hannon, John; Hannon, Edward; Harrin, Edward; Hickey, Charles; Keane, Manus; Kenny, Patrick S; Logan, John; McDonnell, Francis; McDonough, John; McDonnell, Paul; McGarrigle, Charles; Meehan, Bernard; Malone, James; O'Shea, John P; O'Rourke, Peter; O'Brien, Thomas; Reilly, Michael; Rooney, Patrick; Ruddy, Joseph; Ralph, Thomas; Redmond, Myles; Ring, MJ; Sammol, Edward; Tunny, Patrick; Walsh, Thaddeus.

58 TO STAFFORD ON 13 MAY 1916

The following prisoners were removed from Richmond Barracks, Dublin, on 12 May and lodged in Stafford Detention Barracks, England, on 13 May. This list was issued on 17 May:

Barrett, Christopher; Burke, Patrick; Cahill, Michael; Callinan, Thomas; Caulfield, Charles; Cleary, Joseph; Cleary, Thomas B; Coady, William; Commins, Edward; Commins, Michael; Commins, William; Conniffe, Michael; Costello, Martin; Costello, Michael; Costello, Patrick; Coyle, Martin; Cullinane, John J; Dunleary, Michael; Fahy, Lawrence; Fallon, Michael; Favrell, Michael; Feeney, James; Freaney, Michael; Freaney, William; Galvin, Jeremiah; Gardiner, James; Glynn, Michael; Grealish, Patrick; Henegan, Patrick; Henegan, Peter; Higgins, William; Howley, Michael; Howley, William; Hughes, Patrick; Hynes, Martin; Kane, Michael; Kane, Patrick; Kennedy, Patrick; Kennedy, Martin; Kenny, Patrick; King, John; King, Peter; Lynskey, Patrick; McEvoy, Martin; McKeon, Peter; Monaghan, John; Mulryan, William;

Murphy, John; Murphy, Philip; Newell, Thomas; O'Flaherty, Joseph; O'Leary, Michael; Ryan, John; Silk, Thomas; Sweeny, Peter; Waldron, John; Walsh, Martin; Wilson, Richard.

273 TO WAKEFIELD ON 13 MAY 1916

The following prisoners were removed from Richmond Barracks, Dublin, on 12 May and lodged in Wakefield Detention Barracks, England, on 13 May. This list was issued on Thursday, 13 May:

Atkinson, William; Barry, Denis; Begley, Joseph; Behan, Thomas; Birrell, Lawrence; Blaney, John; Bowen, Bartholomew; Boyce, Lawrence; Brady, James; Brett, P; Brown, Charles; Buckley, James; Buckley, William; Buren, Christopher; Burke, Fintan; Burke, Patrick; Byrne, John; Byrne, Martin; Byrne, Nicholas; Callaghan, John; Carmody, Patrick; Casey, William; Clegg, James; Cogan, Robert; Collins, Edward; Comerford, E; Connors, Michael; Corkerry, Daniel; Cox, Edward J; Cox, JE; Coyne, James; Crowe, Martin; Crowley, John; Crowley, Michael; Crowley, Patrick; Crowley, Tim; Crowley, William; Daly, Francis; Davies, James J; de Loughrey, Lawrence; Deban, Patrick; Deene, Conor; Degan, M; Dempsey, James; Dempsey, Patrick; Denn, W; Desmond, Denis; Dobbyn, Henry; Dobbyn, James; Donnelly, Michael; Donovan, John; Donovan, Peter; Doorley, Edward; Doorley, JJ; Doyle, Charles; Doyle, John; Doyle, Michael; Doyle, William; Driscoll, Thomas; Duffy, Edward J; Duncan, Patrick; Dwyer, Stephen; Evoy, Daniel; Fanning, John; Finegan, John; Fitzgerald, James; Fitzgerald, John; Fitzgerald, Thomas; Foley, Michael; Fortune, Daniel; Franklin, James; Furlong, Richard; Furlong, Thomas; Gallagher, John; Gallon, Patrick; Gibbons, John; Grehan, Patrick; Gribban, Hugh; Grieve, James; Haden, Patrick; Hales, Robert; Hales, William; Hall, Samuel; Hamill, Thomas; Hamilton, Christopher; Hanley, Daniel; Hannigan, James; Hanratty, James; Harrington, Daniel; Hart, Bernard; Hart, John; Hartley, J; Healy, Denis; Heber, John; Hedley, James; Heduvan, Laurence; Hegarty, Daniel; Hegarty, Patrick; Hehoe, Tim; Henderson, Leo; Higgins, Maurice; Hughes, Gilbert; Hunt, Hubert; Hunt, William; Hyde, John; Hyde, Joseph; Hyde, Michael; Hyde, Patrick; Jordan, Daniel; Kavanagh, John; Kealey, Martin; Kealy, Matt; Kearns, John; Keegan, Michael; Keirse, Thomas; Kelly, Daniel; Kelly, James; Kelly, John E; Kelly, John; Kelly, John; Kelly, Robert; Kenny, Christopher; Kenny, Joseph; Kenny, Michael; Kenny, Patrick; Kenny, Patrick; Kent, John; Kerr, Patrick; Kiniry, Martin; Kiniry, Martin; Lalor, James; Lennon, William;

Lynch, John; Lynch, Lawrence; Lynch, Patrick; Lynch, Tim; Lyng, James; MacGough, O; Madigan, James; Marmion, Tim; Martin, Edward; May, Patrick; McAllister, Dan; McCarthy, John; McCarthy, Joseph; McCormack, Michael; McCrann, Alfred; McDermott, Edward; McDonnell, William; McGrath, M; McGrath, T; McGuinness, Francis; McGuirk, Anthony; McInerney, Thomas; McLoughlin, Fred; McMahon, Edward; McQuill, Joseph; McQuillan, Phil; Mooney, Patrick; Mooney, Thomas; Moran, Edward; Moran, Louis; Mullally, Antony; Mullany, John, J; Murphy, D; Murphy, Edward J; Murphy, Francis; Murphy, James; Murphy, Jer; Murphy, John; Murphy, John; Murphy, William; Murray, James; Murray, Peter; Murthagh, Peter; Neary, Thomas; Neill, John; Noctor, John; Noonan, John; Noonan, William; Nowlan, James; O'Breslin, Charles; O'Brien, James; O'Brien, John; O'Brien, John; O'Brien, John; O'Brien, William; O'Brien, William; O'Connell, Christopher; O'Connell, John; O'Connor, James; O'Connor, Patrick; O'Connor, Patrick; O'Connor, Stephen; O'Doherty, Andrew; O'Doherty, Joseph; O'Dwyer, Michael; O'Dwyer, Patrick; O'Halloran, John; O'Halloran, Tim; O'Keeffe, Michael; O'Kelly, Michael; O'Kennedy, John; O'Kennedy, Michael J; O'Kennedy, Philip A; O'Leary, James; O'Leary, John; O'Leary, S; O'Neill, Arthur; O'Neill, J; O'Neill, Michael; O'Shea, Patrick; O'Sullivan, Patrick; O'Toole, W; Parsons, Patrick; Prendergast, James; Purcell, Michael; Quigley, James; Quinn, Thomas; Quinn, George; Rearden, Tim; Reardon, John; Richardson, Joseph; Riordan, Jeremiah; Riordan, Michael; Roche, John; Roche, John; Rodgers, Hugh; Ruttle, SM; Ryan, M; Rynne, William; Savage, Michael; Selby, Joseph; Shane, Robert; Shannon, MJ; Sheehan, Michael; Sheehan, Michael; Shiels, Patrick; Smith, Louis; Smith, Patrick; Smyth, Charles; Southwell, John; Spillane, John; Stephens, W; Stokes, John; Sullivan, Edward; Sunderland, John; Sweeney, Owen; Synnott, Michael; Synnott, Pierce; Thornton, Joseph; Toomey Richard; Toomey, James; Travers, John; Travers, Martin; Tuite, Daniel; Waldron, Edward; Wall, James; Wallace, John W; Walsh, James; Walsh, James; Walsh, Lawrence J; Walsh, Lawrence; Walsh, Redmond; Walshe, Daniel P; Warner, Peter; Wickham, Mark; Wilson, HJC; Windram, SW.

197 TO GLASGOW AND PERTH ON 20 MAY 1916

On Wednesday, 24 May, two lists were issued containing the names of the prisoners who were removed from Dublin on 19 May to Barlinnie Detention

Republican prisoners in Stafford Jail, 1916.

Barracks, Glasgow, and Perth Detention Barracks:

To Perth: Boland, Patrick; Browne, John; Burke, Edward; Burke, Thomas; Burns, Michael; Carroll, James; Coen, James; Coen, Martin; Collohan, Patrick; Collohan, Thomas; Conner, Bryan; Connolly, Thomas; Corbett, Patrick; Corbett, Peter; Corbett, Thomas; Coughlan, Charles; Coy, James; Coy, Michael; Coy, Patrick; Coy, Patrick; Craven, John; Cunniffe, Michael; Cunniffe, Patrick; Cunniffe, Thomas; Currin, James; Delahunty, Michael; Dempsey, Patrick; Donnellan, Patrick; Doyle, Thomas; Duffy, William; Earl, Joseph; Egan, Martin; Egan, Michael; Fahey, John; Fahey, Michael; Fahey, Patrick; Flynn, James; Forde, John; Forde, Michael; Forde, Patrick; Frowley, John; Gardiner, James; Gegan, Michael; Gilligan, Patrick; Grealish, Thomas; Greene, Martin J; Haniffy, James; Haniffy, Michael; Haverty, Richard; Healy, Michael; Hession, Michael; Higgins, Patrick; Hynes, Denis; Hynes, John; Hynes, Michael; Keane, James; Kearns, Daniel; Keating, Joseph; Keating, Michael; Kellahen, James; Kelleper, Daniel; Kellerker, Martin; Kelly, Michael; Kelly, Michael; Kelly, William; Kennedy, Martin; Lawless, John; Lawless, Patrick; Loughery, John; Lyons, William; Maloney, John; Maloney, Thomas; Martin, Patrick; McGigne, Patrick; McGlynn, Martin; McGlynn, Michael; McNamara, Thomas; Melody, Michael; Molloy, Michael; Moloney, John; Moran, Martin; Mullins, Thomas; Naughton, Patrick; Nestor, Michael; O'Brien, Augustus; Roche, Edward; Roughan, Peter; Rudy, HC; Stafford,

Mat; Sweeney, Patrick; Walsh, Patrick; Walsh, Walter; Ward, James; White, Joseph; White, Patrick.

To Glasgow: Benn, W; Berry, John; Blake, Michael; Brennan, M; Brennan, M; Burke, S; Burke, William; Burns, James; Burns, Michael; Burns, Patrick; Casserly, Martin; Clifford, Peter; Connolly, John; Connolly, John; Connolly, Robert; Connor, James; Cooney, Dominick; Corteen, Joseph; Cullinan, John; Cunniff, Thomas; Cunningham, P; Dalton, LJ; Daly, Patrick; Deely, Jeremiah; Drohan, F; Egan, J; Fahy, John; Fahy, Michael; Fallon, Bernard; Flanagan, Patrick; Foley, Edward; Forde, P; Forde, William; Garvey, Law; Glynn, James; Golding, Patrick; Greany, Hugh; Halpin, Thomas; Hassett, Daniel; Haverty, James; Hawkins, Thomas; Healy, Patrick; Heffernan, J; Hilton, Thomas; Hughes, Patrick; Hynes, William; Ivers, Thomas; Joyce, Michael; Joyce, P; Keane, D; Keane, Martin; Kearney, Francis; Kelly, James; Kelly, James; Kelly, Patrick; Kelly, Thomas; Kelly, William; Kennedy, John; Kennedy, Patrick; Kilkelly, P; Mackey, D; Maloney, PJ; McGuire, John; McKenna, John; Mitchell, John; Moloney, Martin; Moore James; Moran, B; Morin, John; Morris, M; Morrissey, Gilbert; Morrissey, J; Morrissey, Patrick; Morrissey, Richard; Mullen; Murphy, John; Murphy, Martin; Murphy, Thomas; Nelly, JJ; Newell, Martin; Noone, James; Noone, Patrick; O'Connor, Matthew; O'Hanlon, P; O'Kennedy, TJ; O'Reilly; Piggett, P; Quinn, John; Rogers, TF; Rooney, John; Rooney, Martin; Ryan, J; Ryan, WE; Stephenson, T; Tally, Thomas; Toole, Martin; Trayers, M; Walsh, D; Walsh, Patrick.

40 TO WOKING ON 20 MAY 1916

It was announced on Thursday, 25 May, that these prisoners were moved from Richmond Barracks, Dublin, on May 19 and lodged in Woking Detention Barracks, England, on the following day:

Barrett, Pat; Burke, Patrick; Burke, Peter; Cleary, James; Cleary, Thomas; Connolly, Patrick; Cullen, James Joseph; Cullen, James; Daley, John; Devereux, Eugene; Doherty, John; Dolan, James N; Dooley, John; Dooley, Michael; Doyle, Patrick; Dwyer, Peter; Egan, Thomas; Fahy, Thomas; Fenlon, William; Flanagan, James; Gardiner, John; Gilgan, Bryan; Gilgan, Thomas; Henehan, Patrick J; Hynes, Martin; Hynes, Patrick; Kenny, John; Larden, James; Lawless, Peter; Mahon, Peter; Murphy, James; Murphy, Michael; O'Connor, R; O'Loughlin, James; O'Loughlin, Thomas; Rooney, Joseph; Rossiter, Edward; Wafer, John; Walsh, Michael; Young, Joe.

59 TO LEWES ON 20 MAY 1916

The following prisoners were removed from Richmond Barracks on 19 May and lodged in Lewes Detention Barracks the following day:
Abernatty, Henry; Burke, Martin; Byrne, Alphonsus; Cassidy, John; Coleman, JJ; Concannon, Patrick; Connolly, Thomas; Culligan, Bernard; Cummins, Patrick; Cunniffe, James; Daly, Patrick; Daly, Thomas; Darcy, James; Darcy, John; Davis, John; Doherty, Daniel; Doyle, Michael; Flannery, BJ; Fox, John; Goen, John; Grealy, Peter; Hyland, Matthew; Jennings, James; Kavanagh, James; Kelly, Joe; Kelly, WJ; Kyne, Michael; Lennon, Philip; Loughran, WJ; Martin, Thomas; McCormick, Thomas; McGrath, Patrick; McKenna, B; Molloy, John; Morley, JF; Murphy, Arthur; Murphy, F; Murphy, Michael; Neeson, John; Nolan, Thomas; O'Byrne, Thomas; O'Brien, James; O'Brien, John; O'Connor, Denis; O'Donnell, A; O'Gara, Bartley; O'Hara, TF; O'Neill, James; O'Reilly, Pat; Quill, Michael; Raul, Laurence; Ryan, Patrick J; Sargeant, Philip; Sinnott, Patrick; Tobin, Patrick; Trimble, Joseph; Wade, Michael; Ward, Thomas; Watkins, Thomas.

100 TO WAKEFIELD ON 2 JUNE 1916

On Saturday, 3 June, it was announced that these prisoners had been removed from Richmond Barracks, Dublin, on 1 June and lodged in Wakefield Detention Barracks, England, on the following day:
Ahern, Con; Ahern, M; Barrett, Edward; Brennan, John; Burke, Thomas; Burns, Peter; Butterly, John; Collins, David; Conway, Michael; Cornan, John; Cotton, AW; Curtin, Thomas; De Loughey, Peter; Duggan, William; Fahey, John J; Fahey, John; Fahey, Patrick; Fahey, Peter; Fahy, John; Fergus, Tim; Flaherty, M; Flannery, Michael; Fleming, George; Fleming, Patrick; Fury, Michael; Fury, Stephen; Gantley, Patrick; Geraghty, George; Gill, Joseph; Glynn, James; Grealish, John; Grealish, Pat; Gregan, Edward; Gregan, James; Griffing, M; Halloran, Denis; Hanley, John; Hanniffy, Martin; Hanrahan, Edward; Harris, MJ; Harris, TF; Harte, Pat; Haskins, Robert; Henlon, David; Heron, Sam; Higgins, James; Hourihane, John; Howley, Patrick; Hurley, John; Hynes, Thomas; Jordan, Pat; Keane, Pat; Kelly, James; Kelly, T; Kelly, Thomas; Kelly, Thomas; King, Pat; Langley, WT; Layng, Joseph; Leahy, M; Lynch, M; MacSwiney, TJ; Mahon, Pat; Mahon, Thomas; Malinn, Peter; Malone, James; Manning, Daniel; Manning, Denis; McBride, Joseph; McKeever, Andrew; Meade, JW; Meade, WJ; Mulroyan, Bart; Mulroyan, John; Mulroyan, William;

Murphy, J; Murphy, Michael; Murray, James; Newell, James; Newell, William; O'Dea, John; O'Driscoll, J; O'Dwyer, Edward; O'Hourihan, Peter; O'Leary, Joseph; O'Loughlin, T; O'Madden, PL; O'Mahony, C; O'Mahony, John; O'Shea, P; O'Shea, T; O'Sullivan, M; Rickard, James; Ruane, Michael; Scullen, Patrick; Tomkins, Patrick; Tracey, M; Tracey, T.

49 TO WANDSWORTH ON 2 JUNE 1916

On Saturday, 3 June, it was announced that the following prisoners had been removed from Richmond Barracks, Dublin, on 1 June and lodged in Wandsworth Detention Barracks, England, on the following day:

Bindon, John; Byrne, Joseph; Casserly, Peter; Collins, J; Cuffe, Thomas; Cullaghan, Unknown; De Bourca, P; Donnelly, Patrick; Donoghue, D; Feeney, Patrick; Ferguson, Michael; Fitzgerald, R; Foley, J; Hanlon, James; Hennessy, W; Horgan, William; Larkin, John; Lyons, John; Maguire, Bernard; Malone, Thomas; Martin, Ambrose; McArten, B; McCrory, Hugh; Minahan, James; Mullen, D; Murphy, M; Newell, Edward; Newell, Michael; Neyland, Thomas; Nogan, J; Nolan, Bartholomew; O'Brien, Patrick; O'Connell, J; O'Connor, B; O'Dea, Michael; O'Donovan, Thomas; O'Hehir, Hugh; O'Keeffe, Pat; O'Kelly, John T; O'Leary, J; O'Neill, John; O'Neill, John; O'Sullivan, S; Raffley, Michael; Scullen, JJ; Shannon, Charles; Smyth, Michael; Ward, P.

50 TO KNUTSFORD ON 2 JUNE 1916

On Saturday, 3 June, it was announced that the following prisoners had been removed from Richmond Barracks, Dublin, on 1 June and lodged in Knutsford Detention Barracks, England, on the following day:

Bindon, Thomas; Birrell, PT; Booth, Frank; Connell, John; Fallon, Bernard; Foran, T; Hessin, Michael; Johnson, James; Keane, John; Keigheny, M; Kelly, William; Kilkelly, John; Lally, Frank; Larkin, Joseph; Lynch, Michael; Mannion, Michael; Mason, Thomas; McCann, Pierce; McCullough, Denis; McDowell, Charles; McInery, Thomas; McNally, Peter; Merriman, Thomas; Mitchell, Pat; Monaghan, Pat; Neasly, Frank; Nolan, James; O'Dea, John; O'Neill, Felix; Quirke, Martin; Ronan, Pat; Rourke, James; Ryder, Michael; Shaughnessy, Michael; Silver, Patrick; Smith, James; Stanley, JM; Stanton, Michael; Tanner, William; Thompson, Martin; Thompson, Martin; Thompson, William; Wall, Martin; Walsh, Michael; Walsh, Michael; Walsh, Thomas; Ward, Joseph; Wilson, Thos.

41 TO KNUTSFORD ON 7 JUNE 1916

On Thursday, 15 June, it was announced that the following prisoners were removed from Richmond Barracks, Dublin, on 6 June and lodged in Knutsford Detention Barracks, England, on the following day:

Barrett, James; Brennan, James; Byrne, Joseph; Cleary, John; Connell, Thomas; Connolly, Alex; Connolly, Joseph; Connors, Joseph; Daly, Thomas; Duggan, Thomas; Dundon, Edward; Dunne, Arthur; Fury, Thomas; Healy, FF; Howlett, John; Kennedy, Luke; Lalor, Patrick; McCarthy, Daniel; McLinn, Joseph; Milroy, John; Monaghan, Philip; Morris, William; Morrissey, Martin; Murphy, Con; Murphy, Eugene; Murphy, NJ; O'Brien, William; O'Connor, MJ; O'Keefe, Eugene; O'Reilly, Paul; Redmond, Lawrence; Roughan, Bryan; Ryan, John; Sexton, Timothy; Silver, Michael; Spillane, Michael; Sullivan, Con; Supple, Patrick; Wall, John; Walsh, John; Walsh, Michael.

25 TO KNUTSFORD ON 16 JUNE 1916

On Wednesday, 21 June, it was announced that the following prisoners, who were removed from Richmond Barracks, Dublin, on 15 June were lodged in Knutsford Detention Barracks, England, on the following day:

Costello, Martin; Donoghue, Con; Donoghue, Patrick; Fahy, Patrick; Finlay, John; Freaney, Michael; Hales, John; Halpin, William Robert; Halpin, William Thomas; Hanratty, James; Hearne, Edward; Herty, Thomas; Jourdan, Stephen Joseph; Kelly, John; Kelly, Michael; Larkin, Stephen; McCrave, Thomas; Murphy, Richard; Nielan, Martin; Nolan, Patrick Joseph; O'Dea, Patrick Francis; O'Dea, Thomas; Reilly, Francis; Stokes, Thomas Joseph; Thornton, Joseph.

211 DETAINED AT RICHMOND BARRACKS

The following official list of the persons confined at Richmond Barracks was issued on Saturday, 20 May 1916:

Allen, James; Allen, Thomas; Allen, William; Balfe, Robert; Biggs, Patrick; Bindon, Thomas; Birrell, PJ; Booth, Frank; Bracken, Peter; Brennan, F; Brennan, JM; Brennan, John; Brennan, MJ; Brennan, Patrick; Brennan, Thomas; Broderick, J; Burke, James; Burke, Michael; Burke, TF; Burke, Thomas; Butterly, John; Butterly, Nicholas; Byrne, Joseph; Byrne, Peter; Byrne, Thomas; Campbell, J; Carr, Martin; Casserly, Patrick; Cassidy, Michael; Chardyce, Bertie; Clarke, James; Cleary, TV; Coen, Michael; Collins, John; Connolly, Alex; Connolly, Joseph; Connor, Thomas; Cooney, John; Corbett, Dominick;

Corbett, John; Costello, Michael; Cotton, AW; Cowley, John; Cuffe, Thomas; Cullen, C; Cullen, James; Cusack, Paul; Daffy, Pat; Daly, Matt; De Bourca, P; De Loughrey, Peter; Delaney, John; Dillon, Hubert; Dixon, Henry; Donoghue, Peter; Dorris, Patrick Joseph; Duggan, Thomas; Duggan, Thomas; Dundon, Edward; Dunlevy, Patrick; Elliott, JJ; Fahey, James; Fahey, Martin; Fahey, Michael; Fallon, Michael; Fallow, Bernard; Faran, T; Feeney, Patrick; ffrench-Mullen, Douglas; Figgis, Darrell; Fitzgerald, T; Fogan, Michael; Fogan, Thomas; Gaffney, Joseph; Garland, P; Gerathy, George; Gill, Joseph; Graham, Joseph; Grealish, John; Grealish, Patrick; Gregan, James; Grelish, Bernard; Hanley, Edward; Harris, FF; Harris, M.J; Harte, Patrick; Harte, William; Haskin, Robert; Heely, FJ; Heron, Sam; Herty, Thomas; Higgins, James; Hogan, Thomas; Holland, Patrick; Hughes, Charles; Hurley, John; Hynes, Thomas; Inskipp, Peter; Johnston, J; Jordan, Patrick; Kavanagh, John; Keene, Patrick; Kelly, James; Kelly, T; Kelly, Thomas; Kennedy, Luke; King, Patrick; Kirwin, W; Lally, Michael; Larkin, J; Larkin, J; Layng, James; Lehey, Denis; Lehey, Michael; Loughley, W; Lynch, M; Lyon, John; Mahon, Patrick; Mahon, Patrick; Mahoney, Abel; Malin, Joseph; Malone, James; Malone, Thomas; Manning, Patrick; Maron, John; McBride, Joseph; McCarten, B; McCarthy, JJ; McCrory, Hugh; McCullough, Denis; McDowell, Charles; McGuire, Bernard; McLaughlin, Patrick; McNally, Henry; Melinn, Peter; Mellowes, H; Milroy, John; Minahan, Joseph; Molone, Thomas; Monaghan, Phil; Mooney, Joseph; Morris, Joe; Morrissey, Patrick; Mulroy, Bartholomew; Mulroy, John; Mulroyan, William; Murphy, M; Murray, Frank; Murray, Joseph; Neasey, Frank; Newell, Ed; Newell, Jas; Newell, Michael; Newell, William; Nolan, Bartholomew; O'Donovan, Thomas; O'Keefe, Patrick; O'Reilly, Paul; O'Brien, Patrick; O'Brien, W; O'Connell, J; O'Connor, B; O'Connor, John; O'Connor, NJ; O'Dea, J; O'Donnell, Philip; O'Dwyer, Ed; O'Hehir, Hugh; O'Hourihane, Peter; O'Kelly, TG; O'Leary, Patrick; O'Loughlin, T; O'Madden, PL; O'Mahoney, John; O'Neill, Felix; O'Neill, JJ; O'Neill, John; O'Neill, John; O'Neill, John; O'Reilly, John; O'Rourke, B; O'Sullivan, G; Parker, Thomas; Purcell, Jer; Quigley, James; Quinn, Chas; Raffly, Michael; Ruane, Martin; Ruane, Michael; Ryan, Michael; Ryan, Thomas; Sally, James; Scullen, JJ; Scullen, Patrick; Shannon, Charles; Sheridan, F; Smith, James; Smythe, Michael; Somerly, Thomas; Stack, Austin; Stanley, Joseph M; Sweeney, Terence; Tracey, I; Treacy, Michael; Wall, John; Walsh, Thomas; Ward, P; Warwick, James; Weston, Thomas; Whelan, James; Wilson, Thomas.

Section Twelve: 1916 around Ireland

Diarmuid Lynch, who was on the Supreme Council of the IRB, wrote that the initial plans for the Rising around the country were as follows: 'Cork was to hold the County to the south and west of the Bogger-agh Mountains – left flank contacting the Kerry Brigade which was to extend eastwards from Tralee; Limerick was to contact Kerry on the south, Clare and Galway to the north; Limerick, Clare and Galway were to hold the line of the Shannon to Athlone.'[1]

Lynch also noted: 'Thus, these provincial Brigades would be in occupation of pre-selected positions on Easter Sunday ... From the German shipload of arms and ammunition expected to arrive at Tralee Bay, the scanty military equipment of the Kerry Volunteers on the spot was to be augmented; trains and other transport were to be commandeered to ensure distribution throughout the country.'[2]

The failure of the arms to land due to the capture of the *Aud*, the arrest of Roger Casement, and the subsequent countermanding order of Eoin MacNeill, resulted in indecisiveness in the country. Dublin would rise, mainly due to the drive of the leaders in the city but also because it was easier to remobilise there, since messages from the IRB Military Council could physically reach the Dublin Battalions before places further afield.

Also, there was a decent supply of Howth Mausers in Dublin, but other parts of the country were relying heavily on the expected ship-ment of arms on the *Aud*. Their orders centred around the distribution of these arms. When it transpired that there were no guns to land, their orders seemed irrelevant; lacking a plan B, they simply demobilised.

ASHBOURNE, CO. MEATH

The Fifth Battalion, or Fingal Volunteers, under Thomas Ashe numbered about sixty. Ashe appointed Richard Mulcahy as his second-in-command, and the Fingal Quartermaster was Frank Lawless. Orders came from Connolly to send some Volunteers (twenty) to the GPO; the remainder should attack RIC barracks and disrupt the railways. Successful attacks on the rail and telegraph lines in Donabate and Swords also saw reinforcements from those areas joining the main group. A number of raids were carried out on RIC stations and barracks, culminating in the decision to wreck the railway lines of the Midland Great Western Railway near Batterstown.

The Volunteers were split into four sections of about a dozen; three groups headed towards the railway on Friday, 28 April. Ashe decided it would be worth making an attempt on Ashbourne RIC barracks, as it was occupied and was in their line of retreat from Batterstown.

Half an hour into the attack on the barracks, the police offered a white flag after a home-made bomb was thrown by a Volunteer. Within minutes, the flag was withdrawn as twenty-four cars laden with RIC arrived on the scene. Firing from Volunteers made the police stop short of the barracks and abandon their cars. The Volunteers were heavily outnumbered and had little ammunition, but a firefight ensued and lasted for over four hours. Eleven police surrendered to two Volunteers. A District Inspector called Harry Smyth killed Frank Crennigan but was himself shot dead by Frank Lawless.

Reinforced by the arrival of the fourth section, the Volunteers made a charge and the police, fifteen of whom were wounded, decided to surrender. Eight RIC lay dead, and many were injured. When word came from Pearse to surrender, the Fingal Volunteers were taken to Richmond Barracks. Ashe was sentenced to death, but this was commuted to life in prison. He died after being force-fed during a hunger strike in Mountjoy Jail in September 1917.

ENNISCORTHY, CO. WEXFORD

Confusion as to whether the Rising was cancelled or not resulted in a lack of action in Wexford until Wednesday of Easter Week. The fear was that adjoining counties were not in action, so plans to link up would be impossible. However, on Wednesday a message arrived from James Connolly via Vice-Commandant PP Galligan ordering the Volunteers of Enniscorthy to hold the railway line from Rosslare to prevent British reinforcements from arriving in Dublin.

The following morning, Thursday, the Enniscorthy Volunteers, Fianna and Cumann na mBan, numbering hundreds, decided to seize the town of Enniscorthy and made their headquarters in the Athenaeum in Castle Street under Commandant Robert Brennan. There was sporadic firing in the town, but the RIC were essentially confined to barracks. PP Galligan set up an outpost at Ferns with fifty men who occupied the vacated RIC Barracks. On Saturday, a deputation of businessmen and a priest tried to encourage the garrison to surrender. Volunteer Second Lieutenant Seamus Doyle and Seán Etchingham went to Dublin under British protection. They met Pearse at Arbour Hill, and he told them to surrender. The Enniscorthy surrender document was signed by Robert Brennan, Seamus Doyle, Seán Etchingham, Micheál de Lacy and RF King.

CASTLEBELLINGHAM, CO. LOUTH

Desmond Ryan wrote about the part Louth played in his book on the Rising: 'On Easter Monday County Louth Volunteers mobilized and entered the North Dublin area. One section marched towards Dundalk through Castlebellingham where some RIC men were arrested; one constable was shot, apparently accidentally, and at the same time a British officer was severely wounded when cars on the main road were stopped and seized. Some of the Louth Volunteers then proceeded to Dublin, and took part in the GPO fighting.'[3]

CO. LAOIS

Captain PJ Ramsbottom of the Portlaoise Irish Volunteers stated that 'the duties assigned to our Company were the demolition in our area of the railway lines from Waterford to Dublin with the object of holding up and delaying the advance of enemy troops that might be sent to Dublin that way from Britain via Rosslare or Waterford. After carrying out those duties we were to proceed to the Scollop Gap near Borris, County Carlow, where we would link up with other forces and receive further orders.' [4]

Ramsbottom, Laurence Brady, Thomas Brady, John Muldowney, Patrick Muldowney, Michael Sheridan and Colum Holohan went to Colt Wood on Easter Sunday at 6.50pm and commenced sawing down telegraph poles and pulling up railway lines. At 10pm they observed a railway employee inspecting the situation with a lamp. He was ordered to halt but didn't, so Ramsbottom fired over his head – the very first shots of the Easter Rising.

Meanwhile Officer Commanding Eamon Fleming, Michael Gray and Michael Walsh made their way to Athy, cut down a telegraph pole and laid it across the railway tracks. A disappointing turnout and a lack of decent tools meant they could do little else.

The next day, five RIC men and three railwaymen on board a train were lucky to escape with their lives when it was derailed by the work the Laois Volunteers had carried out at Colt Wood. Later on the Great Southern and Western Railway applied for compensation for the destruction of 60 yards of railway line, twelve 30-foot rails, 66 sleepers, 208 bolts and one locomotive engine. [5]

CO. GALWAY

Liam Mellows, freshly escaped from house arrest in England, led the Galway Irish Volunteers. Larry Lardiner was Brigade Commandant; Alf Monaghan was Volunteer Organiser; Eamonn Corbett was Vice-Commandant;

Matty Nieland was Adjutant and Sean Broderick was Quartermaster. Having stood down after receiving MacNeill's countermanding order, Galway rose instead on the evening of Easter Monday. Headquarters were established in Killeeneen, near Craughwell, and around five hundred Volunteers and Cumann na mBan were mustered.

Alf Monaghan (brother of Charlie Monaghan, drowned at Ballykissane) recalled that on 'Tuesday morning several RIC barracks were attacked, including Gort and Oranmore barracks. The police succeeded in escaping from Gort, but Oranmore was defended until reinforcements arrived from Galway. Many RIC men were made prisoners. Liam Mellows himself covered the retirement of the Volunteers from Oranmore, he scattered the reinforcements from Galway, and it is said that eleven RIC men were wounded.' [6]

They then went to Athenry and linked up with more Volunteers. They encamped at the Model Farm and occupied the town hall for a while. It is often said that the HMS *Gloucester* in Galway Bay succeeded in scattering the Volunteers. However, Alf Monaghan maintained that not one shell landed within five miles of them.

Meanwhile on Wednesday, at Carnmore Cross, a large convoy of police and soldiers were seen driving towards the Castlegar Volunteers. Captain Brian Molloy told them to take cover behind some walls. They were fired upon and the police approached their position. Constable Whelan was pushed by District Inspector Herd up on top of the wall. Whelan shouted, 'Surrender, boys, I know ye all.' He was shot dead. Michael Newell recalled that the 'enemy then made an attempt to outflank our position but were beaten back'.[7] The Castlegar Volunteers then made their way to Athenry and joined Mellows at the Model Farm.

On Wednesday Mellows and his troops marched to Moyode Castle, a couple of miles south of Athenry. That night a council of war was held at Moyode after reports came in of a huge British presence in the area, and about two hundred Volunteers went home. On Friday, hearing that nine hundred British soldiers were in the area, Mellows sent many of the married men home. The decision was made to retreat, and the column left Athenry with the intention of heading for Co. Clare. At Limepark, a priest called Fr. Thomas Fahy informed Mellows that Dublin was in flames, that the country had not risen, and that hundreds of British were looking for the (now dwindling) Galway Volunteers. After a long debate at Tulira Castle, with Mellows and Monaghan arguing against it, the majority of Volunteer officers decided to disband. The last three to disband, Alf Monaghan, Frank Hynes and Liam Mellows, spent many months on the run.[8]

Galway is a fine example of how the loss of the weapons from the *Aud* affected the Rising. Alf Monaghan said the Volunteers expected as many as 3,000 rifles to be delivered, and that there would have been a man for each one. 'Over 500 men assembled at the Model Farm, but a great part of them had no firearms of any sort. In fact, there were only 35 rifles, and 350 shotguns, all told.'[9]

CO. LIMERICK

Despite the large number of Volunteers willing to participate on Easter Sunday, the cancellation of the Rising by Eoin MacNeill was taken as the final order by Michael Colivet and other officers in Limerick. On Easter Monday at 1.30pm, Agnes and Laura Daly delivered a message to Colivet that read, 'Dublin Brigade goes into action today. Carry out your orders.' Colivet called a meeting of his Volunteer officers. They decided that, as the orders relating to Limerick were based upon the arrival of arms from the *Aud*, it was now impossible to carry them out. Aside from the lack of arms, the British Army had taken complete charge of Limerick very quickly. On Tuesday, 25 April, when word again came that Dublin was 'out', Colivet called another meeting of Volunteer staff. It was decided by a majority of ten to six that nothing could be done. On 5 May 1916, the Limerick Volunteers surrendered their arms to the mayor in the town hall; he in turn gave them to the British military who were present.

CO. KERRY

Plans for Kerry began to go wrong with the arrival of the *Aud* before the Kerry Volunteers expected it. Then there was the arrest of Roger Casement on Good Friday, followed by the arrest of Commandant Austin Stack of the Kerry Volunteers when he voluntarily went to Tralee RIC Barracks.

Robert Monteith, who had arrived on the *U-19* with Casement, had made contact with Stack and told him that Casement was trying to stop the Rising from going ahead. After Stack's arrest, Monteith told the Volunteer Vice-Commandant, PJ Cahill, that he should take charge. Cahill told Monteith that he would make a better Commandant. Monteith then arranged a meeting of Kerry Volunteer officers, where he was informed that Stack was the only one who knew what the plans for the Kerry Volunteers were. The others had just a general idea that they were to unload weapons from the arms ship, seize the railway and dispatch arms to Limerick and Galway.

On Sunday, about 320 Volunteers mustered at Tralee. Patrick Whelan arrived from Limerick with MacNeill's countermanding order, and Monteith decided to hand control of the Volunteers back to Cahill and get out of Tralee. He went on the run for months and eventually made it to the US.

CO. CORK

Just over 1,100 Irish Volunteers were mustered throughout Cork on Easter Sunday. Having received the countermanding order from Eoin MacNeill, the Commandant in Cork, Tomás Mac Curtain, and his second, Terence MacSwiney, set out for the Cork-Kerry border to inform Volunteers to stand down.[10]

On Easter Monday they were still out of the city when Marie Perolz arrived at about 12.30pm with a message from Pearse, written into the flyleaf of a small pocket diary: 'We go into action today. P.H.P.' The Brigade

Commandants did not return to town until 8pm that night. Some confusion arose over the fact that Pearse had initialled the order as opposed to signing it. Also, their orders were to meet the Kerry Volunteers and distribute the weapons from the *Aud*, just as in Limerick. There seemed little point in the enterprise as the ship had been sunk, and therefore the Cork Brigade did not come out.

FERMOY, CO. CORK

When news of the Rising in Dublin reached the Kent brothers at their home in Bawnard House, Castlelyons, they waited in some neighbouring houses for orders to mobilise.[11] By Tuesday, 2 May, four of the brothers – Thomas, William, Richard and David – returned to Bawnard House. At dawn, the police came with orders to arrest the whole family. They surrounded the house and for the next three hours, a battle ensued. The Kents had only three shotguns and one rifle, and they eventually ran out of ammunition. One of the brothers, David, was wounded, and Head-Constable William Rowe was killed.

In the confusion of the Kents' surrender, the athletic Richard – who had suffered some mental health problems in his past – made a dash for the woods. He was killed in a fusillade of RIC rifle fire. The constables were enraged and threw William and Thomas against a wall. They would have shot them but for the intervention of a military officer. On 4 May William and Thomas were court-martialed. William was acquitted, but Thomas was convicted and sentenced to death. He was executed in Cork Detention Barracks on 9 May 1916.

CO. TIPPERARY

In May 1916, the *Police Gazette, Hue and Cry* carried a description of Volunteer Michael O'Callaghan of Tipperary, who was 'armed and highly dangerous; supposedly mentally deranged'. O'Callaghan, it seems, had been harassed in Tipperary town by a hostile, pro-British crowd who were against the Volunteers. Fearing for his safety, O'Callaghan shot into the crowd and wounded one, Patrick Ryan. On Wednesday, 28 April, the RIC entered a house in Monour, Galbally, where they found O'Callaghan. He drew his revolver; Sergeant Thomas O'Rourke was shot in the stomach and died the following day. Constable John Hurley died at the scene from multiple bullet wounds.[12] O'Callaghan went on the run for months, until he eventually escaped to the US.

CO. TYRONE AND BELFAST

Denis McCullough, President of the Supreme Council of the IRB, was central to the Belfast Volunteers not engaging the British in 1916. A few days before Easter, McCullough gave a large sum of money to Archie Heron, who, by disguising his political allegiance, bought a great deal of military equipment in the Ulster Volunteers' Stores, a shop that sold military equipment to the UVF. The equipment was distributed to 132 Irish Volunteers at their HQ on the Falls Road. Each Volunteer was also given the money for a single train ticket to Dungannon so they could join forces with the Tyrone Volunteers.

They mobilised on Saturday, 22 April, and made their way to Dungannon. According to McCullough, he received orders from Pearse and Connolly that they should all head for Galway and join up with Liam Mellows. McCullough went to visit Pat McCartan, Commandant of the Tyrone Volunteers, and a number of other Volunteer officers at McCartan's home near Carrickmore. They refused to leave Tyrone and insisted that they should stay and fight in their territory.

When the Belfast Volunteers and Cumann na mBan reached Dungannon, they were billeted in the Parochial Hall in Coalisland, four miles away. McCartan drove to Dublin to meet Tom Clarke, who reinforced the order that the Tyrone and Belfast Volunteers should not fire a shot in their area but should proceed to Galway. When McCartan returned to Coalisland, McCullough decided that 'the Tyrone men were not prepared to carry out any orders or to leave their own county and that there was no possibility, or useful purpose, to be served by the Belfast's men's attempting, alone, to march that distance [to Galway] so I took the only course open to me. I ordered the Belfast men and some Cumann na mBan to return to Belfast.'

William Kelly, who was with the Dungannon Volunteers mustered at Donaghmore, recalled that 'Denis McCullough and Herbert Moore Pim arrived by car. McCullough informed us that the Rising was called off by Eoin MacNeill. The news which appeared in the morning papers had not then reached us.'[13] Further news delivered by a messenger from Dundalk confirmed this, and most of the Tyrone Volunteers disbanded.

John Shields, however, recalled engaging in a small piece of action. 'On Thursday night of Easter Week I took some of my Company into Dungannon and joined up with three men of the Dungannon Companies. We raided St. Patrick's Hall, Dungannon, the H.Q. of the National Volunteers, and seized about 30 old Italian rifles belonging to the National Volunteers.'[14]

Six of the Belfast Cumann na mBan women who were in Coalisland – Nora and Ina Connolly, Kathleen Murphy, Eilis Allen and the two Corr sisters, Elizabeth and Nell – having received some wind of Mac-Neill's countermanding order, got the midnight train to Dublin. They arrived in the early hours of Sunday and made their way to Liberty Hall. Nora assured her father, James Connolly, that the Belfast Volunteers and Tyrone Brigade were all ready for action. Later the women got the train back to Tyrone and made contact with Pat McCartan, but he felt that it was futile to do anything once the Volunteers had demobilised.

Section Thirteen: Statements & Last Letters of the Signatories

PATRICK PEARSE'S LETTERS TO HIS MOTHER

Arbour Hill Barracks, Dublin.
1st May 1916.
My dear Mother,
You will I know have been longing to hear from me. I do not know how much you have heard since the last note I sent you from the G.P.O.

On Friday evening the Post Office was set on fire and we had to abandon it. We dashed into Moore Street and remained in the houses in Moore St. on Saturday evening. We then found that we were surrounded by troops and that we had practically no food.

We decided in order to prevent further slaughter of the civilian population and in the hope of saving the lives of our followers, to ask the General Commanding the British Forces to discuss terms. He replied that he would receive me only if I surrendered unconditionally and this I did.

I was taken to the Headquarters of the British Command in Ireland and there I wrote and signed an order to our men to lay down their arms.

All this I did in accordance with the decision of our Provisional Government who were with us in Moore St. My own opinion was in favour of one more desperate sally before opening negotiations, but I yielded to the majority, and I think now that the majority was right, as the sally would have resulted only in losing the lives of perhaps 50 or 100 of our men, and we should have had to surrender in the long run as we were without food.

I was brought in here on Saturday evening and later all the men with us in Moore St. were brought here. Those in the other parts of the City have, I understand, been taken to other barracks and prisons.

All here are safe and well. Willie and all the St. Enda's boys are here. I have not seen them since Saturday, but I believe they are all well and that they are not now in any danger.

Our hope and belief is that the Government will spare the lives of all our followers, but we do not expect that they will spare the lives of the leaders. We are ready to die and we shall die cheerfully and proudly. Personally I do not hope or even desire to live, but I do hope and desire and believe that the lives of all our followers will be saved including the lives dear to you and me (my own excepted) and this will be a great consolation to me when dying.

You must not grieve for all this. We have preserved Ireland's honour and our own. Our deeds of last week are the most splendid in Ireland's history. People will say hard things of us now, but we shall be remembered by posterity and blessed by unborn generations. You too will be blessed because you were my mother.

If you feel you would like to see me, I think you will be allowed to visit me by applying to the Headquarters, Irish Command, near the Park. I shall I hope have another opportunity of writing to you.

Love to W.W., M.B., Miss Byrne, . . . and your own dear self.

P.

P.S. I understand that the German expedition which I was counting on actually set sail but was defeated by the British.

Kilmainham Prison, Dublin. 3 May, 1916.
Mrs. Pearse,
St. Enda's College, Rathfarnham;
or Cullenswood House, Oakley Road, Ranelagh.
My Dearest Mother,
I have been hoping up to now that it would be possible to see you again,

but it does not seem possible. Goodbye, dear, dear Mother. Through you I say good-bye to Wow Wow, M.B., Willie, Miss Byrne, Mícheál, Cousin Maggie, and every one at St. Enda's. I hope and believe that Willie and the St. Enda boys will be safe.

I have written two papers about financial affairs and one about my books, which I want you to get. With them are a few poems which I want added to the poems of mine in MS in the large bookcase. You asked me to write a little poem which would seem to be said by you about me. I have written it, and one copy is in Arbour Hill barracks with the other papers and Father Aloysius is taking charge of another copy of it.

I have just received Holy Communion. I am happy except for the great grief of parting from you. This is the death I should have asked for if God had given me the choice of all deaths – to die a soldier's death for Ireland and for freedom.

We have done right. People will say hard things of us now, but later on they will praise us. Do not grieve for all this, but think of it as a sacrifice which God asked of me and of you.

Good-bye again, dear, dear Mother. May God bless you for your great love for me and for your great faith, and may He remember all that you have so bravely suffered. I hope soon to see Papa, and in a little while we shall all be together again.

Wow-Wow, Willie, Mary Brigid, and Mother, goodbye. I have not words to tell my love of you and how my heart yearns to you all. I will call to you in my heart at the last moment.

Your son, Pat

LAST STATEMENT OF JAMES CONNOLLY

To the Field General Court Martial, held at Dublin Castle, on May 9th, 1916:
I do not wish to make any defence except against charges of wanton cruelty to prisoners. These trifling allegations that have been made, if they record facts that really happened deal only with the almost unavoidable incidents of a hurried uprising, and overthrowing of long established authorities, and no where show evidence of a set purpose to wantonly injure unarmed prisoners.

We went out to break the connection between this country and the British Empire and to establish an Irish Republic. We believe that the call we thus issued to the people of Ireland was a nobler call in a holier cause than any call issued to them during this war, having any connection with the war.

We succeeded in proving that Irishmen are ready to die endeavouring to win for Ireland their national rights which the British Government has been asking them to die to win for Belgium. As long as that remains the case, the cause of Irish freedom is safe. Believing that the British Government has no right in Ireland, never had any right in Ireland, and never can have any right in Ireland, the presence in any one generation of even a respectable minority of Irishmen, ready to die to affirm that truth, makes that Government for ever a usurpation and a crime against human progress.

I personally thank God that I have lived to see the day when thousands of Irish men and boys, and hundreds of Irish women and girls, were ready to affirm that truth and to seal it with their lives if necessary.

James Connolly,

Commandant-General, Dublin Division, Army of the Irish Republic [1]

MESSAGE FROM TOM CLARKE TO THE IRISH PEOPLE

I and my fellow-signatories believe we have struck the first successful blow for Freedom. The next blow, which we have no doubt Ireland will strike, will win through. In this belief we die happy. [2]

Thomas J Clarke, Kilmainham Gaol, 3 May, 1916.

THOMAS MACDONAGH'S LAST LETTER

Kilmainham Gaol, Midnight, Tuesday 2nd May, 1916

I, Thomas MacDonagh, having now heard the sentence of the Court Martial held on me today, declare that in all my acts – all the acts for which I have been arraigned – I have been actuated by one motive only, the love of my country, the desire to make her a sovereign independent state, I still hope and pray that my acts may have for consummation her lasting freedom and happiness.

179

I am to die at dawn, 3:30 a.m., 3rd. May. I am ready to die, and thank God that I die in so holy a cause. My country will reward my dust richly.

On April 30th I was astonished to receive by a messenger from P.H. Pearse, Commandant General of the Army of the Irish Republic, an order to surrender unconditionally to the British General. I did not obey the order as it came from a prisoner. I was then in supreme command of the Irish Army, consulted with my second in command and decided to confirm the order. I knew that it would involve my death and the deaths of other leaders. I hoped that it would save many true men among our followers, good lives for Ireland. God grant it has done so and God approve our deed. For myself I have no regret. The one bitterness that death has for me is the separation it brings from my beloved wife Muriel, and my beloved children, Donagh and Barbara. My country will then treat them as wards, I hope. I have devoted myself too much to National work and too little to the making of money to leave them a competence. God help them and support them, and give them a happy and prosperous life. Never was there a better, truer, purer woman then my wife Muriel, or more adorable children than Don and Barbara. It breaks my heart to think that I shall never see my children again, but I have not wept or mourned. I counted the cost of this and am ready to pay it. Muriel has been sent for here. I do not know if she can come. She may have no one to take the children while she is coming. If she does –

My money affairs are in a bad way. I am insured for £200 in the New York Life Co. but have borrowed £101, I think. I am insured for £100 in the Alliance Co., but have a bank debt for £80. That brings less than £120 from these sources, if they produce anything. In addition I have insured my two children for £100 each in Mutual Co. of Australasia, payment of premiums to cease at my death the money to be paid to the children at the age of twenty one. I ask my brother Joseph MacDonagh and my good and constant friend David Houston to help my poor wife in these matters. My brother John, who came with me and stood by me all last week has been sent away from here, I do not know where to. He, if he can, will help my family too. God bless him and my other sisters and brothers.

Assistance has been guaranteed from funds in the hands of Cumann na mBan and other funds to be collected in America by our fellow countrymen there in provision for the dependents of those who fall in the fight. I appeal without shame to the persons who control these funds to assist my family. My wife and I have given all for Ireland.

I ask my friend David Houston to see Mr. W.G. Lyon, publisher of my latest book, *Literature in Ireland*, and see that its publication may be useful for my wife and family. If Joseph Plunkett survives me and is a free man I make him, with my wife, my literary executor. Otherwise my wife and David Houston will take charge of my writings. For the first time I pray that they may bring in some profit at last. My wife will want money from every source.

Yesterday at my Court Martial in rebutting some trifling evidence, I made a statement as to the negotiations for surrender with General Lowe. On hearing it read after it struck me that it might sound like an appeal. It was not such. I make no appeal, no recantation, no apology, for my acts. In what I said I merely claimed that I act honourably and thoroughly in all that I set myself to do. My enemies have, in return, treated me in an unworthy manner. But that can pass. It is a great and glorious thing to die for Ireland and I can well forget all petty annoyances in the splendour of this. When my son, Don, was born I thought that to him and not to me would this be given. God has been kinder than I hoped. My son will have a great name.

To my son Don. My darling little boy remember me kindly. Take my hope and purpose with my deed. For your sake and for the sake of your beloved mother and sister I would wish to live long, but you will recognise the thing I have done and see this as a consequence. I still think I have done a great thing for Ireland, and with the defeat of her enemy, won the first step of her freedom. God bless you, my son.

My darling daughter, Barbara, God bless you. I loved you more than ever a child has been loved.

My dearest love, Muriel, thank you a million times for all that you have been to me. I have only one trouble in leaving life – leaving you so. Be sure, Darling, God will assist and bless you. Goodbye. Kiss my darlings for me. I send you the few things I have saved out of this war. Goodbye my love, till we meet again in heaven. I have a sure faith in our union there. I kiss this paper that goes to you.

I have just heard that they have not been able to reach you. Perhaps it is better so. Yet Father Aloysius is going to make another effort to do something. God help and sustain you, my love. But for your suffering this would be all joy and glory.

Your loving husband, Thomas MacDonagh.

Good bye. I return the darlings' photographs. Good bye, my love.[3]

LAST STATEMENT OF SEÁN MACDIARMADA

I, Seán MacDiarmada, before paying the penalty of death for my love of country and hatred of her slavery, desire to leave this message to my fellow-countrymen:

That I die as I have lived, bearing no malice to any man, and in perfect peace with Almighty God. The principles for which I give my life are so sacred that I now walk to my death in the most perfectly calm and collected manner.

I go to my death for Ireland's cause as fearlessly as I have worked for that sacred cause during all my short life.

I have asked the Reverend Eugene McCarthy, who has prepared me to meet my God, and who has given me courage to undergo this ordeal, to convey this message to my fellow-countrymen.

God save Ireland.[4]

Seán MacDiarmada, Kilmainham Prison, 12 May, 1916

ÉAMONN CEANNT'S LAST LETTERS

Cell 88, Kilmainham Gaol, May 1916
I leave for the guidance of the other revolutionaries who may tread the path which I have trod this advice: never to treat with the enemy, never to surrender to his mercy but to fight to a finish. I see nothing gained but grave disaster caused by the surrender which has marked the end of the Irish Insurrection of 1916 – so far at least as Dublin is concerned. The enemy has not cherished one generous thought for those who, with little hope, with poor equipment and weak in members withstood his forces for one glorious week. Ireland has shown that she is a nation. This generation can claim to

have raised sons as brave as any that went before and in the years to come
Ireland will honour those who risked all for her honour at Easter 1916.
I bear no ill-will towards those against whom I fought. I have found the
common soldiers and the higher officers humane and companionable, even
the English who were actually in the fight against us. Thank God soldiering
for Ireland has opened my heart and helped me to see pure humanity where
I expect to find only scorn and reproach. I have met the man who escaped
from me by a ruse under the Red Cross but I do not regret having with-
held my fire. He gave me cakes. I wish to record the magnificent gallantry
and fearless calm determination of the men who fought with me. All were
simply splendid. Even I knew no fear or panic and shrunk from no risk even
as I shrink not now from the death that faces me at day-break. I hope to see
the face of God even for a moment in the morning. His will be done. All
here are very kind.

My poor wife saw me yesterday and bore up; so the warder told me, even
when she left my presence. Poor Áine, poor Rónán, God is their only shield
now that I am removed and God is a better shield that I. I have seen Áine,
Nell, Richard and Mick and bid them conditional goodbye. Even now they
have hope.

Éamonn Ceannt [5]

My dearest wife Áine,
Not wife but widow before these lines reach you. I am here without hope
of this world and without fear, calmly awaiting the end. I have had Holy
Communion and Fr. Augustine has been with me and will be back again.
Dearest 'silly little Fanny'. My poor little sweetheart of – how many – years
ago. Ever my comforter, God comfort you now. What can I say? I die a
noble death, for Ireland's freedom. Men and women will vie with one
another to shake your dear hand. Be proud of me as I am and ever was of
you. My cold exterior was but a mask. It has saved me in these last days.
You have a duty to me and to Rónán, that is to live. My dying wishes are
that you shall remember your state of health, work only as much as may be
necessary and freely accept the little attentions which in due time will be
showered upon you. You will be – you are, the wife of one of the Leaders

of the Revolution. Sweeter still you are my little child, my dearest pet, my sweetheart of the hawthorn hedges and Summer's eves. I remember all and I banish all that I may be strong and die bravely. I have one hour to live, then God's judgement and, through his infinite mercy, a place near your poor Grannie and my mother and father and Jem and all the fine old Irish Catholics who went through the scourge of similar misfortune from this Vale of Tears into the Promised Land. Bíodh misneach agat a stóirín mo chroidhe. Tóig do cheann agus bíodh foighde agat go bhfeicfimid a chéile arís I bhFlaithis Dé – tusa, mise agus Rónán beag bocht.

Adieu,

Éamonn

JOSEPH PLUNKETT'S LETTER TO HIS NEW WIFE

Richmond Barracks,
Tuesday, May 2nd, 1916
My darling child,
This is my first chance of sending you a line since we were taken. I have no notion what they intend to do with me but have heard a rumour that I am to be sent to England.

The only thing I care about is that I am not with you – everything else is cheerful. I am told that Tomás was brought in yesterday. George and Jack are both here and well. We have not had one word of news from outside since Monday 24th April except wild rumours. Listen – if I live it might be possible to get the Church to marry us by proxy – there is such a thing but it is very difficult I am told. Father Sherwin might be able to do it. You know how I love you. That is all I have time to say. I know you love me and so I am very happy.

Your own, Joe
Miss Grace M V Gifford,
8 Temple Villas,
Palmerston Rd.,
Rathmines[6]

Section Fourteen: Medals & Recipients

1916 ARMBAND

At commemorations and marches, the men and women who took part in the Rising wore a green and orange armband with '1916' and the star-and-flame 'FF' badge of Óglaigh na hÉireann in gold lettering. The 'FF' stands for Fianna Fáil, the Soldiers of Destiny. This term predated the foundation of the political party. These armbands were presented in a commemorative ceremony in the Rotunda Rink on the nineteenth anniversary of the Rising in 1935. They were made by Bergins, and are of 'real Irish poplin'.

1916 MEDAL

On 24 January 1941 it was decided by the government that a medal would be a more appropriate way to recognise those who fought in the

Rising. Its design is based upon the Irish Army crest and depicts the dying figure of Cúchulainn. It is 38 millimetres in diameter, bronze, and is made up of a circle of flames beneath an eight-pointed star. On the reverse it reads 'Seachtain na Cásca 1916' ('Easter Week 1916'). The poplin ribbon is green and orange, in two vertical panels, and the bronze suspension bar has a Celtic interlaced design.

SERVICE MEDAL (1917–21)

On 26 May 1942 a decision was made by the government to issue a medal to those who had fought during the conflict after 1916. The design is a circular bronze of 39 millimetres bearing the arms of the four provinces of Ireland around the word 'Éire'. A Volunteer stands erect above the words 'Cogadh na Saoirse' ('The Fight for Freedom'). The poplin ribbon is of two vertical stripes of black and tan-brown. The suspension bar is a Celtic interlaced design.

A smaller number of medals were issued to those who were in receipt of a Military Pension or who satisfied the Minister for Defence that they were on active service – these have a second bar and the inscription 'Cómhrac' ('Combat'). The medals without the bar were for members of the IRA, Na Fianna, Cumann na mBan or the ICA for the three months ending 11 July 1921.

1916 SURVIVORS' MEDAL

This medal was awarded in 1966, the 50th anniversary of the Rising, to surviving participants. The face is the same as the 1916 medal, but it is a bright-silver gilt 38 millimetres in diameter. The reverse bears the inscription '1916 Cáisc 1966' ('Cáisc' means Easter). The ribbon is green with orange borders, and a thin white strip runs down the centre. The suspension bar is of a Celtic interlaced design.

TRUCE COMMEMORATION MEDAL

To commemorate the 50th Anniversary of the Truce of 11 July 1921, a new medal was struck. It was awarded to veterans of the 1919–21 war who had received the Service Medal and were still alive in 1971. The medal is similar to the Service Medal, but is smaller at 32 millimetres and is of brighter bronze colour. The reverse has the palm leaf design and is inscribed '1921–1971'. The ribbon has green borders followed by two strips of tan with a black stripe running down the centre. The suspension bar is of the usual Celtic interlace.

FAKE MEDALS

There are many fake medals for sale on the Internet. Caution should be exercised when buying a 1916 or Service Medal, especially online.

RECORD OF MEDALS ISSUED UP TO 31 JANUARY 1988

	Issued to Pensioners	Issued to others	Total
1916 Medals	2,390	87	2,477
Service (1917–21) w. bar	13,067	2,119	15,186
Service (1917–21) no bar		51,233	51,233
1916 Survivors (approx.)			c.1,000
Truce Commemoration	7,120	15,312	22,432

VERIFICATION PROCESS

The decision to award medals was not taken lightly, and verification of entitlement involved a rigorous process: 'Each applicant for a medal was required to complete a form stating the names of his former Brigade Commander, Battalion Commander and Company Commander. If these officers were then deceased, emigrated or not willing to cooperate, the forms were sent to not less than two officers or members of the Unit/ sub-Unit named for supporting testimony/signatures. These persons were usually in receipt of service pensions. Initially, applications for the medal without bar were investigated by a Committee of two members of the Military Service Registration Board, and one Interviewing Officer, who had acted for the Referee under the Military Service Pensions Act, 1934.'[1] Almost 13,500 applications for medals were refused or abandoned by the applicants.

Note: The list of medal recipients on the following pages was released by the Military Archives in 2015. Up until 1988, 2,477 medals were awarded to participants of the Rising; over the next few years, 81 more medals were issued. This gives us a total in this list of 2,558 medal recipients.

(D = Dublin)

Adams, John: 13 Gray St., D.

Adams, John Francis: 109 Cork St., D.

Adrien, Mary: Garden View, Oldtown, D.

Agnew, Arthur Patrick: 72 Seatown, Swords, D.

Alexander, Nicholas: 131 Cork St., D.

Allen, Mary: 54 Mountjoy Square, D.

Allen, Thomas: 19 Monck Place, Phibsborough, D.

Allum, Annie: 55 Rotherwood Rd., Putney, London SW15.

Archer, Liam Aloysius: Portobello Barracks, D.

Armstrong, Kate: Caherwilder, Kilcolgan, Galway.

Arnold, James: 125 Hut, Keogh Square, Inchicore, D.

Ashe, Thomas: Kinard, Lispole, Kerry.

Ashton, William Francis: 22 Manor Place, D.

Athy, Michael: Maree, Oranmore, Galway.

Atkins, Thomas R.: 70 South Circular Rd., Portobello, D.

Aungier, Richard: 28A Beresford St., D.

Bailey, Edward: 17 Park St., Dundalk, Louth.

Bailey, Patrick J.: 5 Lwr. Basin St., James's St., D.

Balfe, James: Shannon Hill, Enniscorthy, Wexford.

Balfe, John: 28 Shannon Hill, Enniscorthy.

Balfe, Richard: 13 Pembroke St., Irishtown, D.

Bane, John: Cahertymore, Athenry, Galway.

Banks, Henry: Ceann Coradh, Highfield Pk., Dundrum, D.

Bannon, John: 68 Foley St., D.

Barnes, Michael: Great Southern Railways, North Wall, D.

Barrett, Benedict: 43 Eccles St., D.

Barrett, Christopher: Court Ave., Athenry, Galway.

Barrett, James: 16 Canning Place, Seville Place, North Strand Rd., D.

Barrett, James: Court View, Athenry, Galway.

Barrett, Kathleen: 14 Lwr. Rutland St., D.

Barrett, Michael: Caheroyan, Athenry, Galway.

Barrett, Michael: 9 St Bridget's Terrace, Tuam, Galway.

Barrett, Patrick: Scalp, Ballinagran, Craughwell, Galway.

Barrett, Thomas: Caheroyan, Athenry, Galway.

Barrett, William: 72 Inisfallen Parade, North Circular Rd., D

Barry, John: 2 Spencer St., North Strand, D.

Barry, Leslie Mary: 8 Belgrave Place, Wellington Rd., Cork.

Béaslaí, Piaras: N Block, Portobello Barracks, D.

Beatty, Katie: Claregate St., Kildare.

Beggs, Robert: 8 St. Joseph St., off North Circular Rd., D.

Begley, Daniel Joseph: Beresford Barracks, Curragh Training Camp, Kildare.

Begley, David Timothy: 23 Buckley Rd., High Rd., Kilburn, London NW6.

Begley, Joseph Patrick: 387 North Circular Rd., D.

Behan, James: 24 Botanic Ave., Drumcondra, D.

Bent, John (Senior): 4 Swifts Row, Lwr. Ormond Quay, D.

Bermingham, Andrew J.: 25 Lwr. Glengariff Parade, North Circular Rd., D.

Bermingham, John: Willbrook, Rathfarnham, D.

Bermingham, John Joseph: 24 St Ignatius Rd., Drumcondra, D.

Bermingham, Peter: 589 Wood View Terrace, Rathfarnham, D.

Bernie, James: 46 Church St., Widnes, Lancashire.

Berrill, Patrick Joseph: Williamsons Place, Dundalk, Louth.

Berry, William: 10 Cuffe St., D.

Bevan, Charles Stewart: 9 Geraldine St., D.

Bevan, Thomas Joseph: 9 Geraldine St., Berkeley Rd., D.

Billings, Joseph Patrick: 24 Bayview Ave., North Strand Rd., D.

Bindon, John: Stradbally, Kilcolgan, Galway.

Bindon, Thomas: Castletaylor, Ardrahan, Galway.

Bird, James: 4 Rutland Cottages, Lwr. Rutland St., D.

Bird, Patrick: 1 Ben Edair Rd., Arbour Hill, D.

Birney, Patrick: 7 Byrne's Cottages, Dollymount, D.

Bishop, Thomas: Shannon Hill, Enniscorthy, Wexford.

Black, Edward: 66 John St., Enniscorthy.

Blackburn, Kathleen: 16 North Great George St., D.

Blake, Michael: Cloonacauneen, Claregalway, Galway.

Blake, William: 36 Bangor Rd., Crumlin, D.

Blanchfield, Peter: Ballydowney House, Killarney, Kerry.

Blanchfield, Thomas: 96 Lwr. Mount St., D.

Boland, Edmund: St. Michael's, 315 Clontarf Rd., D.

Boland, Gerald: 102 Howth Rd., Clontarf, D.

Boland, Harry: St. Michael's, 315 Clontarf Rd., D.

Boland, Michael: Lwr. Rathfarnham, D.

Boland, Patrick: Bree, Enniscorthy.

Boland, Patrick James: 12 Lwr. Pembroke St., D.

Bolger, John: Ballinaglough, Wexford.

Bourke, David J: Imly, Knocklong, Limerick.

Bowles, William Patrick: 5 Mountain View Ave., Harold's Cross, D.

Bowman, Joseph: 7A Leslie Ave., Dalkey, D.

Boylan, John: 23 St. Michael's Terrace, Blackpitts, D.

Boylan, Seán: Dunboyne, Meath.

Boylan, Stephen: 17 East James's St., D.

Boylan, Thomas: 45 Frankfort Ave., Rathgar, D.

Boyne, John: Main St., Finglas, D.

Boyne, John: 21 Shannon Hill, Enniscorthy.

Boyne, William: 7 The Shannon, Enniscorthy.

Brabazon, Joseph: 44A Mountjoy St., D.

Bracken, John: 55 Leeson St., D.

Bracken, John: 29 South Dock St., Ringsend, D.

Bracken, Joseph: 5 Wellington Place, Ballsbridge, D.

Bracken, Peadar: The Lawn, Tullamore, Offaly.

Bradley, Luke: Fordstown, Kells, Meath.

Bradley, Patrick: Ballymckeogh, Newport, Tipperary.

Brady, Francis: 24 Annamoe Pk., Cabra, D.

Brady, James Joseph: 71 Bride St., D.

Brady, John: 6 Irish St., Enniscorthy.

Brady, Michael: 74 Lwr. Leeson St., D.

Brady, Michael: 63A Talbot St., D.

Brady, Patrick: 18 Mount Pleasant Place, D.

Brannelly, Michael: Flood St., Galway.

Brannelly, Thomas: Prospect Hill, Galway.

Breen, John: St. Senan's, Templeshannon, Enniscorthy.

Breen, Joseph: Tinnashrule, Ferns, Wexford.

Breen, Mary: 8 Slaney St., Enniscorthy.

Breen, Myles P: Tinnashrule, Ferns, Wexford.

Breen, Seán: 38 Warren St., South Circular Rd., D.

Brennan, James: 59 Bride St., D.

Brennan, James Joseph: 5 Mannix Rd., Glasnevin, D.

Brennan, James Michael: 125 Cabra Rd., D.

Brennan, Laurence: 98 Harold's Cross Cottages, D.

Brennan, Maurice: 34 Shandon Drive, Cabra, D.

Brennan, Michael: Sydney House, Cork.

Brennan, Patrick: Leinster House, Kildare St., D.

Brennan, Patrick: Swamp Hill House, Sundrive Rd., D.

Brennan, Robert: 3842 Cathedral Ave., N.W. Washington, D.C.

Brennan, Thomas: The Weir, Kilcolgan, Galway.

Brennan, Una: 10 Belgrave Rd., D.

Brennan-Whitmore, William James: General Headquarters, Parkgate St., D.

Breslin, Christopher: 9 Mount Temple Rd., off Arbour Hill, D.

Breslin, James: 21 Aungier St., D.

Breslin, Thomas: 22 O' Leary Rd., Kilmainham, South Circular Rd., D.

Breslin, Tobias: 15 Lincoln Place, D.

Bridgeman, Edward: Main St., Celbridge, Kildare.

Brien, John: 181 Malahide Rd., Donnycarney, D.

Broderick, Seán: Athenry, Galway.

Brogan, Patrick: North Commons, Lusk, D.

Brooks, Christina: St Enda's, 17 Bantry Rd., Drumcondra, D.

Brooks, Frederick John: St Enda's, 17 Bantry Rd., Drumcondra, D

Brophy, Daniel: Lusk, D.

Brophy, Thomas: 77 Summerhill, D.

Brougham, James: 10 St. Laurence St., North Wall, D.

Brown, Joseph: Amiens St., D.

Browne, James: 28 Bolton St., D.

Browne, James: Clogher, Gooldscross, Tipperary.

Browne, William: 28 Bolton St., D.

Bruen, William: 23 Clonliffe Ave., Ballybough, D.

Bryan, Thomas: Downings, Prosperous, Naas, Kildare.

Buckley, Donal: Dun Laoghaire.

Buckley, William Joseph: 43 Great Charles St., D.

Bulfin, Eamon: Derrinlough House, Birr, Offaly.

Burke, Bartholomew: Whitechurch Cottages, Rathfarnham, D.

Burke, Edward: 13 Park Terrace, Meath St., D.

Burke, Fintan: 15 Rafter St., Enniscorthy.

Burke, Frank: St Enda's College, Rathfarnham, D.

Burke, James Joseph: 6 Oxford Rd., Ranelagh, D.

Burke, John: Cnocabhudd, Meadhraidhe, Uran Mór, Galway.

Burke, John: Cahermore, Ardrahan, Galway.

Burke, Joseph: Station Rd., Oranmore, Galway.

Burke, Martin: 2702 Woodley Place, N.W., Washington D.C.

Burke, Matthew: 13 Pk. Terrace, Meath St., D.

Burke, Michael: Gárda Síochána, Falcarragh, Donegal.

Burke, Michael: 22 St. Dominick's Terrace, Fairhill, Galway.

Burke, Michael: Doughiska, Galway.

Burke, Nicholas: 21 Holly Rd., Donnycarney, D.

Burke, Patrick: 16 Longford Terrace, Monkstown, D.

Burke, Patrick: Kilcaimin, Oranmore, Galway.

Burke, Peter: Cahermore, Ardrahan, Galway.

Burke, Thomas: Civic Guard Station, Taghmon, Wexford.

Burke, Thomas: 12 St Brendan's Rd., Drumcondra, D.

Burke, William Francis: 174 James St., D.

Burns, James: 1 Finn St., D.

Burns, James: Stradbally, Kilcolgan, Galway.

Burns, John: Stradbally, Kilcolgan, Galway.

Burns, John: Ballinamana, Oranmore, Galway.

Burns, Michael: Licklea, Colemanstown, Ballinasloe, Galway.

Burns, William: Coldwood, Athenry, Galway.

Burns, William: Ross Rd., Killarney, Kerry.

Bushell, Ellen Sarah: 2 New Rd., Inchicore, D.

Butler, Christopher: 61 Emmet Rd., Inchicore, D.

Butler, George: Coolbawn Cottages, Ferns, Wexford.

Butler, George: 24 Lwr. Kimmage Rd., D.

Butler, James: 39 Lombard St. South, D.

Buttner, Patrick: 2 Swifts Row, Ormond Quay, D.

Byrne, Alphonsus: 7 Dodderdale Terrace, Rathfarnham, D.

Byrne, Ambrose: 42 Arran Quay, D.

Byrne, Andrew Joseph: 104 Townsend St., D.

Byrne, Bernard Christopher: 24 Manor Place, D.

Byrne, Charles: 36 Mountpleasant Square, D.

Byrne, Charles Bernard: Bandon Barracks, Cork.

Byrne, Christopher: 45 St. Mary's Rd., Church Rd., D.

Byrne, Christopher: 7 Geoffrey Keating Rd., South Circular Rd., D.

Byrne, Christopher: 27 Ferguson Rd., D.

Byrne, Christopher Columba: 33 St Alban's Rd., South Circular Rd., D.

Byrne, Denis: 13 Seafort Villas, Sandymount, D.

Byrne, Denis: 182 H Block, New Bride St., D.

Byrne, Edward: 31 Duffry Gate, Enniscorthy.

Byrne, George: 6 Petrie Rd., South Circular Rd., D.

Byrne, Gerald: 16 Susan Terrace, Donore Ave., D.

Byrne, Henry: Corps of Engineers, Portobello Barracks, D.

Byrne, James: 31 Lwr. Stephen St., D.

Byrne, James: 38 Storey St., Islington, London N.W. 1.

Byrne, James: Portrane Mental Hospital, Donabate, D.

Byrne, John: 31 Upr. Wellington St., D.

Byrne, John: 54 York St., D.

Byrne, John: 28 Malachi Rd., Manor Place, D.

Byrne, John Joseph: Custume Barracks, Athlone, Westmeath.

Byrne, John Joseph: 7 St Nicholas Place, D.

Byrne, John Joseph: Rose Hill, Convent Rd., Enniscorthy.

Byrne, Joseph: 5 Shelmartin Terrace, Croydon Pk., Fairview, D.

Byrne, Joseph: 2 Boland's Cottages, Church Rd., Fairview, D.

Byrne, Joseph John: Harbour Rd., Howth, D.

Byrne, Laurence: 42 Arran Quay, D.

Byrne, Lillie: 582 North Circular Rd., D.

Byrne, Louis: 23 Summerhill, D.

Byrne, Louis: 47 Lwr. Gardiner St., D.

Byrne, Lucy Agnes: 67 Old Cabra Rd., D.

Byrne, Mary: 28 Malachi Rd., Manor Place, D.

Byrne, Michael: 65A Townsend St., D.

Byrne, Michael: 6 Rehoboth Place, Dolphin's Barn, D.

Byrne, Michael: 4 Bishop St., D.

Byrne, Michael: 47 Dolphin's Barn St., D.

Byrne, Michael: Milltown, D.

Byrne, Patrick: 20 Patrick's Terrace, Inchicore, D.

Byrne, Patrick: 9 Ring Terrace, Inchicore, D.

Byrne, Patrick: 33 St. Alban's Rd., South Circular Rd., D.

Byrne, Patrick: 3 Dolphin's Barn St., D.

Byrne, Patrick Joseph: 38 Lwr. Buckingham St., D.

Byrne, Patrick Joseph: 60 Lwr. Dominick St., D.

Byrne, Peter: 7 Barrow St., Grand Canal St., D.

Byrne, Peter Sylvester: 12 Richmond Cottages, Summerhill, D.

Byrne, Seán: 131 Larkfield Grove, Kimmage, D.

Byrne, Seumas: 6 Whitworth Place, Drumcondra, D.

Byrne, Stasia: 13 Ashworth Place, Harold's Cross, D.

Byrne, Stasia: 131 Larkfield Grove, Kimmage, D.

Byrne, Teresa: 54 St Mary's Rd., Church Rd., D.

Byrne, Thomas: 58 Larkfield Gardens, Kimmage Rd., D.

Byrne, Thomas Francis: 30 Eccles St., D.

Byrne, Vincent: 147 Emmett Rd., Inchicore, D.

Byrne, William: 4 Smithfield Ave., Fairview, D.

Byrne, William: 83 Seafield Rd., Clontarf, D.

Byrne, William: Teach Mhuire, Dundrum Rd., D.

Byrnes, Michael: Tawin, Oranmore, Galway.

Byrnes, Patrick: Cave, Oranmore, Galway.

Caddell, Patrick: Collinstown, Skerries, D.

Caffrey, John: 14 Killarney Parade, North Circular Rd., D.

Caffrey, Matthew: Grove Cottage, Rathfarnham, D.

Caffrey-Keeley, Christina: 17 Church St., North Wall, D.

Cahalan, Patrick: 591 Millmount Ave., D.

Cahill, Arthur John: 82A Lwr. Dorset St., D.

Cahill, James: 22 Merchant's Quay, D.

Cahill, Michael: Shannon Hill, Enniscorthy.

Cahill, William: Shanbally, Craughwell, Galway.

Caldwell, Patrick: Larrigan, Carrickaboy, Cavan.

Callaghan, John: 11831 Mechanical Transport Corps, Gormanstown Camp, Meath.

Callan, Joseph: Military Detention Barracks, Cork.

Callanan, Michael: Killeeneen, Craughwell, Galway.

Callanan, Patrick: Craughwell, Galway.

Callanan, Thomas: Caherdevane, Craughwell, Galway.

Callender, Ignatius: 23 Brookfield Rd., Kilmainham, D.

Campbell, George: 20A Auburn St., D.

Campbell, Michael John: 21 Northbrook Rd., Leeson Pk., D.

Cannon, James: Ballydavid, Athenry, Galway.

Canny, Daniel: 128 Capel St., D.

Canny, Joseph: 2 South Great George's St., D.

Carberry, Christopher: 3 Myrtle Terrace, Church Rd., D.

Carberry, James: 3 Myrtle Terrace, Church Rd., D.

Cardiff, Joseph John: 53 Weafer St., Enniscorthy.

Carley, John: Camolin, Wexford.

Carney, Francis Joseph: 45 Albert Rd., Sandycove, D.

Carney, Winifred: 3 Whitewell Parade, Belfast.

Carpenter, Peter: Tara Hall, Talbot St., D.

Carpenter, Walter Patrick: 169 Parnell St., D.

Carr, Patrick: Cregboy, Claregalway, Galway.

Carrick, Patrick: Gurrane, Maree, Oranmore, Galway.

Carrigan, Charles E.: Irish American Alliance Hall, 28 North Frederick St., D.

Carrigan, James: 24 North Clarence St., D.

Carroll, Bartholomew Leo: 84 Leinster Rd., Rathmines, D.

Carroll, Dudley: 17 Clarendon St., D.

Carroll, James: 23 Fitzgerald St., Harold's Cross, D.

Carroll, John: 27 Irish St., Enniscorthy.

Carroll, Joseph: Irish St., Enniscorthy.

Carroll, Michael: 18 Upr. Erne St., D.

Carroll, Patrick: 116 Leix Rd., Cabra, D.

Carroll, Peter: 41 Buckingham Buildings, D.

Carroll, Robert J.: 8 Lwr. Skerrard Rd., D.

Carron, Maíre: 36 Nelson St., D.

Carton, Eugene: 21 Temple St., D.

Carty, Patrick: Drumgoold, Enniscorthy.

Carty, Thomas: Carpenterstown, Castleknock, D.

Casement, Roger: 15 Nerotal, Wiesbaden.

Casey, Hugh: 61 St. Ignatius Rd., Drumcondra, D.

Casey, James Joseph: 3 Windsor Terrace, Portobello, D.

Casey, Leo: 60 Shelbourne Rd., Ballsbridge, D.

Cassels, James: 42 Lwr. Mayor St., North Wall, D.

Casserly, Martin Henry: 42 Wellington Rd., Paekakariki, New Zealand.

Casserly, Michael: Cregboy, Claregalway, Galway.

Casserly, Peter: Grealishtown, Galway.

Cassidy, James Philip: 33 Pearse St., D.

Cassidy, Thomas: 13 Denzille St., D.

Cassidy, Thomas: 22 Bolton St., D.

Catlin, John Patrick: 5 Lwr. Sean McDermott St., D.

Cauldfield, Christopher: 97B Calumet St., Roxbury, Massachusetts, USA.

Ceannt, Éamonn: 44 Oakley Rd., Ranelagh, D.

Chadwick, Mary: 92 Caledon Rd., Church Rd., D.

Chambers, Daniel Francis: Botanic Rd., Glasnevin, D.

Chaney, Patrick: 5 Northcourt Ave., Church Rd., D.

Chaney, William: 3 Upr. Rutland St., D.

Charlton, Michael: 55 Saint Alban's Rd., South Circular Rd., D.

Christian, William: 52 York St., D.

Christie, Peter: Artane, D.

Claffey, Joseph: 40 Great Western Villas, Phibsborough, D.

Clancy, Peadar: "Republican Outfitters", Talbot St., D.

Clarke, Joseph: 33 Bath Ave., Sandymount, D.

Clarke, Kathleen: 40 Merlyn Rd., Ballsbridge, D.

Clarke, Liam: Churchtown Pk., Dundrum, D.

Clarke, Philip: 65 Cork St., D.

Clarke, Robert John: Greenan, Saskatchewan, Canada.

Clarke, Thomas: 16b D'Olier St., D.

Cleary, James: Shannon Hill, Enniscorthy.

Cleary, James: Abbey Row, Athenry, Galway.

Cleary, John: Abbey Row, Athenry, Galway.

Cleary, Thomas B.: Abbey Row, Athenry, Galway.

Clifford, Owen: 305 East 78 St., New York, USA.

Clifford, Peter: Castletown Rd., Dundalk, Louth.

Clifford, Thomas: Quarry House, Ballinasloe, Galway.

Clince, Maria: 15 Wolseley St., D.

Clinch, Patrick Joseph: "St. Enda's", Dublin Rd., Sutton, D.

Cloonan, Michael H.: Portmagee, Killarney, Kerry.

Cloonan, Patrick Edward: Ballinacloughy, Oranmore, Galway.

Cloonan, Thomas: Ballinacloughy, Oranmore, Galway.

Cloonan, Timothy: Tawin, Oranmore, Galway.

Clune, Conor: Quinville, Quin, Clare.

Coade, Seán: 2 Fitzgibbon St., D.

Coady, Aidan: 22 Irish St., Enniscorthy.

Coady, James: Rectory Rd., Old Church, Enniscorthy.

Coady, John: 60 Irish St., Enniscorthy.

Coady, Patrick: Irish St., Enniscorthy.

Coady, William: 33 King's Inns St., D.

Coady, William: Clogher, Claregalway, Galway.

Coates, Peter: 12 Gordon St., Ringsend, D.

Coates, Peter: 2 Spencer St., Leinster Ave., North Strand, D.

Coburn, Francis: 2 Pk. View, Demesne, Dundalk.

Cody, Liam: The Little House, 17 Wilby Mews, London W11 3NP.

Cody, Seán: 85 Strand St., Skerries, D.

Coen, Martin: Cartymore, Athenry, Galway.

Coen, Thomas: Carnane, Athenry, Galway.

Coffey, Joseph: 34 Botanic Rd., Glasnevin, D.

Coghlan, Francis Xavier: Newbrook, Rathfarnham, D.

Colbert, Cornelius: 7 Clifton Terrace, Ranelagh Rd., D.

Colbert, Seán: 58 Botanic Ave., Drumcondra, D.

Cole, Patrick: Arodstown, Summerhill, Meath.

Cole, Thomas: 21 Upr. Dorset St., D.

Coleman, Richard: 32 St Peter's Rd., Phibsborough, D.

Coleton, Elizabeth: 2 Croydon Pk. Ave., Fairview, D.

Colfer, Mark: 50 St John's Villas, Enniscorthy.

Colgan, Daniel: 5 Lwr. Annaville, Ranelagh, D.

Colgan, Michael John: 10 Valentia Parade, North Circular Rd., D.

Colgan, Patrick: Maynooth, Kildare.

Colley, Henry Edward: 69 Clonliffe Rd., D.

Collins, Charles Tottenham: 508 Auburn Ave., Buffalo New York, USA.

Collins, John: 241 School St., Somerville, Massachusetts, USA.

Collins, John: Carnmore, Oranmore, Galway.

Collins, Maurice John: 65 Parnell St., D.

Collins, Michael: Mount Carmel, Magazine Rd., Cork.

Comber, Eamon: 66 Lwr. Mount St. , D.

Comerford, Andrew: 7 Upr. Kevin St., D.

Commins, Edward: Tarmuid, Kilcolgan, Galway.

Commins, Edward: Carnmore, Oranmore, Galway.

Commins, Michael: Cregmore, Claregalway, Galway.

Commins, Michael: Kilgraigue, Dunboyne, Meath.

Commins, Michael: Glaniscaul, Oranmore, Galway.

Commins, Patrick: Derrydonnell, Athenry, Galway.

Commins, Thomas: Tarmuid, Kilcolgan, Galway.

Commins, William: Coldwood, Athenry, Galway.

Concannon, John: Montiagh, Claregalway, Galway.

Concannon, Michael: Rinnaharney, Currandulla, Galway.

Concannon, Patrick: Cregboy, Claregalway, Galway.

Condron, Luke: 4 Blackhall Parade, D.

Condron, William: 3 Mullins Terrace, Grove Rd., Harold's Cross, D.

Conlon, Martin: 342 North Circular Rd., D.

Conlon, Peig: 11 Cabra Pk., D.

Connaughton, Patrick: 19 Merton Ave., South Circular Rd., D.

Conneely, John: Carnmore, Oranmore, Galway.

Connell, John: Clarenbridge, Galway.

Conniffe, Thomas Pat: Tawin, Oranmore, Galway.

Connolly, Brid: Kilmore, Artane, D.

Connolly, George: 13 Buckingham Terrace, Buckingham St., D.

Connolly, James: 36 Belgrave Square, Rathmines, D.

Connolly, John: Birchgrove, Athenry, Galway.

Connolly, John: Kiltulla, Oranmore, Galway.

Connolly, Joseph William: Central Fire Station, Tara St., D.

Connolly, Martin: 3 Old Market St., Sligo.

Connolly, Matthew: The Lodge, Kilbarrack House, Raheny, D.

Connolly, Patrick: Terryland House, Galway.

Connolly, Robert: Currantarmid, Monivea, Athenry, Galway.

Connolly, Roderick: Inishowen, Bray Head, Bray, Wicklow.

Connolly, Seán: 3 Mountjoy Square, D.

Connolly, Terence: Rhinn, Oranmore, Galway.

Connolly, Thomas: Ballinamona Lwr., Ballaghkeene, Enniscorthy.

Connolly-Heron, Ina: 62 Malahide Rd., D.

Connolly-O'Brien, Nora: 39 The Rise, Griffiths Ave., Glasnevin, D.

Connor, James: St. Margaret's Post Office, D.

Connor, Joseph: Tiaquinn, Colemanstown, Galway.

Connor, Mary Kate: The Square, Athenry, Galway.

Connors, Jack: Slieveaun, Clarenbridge, Galway.

Connors, William: Ballyglass West, Ardrahan, Galway.

Conroy, Andrew: 16 Pearse Square, D.

Conroy, Herbert: 4 Marino Ave., Clontarf, D.

Conroy, James (Senior): 14 Richmond Parade, North Circular Rd., D.

Conroy, James Patrick: 14 Richmond Parade, North Circular Rd., D.

Conroy, John: 32 Upr. Rutland St., D.

Conroy, William: 10 Sandford Pk., South Circular Rd., D.

Conway, Michael: Lisheenavalla, Claregalway, Galway.

Conway, Sean Joseph: 31 Rosevale St., Partick, Glasgow, Scotland.

Coogan, Patrick Vincent: Moor View, Bonavalley, Athlone, Westmeath.

Cooley, Patrick: Tonroe, Oranmore, Galway.

Cooling, Joseph: 49 Irishtown Rd., Sandymount, D.

Cooney, Elizabeth: 16A Basin St. Upr., James St. Harbour, D.

Cooney, James: 85 Queen St., D.

Cooper, John Dutton: 33 Lennox St., Portobello, D.

Cooper, Robert: 62 Goldenbridge Ave., Inchicore, D.

Corbally, Laurence: 6 Upr. Gloucester Place, D.

Corbally, Richard: 5 Upr. Gloucester Place, D.

Corbally, Thomas: 38 St Patrick's Cottages, Rathfarnham, D.

Corbett, Dominick: Killeeneen, Craughwell, Galway.

Corbett, Eamon: Killeenmore, Athenry, Galway.

Corbett, John: Leonards Hotel, Galway.

Corbett, Joseph: Shudane Monivea, Athenry, Galway.

Corcoran, Edward: Frenchfort, Oranmore, Galway.

Corcoran, James: 2 Elizabeth Place, Oriel St., D.

Corcoran, Joseph: 45 Bow Lane, James's St., D.

Corcoran, Mary Teresa: 45 Leix Rd., Cabra, D.

Corcoran, Patrick: Oranhill, Oranmore, Galway.

Corcoran, Thomas: Esker, Athenry, Galway.

Corcoran, William: Oranhill, Oranmore, Galway.

Corcoran, William: Lydegan, Claregalway, Galway.

Corket, Thady: Montiagh, Claregalway, Galway.

Corless, Patrick John Christopher: 36 De Courcy Square, Glasnevin, D.

Cormican, Edward: Lake View, Claregalway, Galway.

Corr, Elizabeth: 107 Ormeau Rd., Belfast.

Corrigan, William Patrick: Corrigan & Corrigan, 3 St. Andrew St., D.

Cosgrave, Edward: 65 Lwr. Dominick St., D.

Cosgrave, John: 1 Grattan Court, Lwr. Mount St., D.

Cosgrave, Marcella: 2 Lwr. Bridges Rd., Drumcondra, D.

Cosgrave, Michael: 71 Lwr. Leeson St., D.

Cosgrave, Philip B.: 8 Landsdowne Rd., D

Cosgrave, William T.: 8 Landsdowne Rd., D

Costello, Edward: 3 Castle Lane, Lurgan, Armagh.

Costello, John: Cornamagh, Athlone, Westmeath.

Costello, Martin: Oranbeg, Oranmore, Galway.

Costello, Martin: Gortroe, Athenry, Galway.

Costello, Michael: Rinville, Oranmore, Galway.

Costello, Michael: Gortroe, Athenry, Galway.

Costello, Patrick: Glaniscaul, Oranmore, Galway.

Costigan, Ellen: 53 Quarry Rd., Cabra, D.

Cotter, Joseph Alphonsus Patrick: 32 St Anne's Rd., Drumcondra, D.

Coughlan, James John: 4 Ashfield Ave., Ranelagh, D.

Courtney, Christopher: 5 Weafer St., Enniscorthy.

Courtney, Daniel: 13 Upr. Stephen's St., D.

Courtney, John: 63 Ross Rd., Enniscorthy.

Courtney, John: Ballymurthagh, Enniscorthy.

Courtney, William: 15 Ross Rd., Enniscorthy.

Cowley, Michael P: 22 Braemor Pk., Rathgar, D.

Cox, Redmond: 34 Kirwin St., North Circular Rd., D.

Coyle, Henry: 4 Hanover Parade, Townsend St., D.

Coyle, Thomas: 8 Queens Square, Pearse St., D.

Coyle, William: 55 Summerhill, D.

Coyne, Michael: 21 Cameron Square, Kilmainham, D.

Coyne, Thomas: 7 North Brunswick St., D.

Craven, Thomas: 1055 Clark St., Akron, Ohio, USA.

Cremen, Michael: 128 Lwr. Kimmage Rd., D.

Crenigan, James: Roganstown, Swords, D.

Crenigan, John: Roganstown, Swords, D.

Crimmins, Thomas: 48-20 48 St., Woodside, Long Island, USA.

Cripps, Joseph Aloysius: 2072, 8th Ave., New York City, USA.

Croke, Michael: 4 Millbourne Ave., Drumcondra, D.

Croke, Thomas: 44 Millbourne Ave., Drumcondra, D.

Crosby, Gretta: 11 Myrtle Ave., Old Orchard Beach, Maine, USA.

Crothers, Christopher: 43 Connolly Gardens, Inchicore, D.

Cryan, Thomas William: 136 N16 St., Bloomfield, New York, USA.

Cullen, James: The Quay, New Ross, Wexford.

Cullen, James: 83 Lwr. Leeson St., D.

Cullen, John: 18 Whitehall Cottages, Rathfarnham, D.

Cullen, John Christopher: 67 Percy Place, D.

Cullen, John Francis: 80 Prussia St., D.

Cullen, Joseph: 6 Whitworth Place, Drumcondra, D.

Cullen, Michael: Glen Rd., Delgany, Wicklow.

Cullen, Patrick: 12 Parnell St., D.

Cullen, Peter: 3 Bayview Ave., North Strand, D.

Cullen, Sean: Glen Rd., Delgany, Wicklow.

Cullen, Thomas: 26 Lauderdale Terrace, New Row South, D.

Cullen, Thomas: 80 Prussia St., D.

Cullen, William F: 6 Thomas Lane, O'Connell St., D.

Cullinan, Patrick: Cussane, Athenry, Galway.

Cummins, Mark Joseph: 208B 91st St., Queens, New York, USA.

Cunniff, Thomas: Tawin, Oranmore, Galway.

Cunniffe, Michael: Swangate, Athenry, Galway.

Cunningham, James: 13 Leinster Ave., North

Strand, D.

Cunningham, Michael: 35 Hammond St., Blackpitts, D.

Curran, Francis: Boyhill, Athenry, Galway.

Curran, Joseph Michael: 36 Stella Gardens, Irishtown, D.

Curran, William: 76 Lwr. Beechwood Ave., Ranelagh, D.

Cusack, John: 23 Glengariffe Parade, D.

Cushen, Patrick: Tomfarney, Clonroche, Enniscorthy.

Dalton, Patrick: 36 Upr. Gloucester St., D.

Daly O'Sullivan, Laura: 22 Landsdowne Pk., Ennis Rd., Limerick.

Daly, Denis: Main St., Cahirciveen, Kerry.

Daly, Frank: 56 Collins Ave., Donnycarney, D.

Daly, James: 84 Larkfield Gardens, Kimmage, D.

Daly, John: Ballyboggan, Athenry, Galway.

Daly, Patrick: 8 Tram Cottages, Phibsborough, D.

Daly, Patrick J: 39 Great Brunswick St., D.

Daly, Patrick John: 17 Langrishe Place, Summerhill, D.

Daly, Seumas: 3 Rose Terrace, Wharf Rd., D.

Daly, William Daniel: 156 North Strand Rd., D.

Daly, William Joseph: Oak Lodge, 340 North Circular Rd., D.

Darcy, Charles: 4 Murphy's Cottages, Gloucester Place, D.

Darcy, James: Dew Drop, Milltown, D.

Darcy, John Francis: 38 O'Curry Rd., South Circular Rd., D.

Darcy, Patrick Leo: 'Woodside', Dalkey, D.

Darcy, William: 51 Lwr. Camden St., D.

Darker, William: 15 Rutland Cottages, D.

Darling, Luke: 190 North King St., D.

Davis, John: John St., Enniscorthy.

Davis, Michael: St. Patrick's Place, Enniscorthy.

Davitt, Daniel: 4 Russell St., North Circular Rd., D.

Davys, Richard Patrick: 100 Lindsay Rd., Glasnevin.

de Burca, Aoife: Gleann Tulcann, Richmond Rd., Drumcondra, D.

De Coeur, Robert: 80 Tolka Rd., Ballybough, D.

de Lacey, Michael: Caoimheamhla, 14 Conyngham Rd., D.

de Paor, Nancy: 15 Earlsfort Terrace, D.

De Valera, Eamon: Dáil Éireann, D.

Deere, Cornelius: Gooldscross, Tipperary.

Delaney, Henry: 26 Harold's Cross Rd., D.

Delaney, Michael: 62 Brian Rd., Marino, D.

Delemere, Edward: 10 Michen's St., D.

Dempsey, James: 9 Whitworth Row, Seville Place, D.

Dempsey, James: 26 Guild St., North Wall, D.

Dempsey, Patrick: Lissalondon, Craughwell, Galway.

Dempsey, William: 13 Chaworth Terrace, Meath St., Thomas St., D.

Dennany, Patrick: 9 Buckingham Terrace, off Summerhill Place, D.

Derham, Joseph: 28 Iona Drive, Glasnevin, D.

Derham, Matthias: 72 Church St., Skerries, D.

Derham, Michael: 45 Upr. Gardiner St., D.

Derrington, Seán: 106 North King St., D.

Derrington, William Patrick: 58 Rochester Rd., Earlsdon, Coventry.

Dervin, Paul: 24 Hood St., Ancoats, Manchester.

Deveney, John: 123 Pleasant St., Philadelphia, USA.

Devereux, Eugene: 18 Rafter St., Enniscorthy.

Devereux, Patrick: 49 Summerhill, D.

Devereux, Thomas: Oulartlee, Kilcotty, Enniscorthy.

Devine, Francis: 8 O'Donovan Rd., South Circular Rd., D.

Devine, Frederick Victor: 45 Eardley Rd., London, SW16.

Devine, John: North Commons, Lusk, D.

Devine, Thomas William: The Lodge, Roebuck Grove, Clonskeagh, D.

Devlin, Ann: 24 Synott Place, North Circular Rd., D.

Devoy, James Joseph: 28 Waverly Ave., Fairview, D.

Divilly, Thomas: Laughtenoragh, Colesmanstown, Galway.

Diviney, Thomas: Gurrane, Maree, Oranmore, Galway.

Dixon, Grace: c/o 3 Royse Rd., Phibsborough, D7.

Doggett, Christopher: 15 Rutland Ave., Dolphin's Barn, D.

Doherty, John Christopher: North Gate St., Athenry, Galway.

Doherty, John Joseph: 33 Sandford Ave., South Circular Rd., D.

Dolan, Peter: 18 Hill St., D.

Domican, Seán: 18 Thomas Ashe St., D.

Donelan, Brendan: Athenry, Galway. Rd., Loughrea, Galway.

Donelan, Patrick: Newcastle, Monivea, Athenry, Galway.

Donncada, Tomas: 101 Cabra Rd., D.

Donnelly, Charles: "Glenamoy", Grange Rd., Rathfarnham, D.

Donnelly, James: 68 Amiens St., D.

Donnelly, John: 15 Spencer Ave., Seville Place, D.

Donnelly, Michael: 6 Hanover St. West, D.

Donnelly, Patrick: The Hermitage, Rathfarnham, D.

Donnelly, Simon: 16 Arnott St., South Circular Rd., D.

Donohoe, James: 17 Tramway Terrace, Highfield Rd., D.

Donohoe, Richard: Monasootha, Camolin, Wexford.

Donohoe, Robert: 124 Rathgar Rd., D.

Donohoe, Sylvester: 4 Mountpelier Hill, D.

Donohue, Michael: Rathgoran, Craughwell, Galway.

Donovan, Michael: 101 Mountpleasant Buildings, Ranelagh, D.

Doogan, John: 8 Upr. Rutland St., D.

Doolan, James: 38 John St., Enniscorthy.

Doolan, Joseph: 147 Harold's Cross Rd., D.

Dooley, Ellen: Curmacoo, Colmanstown, Ballinasloe, Galway.

Doran, Bridget: Old Bridge House, Milltown, D.

Doran, Denis: c/o District Court Office, Enniscorthy.

Doran, John: 12 Shannon Hill, Enniscorthy.

Doran, Margaret: Lymington Rd., Enniscorthy.

Doran, Michael: Kilcottymore, Enniscorthy.

Dore, Eamonn Thomas: 9 North Circular Rd., Limerick.

Dore, Nora: 9 North Circular Rd., Limerick.

Dowling, Andrew: Navan Rd., Castleknock, D.

Dowling, James Thomas: 148 North Strand Rd., D.

Dowling, John: Navan Rd., Castleknock, D.

Dowling, John: 68 Lwr. Baggot St., D.

Dowling, Michael: 24 East Essex St., D.

Downey, John: 2A Lauderdale Terrace, New Row South, D.

Downey, Joseph: 3 New Rd., Inchicore, D.

Doyle, Alexander: Effernoge, Ferns, Wexford.

Doyle, Andrew: Old Church, Enniscorthy.

Doyle, Andrew: Shannon Hill, Enniscorthy.

Doyle, Anthony: Ballycarrigeen, Ferns, Wexford.

Doyle, Charles: Woodlands, Ferns, Wexford.

Doyle, Christina Mary: 10 Ita's Rd., Glasnevin, D.

Doyle, Christopher: 51 Nash St., Inchicore, D.

Doyle, Daniel: 21 St John's Villas, Enniscorthy.

Doyle, David: 3 Brook Lawn, Donnybrook, D.

Doyle, Edward: Iveagh House, Bride Rd., D.

Doyle, Gerald: 103 Larkfield Gardens, Kimmage, D.

Doyle, James: Coolree, Ballindaggin, Enniscorthy.

Doyle, James: 4 St John's Villas, Enniscorthy.

Doyle, James Henry: 13 Parliament St., D.

Doyle, James Joseph: 1 Desmond St., Portobello, D.

Doyle, John: 55 Amien St., D.

Doyle, John: 137 McDowell's Ave., Mount Brown, D.

Doyle, John: 40 Cuffe St., D.

Doyle, John: 1 Church St., Ferns, Wexford.

Doyle, John: 21 Valentia Parade, North Circular Rd., D.

Doyle, John Joseph: 4 Summerhill Ave., Dun Laoghaire, D.

Doyle, John William: Wellington Quay, D.

Doyle, Joseph: 37 Anner Rd., Inchicore, D.

Doyle, Joseph: Duffrey Hill, Enniscorthy.

Doyle, Joseph Francis: 22 Chamber St., D.

Doyle, Laurence: 14 Templeshannon, Enniscorthy.

Doyle, Mary Ellen: 5 Lwr. Church St., Enniscorthy.

Doyle, Mary Kate: 25 Templeshannon, Enniscorthy.

Doyle, May: 16 Susan Terrace, Donore Ave., D.

Doyle, Michael: 91 Templeshannon, Enniscorthy.

Doyle, Michael: Concrete, Milltown, D.

Doyle, Patrick: Lusk, D.

Doyle, Patrick: Millmount, Milltown, D.

Doyle, Patrick: Mount Pleasant, Ballinasloe, Galway.

Doyle, Patrick: Kiltulla, Athenry, Galway.

Doyle, Patrick: 79 Marlborough Rd., D.

Doyle, Patrick Joseph: 296A North Circular Rd., D.

Doyle, Peadar Seán: 159 Emmet Rd., D.

Doyle, Peter: 114 St Declan Rd., Marino, D.

Doyle, Richard: 25 Templeshannon, Enniscorthy.

Doyle, Seamus: 23 St Aidan's Pk., Marino, D.

Doyle, Sylvester Joseph: 8 Upr. Digges St., D.

Doyle, Thomas: Engineers Barracks, Curragh Camp, Kildare.

Doyle, Thomas: Walkinstown House, Crumlin, D.

Doyle, Thomas: 106 St. Declan's Rd., Marino, D.

Doyle, Thomas: Capitol Cinema, South Main St., Wexford.

Doyle, Thomas: 49 Ross Rd., Enniscorthy.

Doyle, Thomas: Buckstown, Wexford.

Doyle, Thomas: 58 Rialto Cottages, South Circular Rd., D.

Doyle, Thomas J.: 117 Malahide Rd., Donnycarney, D.

Doyle, William: Lissen Hall, Swords, D.

Drennan, William: 53 Bridgefoot St., D.

Drumm, Thomas: 3 Byrnes Ave., Dollymount, Clontarf, D.

Drury, Patrick Joseph: 8 Annesley Square, North Strand, D.

Duffy, Christopher: River Rd., Castleknock, D.

Duffy, Edward: River Rd., Castleknock, D.

Duffy, Joseph: 71 Philipsburg Terrace, Fairview, D.

Duffy, Patrick Joseph: 7 Imaal Rd., Cabra, D.

Duggan, Daniel: Montiagh, Claregalway, Galway.

Duggan, Eamon J.: 1 Ardenza Terrace, Seapoint, D.

Duggan, Francis: 32 Palmerston St., Moss Side, Manchester, England.

Duggan, Henry: Montiagh, Claregalway, Galway.

Duggan, John: 29 Bohermore, Galway.

Duggan, May/Mary: 1 Ardenza Terrace, Seapoint, D.

Duggan, Thady: Montiagh, Claregalway, Galway.

Duggan, Thomas: Rosshill, Galway.

Duke, Thomas Patrick: 48 Hollybank Rd., Drumcondra, D.

Dunbar, Martin: Castle Place, Ferns, Wexford.

Dunleavy, Michael: Ballygurrane, Athenry, Galway.

Dunleavy, Patrick: Toghermore, Tuam, Galway.

Dunne, Andrew: 208 Pearse St., D.

Dunne, Arthur: The Ave., Gorey, Wexford.

Dunne, Denis: Kincora, Brighton Gardens, Terenure, D.

Dunne, Edward: 82 Irish St., Enniscorthy.

Dunne, Francis: 149 Clonliffe Ave., Ballybough Rd., D.

Dunne, James: 5 Cuchulainn Terrace, Castletown Rd., Dundalk, Louth.

Dunne, John: 5 Magennis Square, Pearse St., D.

Dunne, John: 13 South Dock Place, Ringsend, D.

Dunne, Joseph: 7 Grace Pk. Ave., Drumcondra, D.

Dunne, Margaret: 1 B. Block, Buckingham Buildings, D.

Dunne, Patrick: 116 Cabra Pk., Phibsborough, D.

Dunne, Patrick Joseph: 44 Larkfield Grove, Kimmage, D.

Dunne, Peadar: 5 Madden Rd., Donore Ave., D.

Dunne, Thomas: 83 Sundrive Rd., Kimmage, D.

Dunne, Thomas: 95 North King St., D.

Dunne, Thomas: 56 Casino Rd., Fairview, D.

Dunne, Thomas John: 5 St Joseph's Terrace, Richmond Place, North Circular Rd., D.

Durnin, James: Sunnyside, Lisnawilly, Dundalk, Louth.

Dwan, John: 1 Lwr. Gardiner St., D.

Dwyer, Jack: Tomalosset, Enniscorthy.

Dwyer, James: Tomalosset, Enniscorthy.

Dwyer, James: 69 St. John's Villas, Enniscorthy.

Dwyer, James: 4 Arran Quay, D.

Dwyer, Michael: 10 Buckingham Terrace, Buckingham St., D.

Dwyer, Michael: 49 Cork St., D.

Dyas, Albert: 96 Haddington Rd., D.

Dynan, Christopher: 25 Upr. Cumberland St. North, D.

Earle, Michael: 12 Redmond St., Enniscorthy.

Early, John: 49 Shelmartin Ave., Fairview, D.

Early, Patrick Joseph: 2 Marino Pk. Ave., Fairview, D.

Edwards, John: 5 Greenmount Court, Harold's Cross, D.

Edwards, Michael: 125 The Coombe, D.

Egan, John: Cave, Oranmore, Galway.

Egan, John: Kiltrogue, Claregalway, Galway.

Egan, Joseph: Abbey Row, Athenry, Galway.

Egan, Patrick: 32 South Circular Rd., Kilmainham, D.

Egan, Patrick: Keave, Oranmore, Galway.

Egan, William: 22 C Rd., Fairbrothers Fields, South Circular Rd., D.

Egan, William: Moorpark, Athenry, Galway.

Ellis, Samuel: 68 Eccles St., D.

Elmes, Ellett: 23 St. Jarlath Rd., Cabra, D.

English, Maire: 12 Wigan Rd., D.

English, Patrick: Dubber Lane, Finglas, D.

English, Patrick Francis: 32 Main St., Blackrock, D.

Ennis, Christopher: 27 Temple St., D.

Ennis, Edward: 5 Dromard Ave., D.

Ennis, James: Knockmarshal, Enniscorthy.

Ennis, Lily: 56 St John's Villas, Enniscorthy.

Ennis, Michael: 83 Ballybough Rd., D.

Ennis, Michael: Tomalosset, Enniscorthy.

Ennis, Thomas James: Whitefields, Phoenix Pk., D.

Eustace, Robert: 24 Gloucester St., D.

Evans, Robert: 6 Warrenmount Place, Blackpits, D.

Fagan, Brian: 2 Grattan Parade, Drumcondra, D.

Fagan, James: 10 Havelock Square, Bath Ave., D.

Fagan, John: 32 East Arran St., D.

Fagan, Michael: 32 East Arran St., D.

Fagan, Patrick: 53 North King St., D.

Fagan, Patrick: 32 East Arran St., D.

Fagan, William: Captains Lane, Crumlin, D.

Fahey, Michael Joseph: 2 Winchester Place, Medford, Massachusetts, USA.

Fahy, Anna: Bellevue, Dundrum, D.

Fahy, Frank: Bellevue, Dundrum, D.

Fahy, James: Doughiska, Galway.

Fahy, Margaret: Ballinamana, Oranmore, Galway.

Fahy, Martin: Slieverue, Athenry, Galway.

Fahy, Michael: Tawin, Oranmore, Galway.

Fahy, Mortimer: Slieveroe, Athenry, Galway.

Fahy, Patrick: Craughwell, Galway.

Fahy, Patrick Joseph: Quay St., Kinvara, Galway.

Fahy, Philip: Carnane, Athenry, Galway.

Fahy, Thomas: Caherpeak, Kilcolgan, Galway.

Fahy, Thomas: Tawin, Oranmore, Galway.

Fahy, Thomas James: St. Peter's Presbytery, Surry Hills, Sydney, Australia.

Fallon, Bernard: 18 Atherton St., Roxbury, Massachusetts, USA

Fallon, Michael: Two Mile Ditch, Castlegar, Galway.

Farrell, Denis: 6 Willett Place, Glorney's Buildings, D.

Farrell, James: Currmagine, Whitehall, Longford.

Farrell, John: 12 Cabra Rd., D.

Farrell, John: 101 North Brunswick St., D.

Farrell, Michael: 45 Capel St., D.

Farrell, Patrick: 21 Monck Place, Phibsborough, D.

Farrell, Patrick: 2 Lwr. Church St., Enniscorthy.

Farrelly, Christopher: 18 Temple Cottages, Broadstone, D.

Farrelly, Rose: 66 Goldenbridge Ave., Kilmainham, D.

Farren, Stephen: Cole's Lane, D.

Faulkner, John: 32 Upr. Ormond Quay, D.

Fearon, Peter: 30 Viking Rd., D.

Fee, Brigid: 3 Royse Rd., Phibsborough, D.

Feehan, James: 4 Westhampton Place, Terenure, D.

Feekery, Christopher: 240 Milkwood Rd., Herne Hill, London, SE24.

Feeney, Gerald: Ballaghadreen, Roscommon.

Feeney, Henry Joseph: Shrule, Galway.

Feeney, James: 30 Worth St., San Francisco, California, USA.

Feeney, John: Mountpelier, Monivea, Athenry, Galway.

Feeney, Patrick: c/o Hotel Workers Union, 2 Edward St., Wellington, New Zealand.

Feeney, Timothy: Mullacutta, Claregalway, Galway.

Ferguson, Michael: Castletowncooley, Dundalk, Louth.

Ffrench Mullen, Douglas: 68 Upr. Rathmines, D.

Finegan, Michael: 2 Whites Cottages, Summerhill, D.

Finerty, Martin: Cloonbeggan, Claregalway, Galway.

Finlay, John: 5 Grenville St., Mountjoy Square, D.

Finn, James: Moorpark, Athenry, Galway.

Finn, Patrick: 8 Bethune St., New York, USA.

Fisher, John: 81 St. Ignatius Rd., D.

Fitzgerald, Aine: 15 Adrian Ave., Harold's Cross, D.

Fitzgerald, Desmond: Fairy Hill, Bray.

Fitzgerald, James: "Coolgariff", Stillorgan, D.

Fitzgerald, Leo: 173 Pearse St., D.

Fitzgerald, Theobald Wolfe Tone: 173 Pearse St., D.

Fitzgerald, Thomas: 4 Leeson Pk. Ave., Appian Way, D.

Fitzgerald, William: 173 Pearse St., D.

Fitzharris, James: 16 Collins Ave., Donnycarney, D.

Fitzharris, John: Oriel St., D.

Fitzmaurice, Gerald: 10 Navan Rd., Cabra, D.

Fitzpatrick, Andrew Joseph: 1 Chaworth Terrace, Hanbury Lane, D.

Fitzpatrick, Denis: 6 Usher's Island, D.

Fitzpatrick, Francis: 2 Lwr. Kevin St., D.

Fitzpatrick, James: 194 Owen's Ave., Ceannt's Fort, Mount Brown, D.

Fitzpatrick, Maire: 16 St. John's Villas, Enniscorthy.

Fitzpatrick, Michael: Dromineen, Kanturk, Cork.

Fitzpatrick, Patrick: 16 St. John's Villas, Enniscorthy.

Fitzsimons, Maurice: 8 Blessington Place, off Nelson St., D.

Flaherty, William: Carnmore, Oranmore, Galway.

Flanagan, James: Oranmore, Galway.

Flanagan, James Michael: Rosevilla, Rathfarnham, D.

Flanagan, Mary: St Lawrence Cottage, Strand Rd., Sutton, D.

Flanagan, Matthew: 56 Belmont Ave., Donnybrook, D.

Flanagan, Maurice Daniel: 36 Blessington St., D.

Flanagan, Patrick: Cave, Oranmore, Galway.

Flanagan, Patrick: Sunnyside, Oakley Rd., Ranelagh, D.

Flannery, Michael: Merlin Pk., Galway.

Fleming, Dolly: Church St., Athenry, Galway.

Fleming, Eamon C.: c/o Department of Finance, Government Buildings, D.

Fleming, George: Clarinbridge, Galway.

Fleming, James: 9 Hamilton Row, Westland Row, D.

Fleming, John: Clarinbridge, Galway.

Fleming, Joseph: 211 West 108 St., New York, USA.

Fleming, Michael: 9 Hamilton Row, D.

Fleming, Michael: Shillelagh, Wicklow.

Fleming, Michael: Clarinbridge, Galway.

Fleming, Patrick: R. D. 1, New City, New York, USA.

Fleming, Thomas Joseph: Castle Taylor, Ardrahan, Galway.

Flood, Josephine: 30 Little Mary St., D.

Flood, Seán: Peterhead Prison, Scotland.

Flynn, Ignatius George: 1 Rose Terrace, Wharf Rd., D.

Flynn, John A.: 90 Bushy Pk. Rd., Terenure, D6.

Flynn, Patrick: 38 Mountpleasant Buildings, Rathmines, D.

Fogarty, James: 70 Charlemont St., D.

Fogarty, Joseph: 2 Fagan's Cottages, Newfoundland St., D.

Fogarty, Patrick: 3 Brighton Ave., Clontarf, D.

Fogarty, Thomas: 79 Fitzroy Ave., Drumcondra, D.

Foley, Michael: 5 Cabra Rd., D.

Foley, Michael Patrick: Main St., Edenderry, Offaly.

Foran, James: 4 Dolphin's Barn St., D.

Forde, Daniel: Green St., Wexford.

Forde, John: Caherdevane, Craughwell, Galway.

Forde, Patrick: Rhinn, Kilcolgan, Galway.

Forde, Seán: 10 Dollymount Ave., Clontarf, D.

Forde, Thomas: Carnaun, Athenry, Galway.

Forrestal, Joseph: Shroughmore, Ballindaggin, Enniscorthy.

Fox, James: 18 Hastings St., Ringsend, D.

Fox, James Joseph: 3 Altinure Terrace, Cabra Pk., D.

Fox, Michael: Brass Castle, Chapelizod, D.

Foy, Frederick: 695 Saint Laurence Rd., Chapelizod, D.

Foy, Martin: 21 Little Denmark St., D.

Franklin, John: 30 St. John's Villas, Enniscorthy.

Frawley, Denis: 102 Newgrange Rd., Cabra, D.

Freaney, Michael: Derrydonnell, Athenry, Galway.

Freaney, Michael T: Mountain West, Oranmore, Galway.

Freeney, Michael M: Mountain West, Oranmore, Galway.

Friel, Bernard: 168 William St., Glasgow, Scotland.

Fuery, Michael: Colesgrove, Craughwell, Galway.

Fullam, Thomas: 54 Denzille St., D.

Furey, John: 53 St Alphonsus St., Roxbury, Massachusetts, USA.

Furey, Patrick: Oranbeg, Oranmore, Galway.

Furey, Thomas: Oranbeg, Oranmore, Galway.

Furey, Thomas: Bushfield, Oranmore, Galway.

Furey, Thomas: Rhinn, Oranmore, Galway.

Furlong, John: 32 Charles St., D.

Furlong, Joseph: Portobello Barracks, Rathmines, D.

Gahan, Joseph: 40 Mountjoy Square, D.

Gahan, Matthew: 49 Parnell St., D.

Gahan, Tadhg: 76 Vernon Ave., Clontarf, D.

Gallagher, Patrick: Butterfield Ave., Rathfarnham.

Gallagher, Seán: Bandon Barracks, Cork.

Galligan, Peter Paul: Ballinagh, Cavan.

Gannon, Henry: 10 Main St., Rathfarnham, D.

Gannon, Lawrence: 75 Lake Ave., Yonkers, New York, USA.

Gardner, John: Knockbrack, Athenry, Galway.

Garland, Patrick: 171 McCaffery's Estate, Irishtown, D.

Garrett, James J.: 3 Castleview Pk., Malahide, D.

Gartlan, Patrick: 58 Donore Ave., D.

Gaskin, Francis: 55 Reuben Ave., South Circular Rd., D.

Gaskin, Henry: 105 South Circular Rd., D.

Gaskin, Thomas: 55 Reuben Ave., D.

Gavan, John James: 19 Leinster Ave., North Strand, D.

Gay, Tomás Ernán: 8 Haddon Rd., Clontarf, D.

Gaynor, Arthur: 9 Aughrim Villas, Aughrim St., D.

Geoghegan, George: 27 Upr. Dorset St., D.

Geoghegan, John Joseph: Adare, Limerick.

Geraghty, Christopher: Aughrim Lane, Aughrim St., D.

Geraghty, Sean: 83 Terenure Rd. West, D.

Gibson, Edward: 31 St Michael's Terrace, Blackpits, D.

Gibson, Michael: 12 Dean St., D.

Gibson, Richard: 47 Harold Rd., Manor Place, D.

Giffney, Michael: 10 East Rd., D.

Gifford-Donnelly, Nellie: 39 Carlingford Rd., Drumcondra, D.

Gill, James: 3 Lauderdale Terrace, New Row, D.

Gilligan, Robert: 198 Philipsburg Ave., Fairview, D.

Gilsenan, Patrick: 63 Dowth Ave., Cabra, D.

Girvan, John: Carnmore, Oranmore, Galway.

Gleeson, Daniel Patrick: Berkerley St., D.

Gleeson, James: 8 Esmonde St., Gorey, Wexford.

Gleeson, Joseph: 10A Aungier St., D.

Gleeson, Martin: 10A Aungier St., D.

Gleeson, William: 37 Marino Green, Croyden Pk., Fairview, D.

Glynn, George: Lydican, Claregalway, Galway.

Glynn, James: 47 Victoria St., South Circular Rd., D.

Glynn, John: Dooras, Kinvara, Galway.

Glynn, Patrick: Kiltulla, Oranmore, Galway.

Goff, Bridget: 26 Little Mary St., D.

Goff, Henry: 6 New Range, Shannon, Enniscorthy.

Gogan, John Gerard: 11 Maxwell Rd., Rathgar, D.

Gogan, Richard P.: 43 Leix Rd., Cabra, D.

Gogan, Vincent Joseph: 371 North Circular Rd., D.

Golden, David Thomas: 2 Victoria St., South Circular Rd., D.

Golden, Jerry: 49 Croydon Pk. Ave., Fairview, D.

Golding, Patrick: Ballywinna, Craughwell, Galway.

Good, Alfred Joseph: 109 Richmond Rd., Drumcondra, D.

Goodall, James: 58 John St., Enniscorthy.

Goodall, Joseph: 2 Maudlins Folly, Enniscorthy.

Goode, Michael: North Gate St., Athenry, Galway.

Gordon, Edward: 25 Annamoe Drive, Cabra, D.

Gough, James: Collinstown House, Lusk, D.

Gough, James: 16 Station Rd., Baldoyle, D.

Goulding, Charles: 15 Cadogan Rd., Fairview, D.

Goulding, James: 176 Richmond Rd., Fairview, D.

Grace, James Joseph: 3 Stanley's Cottages, Mespil Rd., D.

Graham, Thomas: 33 Black Pitts, D.

Grange, Annie: 12 Upr. Grand Canal St., D.

Grant, Patrick: Gaoth Anair, North Rd., Finglas, D.

Grattan, Richard: 35 Upr. Erne St., D.

Graves, John: Brewery Place, Rathdrum, Wicklow.

Gray, Mary: Carley's Bridge, Enniscorthy.

Grealish, Bernard: Killeenan, Craughwell, Galway.

Grealish, Henry: Kiltrouge, Claregalway, Galway.

Grealish, James: Carnmore, Oranmore, Galway.

Grealish, James Peter: Carnmore, Oranmore, Galway.

Grealish, John: Caherdine, Craughwell, Galway.

Grealish, Martin: Carnmore, Oranmore, Galway.

Grealish, Martin: 4 Davis St., Wellington, New Zealand.

Grealish, Patrick: Lisheencoyle, Athenry, Galway.

Grealish, Patrick: Curragreen, Merlin Pk., Galway.

Grealish, Patrick: Carnmore, Oranmore, Galway.

Grealish, Thomas: Kiltulla, Oranmore, Galway.

Greally, James: Cregboy, Claregalway, Galway.

Greally, Patrick: Clonbresk, Athenry, Galway.

Grealy, Margaret Rose: Rocklawn, Galway.

Grealy, Peter: Glanascual, Oranmore, Galway.

Green, Patrick: 83 Lwr. Dorset St., D.

Greene, Arthur: 40 North Mary St., Dundalk, Louth.

Greene, Josephine: 366 Lwr. Kimmage Rd., Terenure, D.

Greene, Owen: Welaskiwin, Alberta, Canada.

Greene, William: 35 Aungier St., D.

Gregory, John: 14 Charleville Ave., North Strand, D.

Grehan, James: 20 The Hollow, Dolphin's Barn, D.

Griffin, Florence: Glenburn, Sutton, D.

Griffin, Gerald: Glenburn, Sutton, D.

Griffin, Martin: 96 Rialto Cottages, South Circular Rd., D.

Griffin, Michael: The Weir, Kilcolgan, Galway.

Griffith, William: 137 Merrion Rd., D.

Grimley, Michael: 113 Middle Abbey St., D.

Guilfoyle, Joseph: 101 Ceannts Fort, Mount Brown, D.

Guilfoyle, Sean: Portobello Barracks, D.

Habernatty, Henry: Shannon Hill, Enniscorthy.

Hackett, Rosana: 115 Brian Pk., Croydon Pk., Marino, D.

Hall, Samuel Kevin: 44 Portland Row, D.

Halloran, John: Oranmore, Galway.

Halpenny, Peter: 8 Burns Row, Dundalk, Louth.

Halpin, John: 183 Parnell St., D.

Halpin, Patrick E.: 11725 S. Walnut, Orange, California, USA.

Halpin, William: 12 Moore St., D.

Halpin, William: 6 St Valentine's Terrace, Church Rd., Fairview, D.

Hamill, Thomas: 37 Broughton St., Dundalk, Louth.

Hamill, Thomas: 92 Francis St., D.

Hampton, James: 18 Mary's Abbey, D.

Hand, Matthew: 26 Summerhill, D.

Hanify, Murty: Tarmud, Kilcolgan, Galway.

Hanley, John: 155 West 91st St., New York, USA.

Hanlon, David: Loughcurra, Kinvara, Galway.

Hanlon, Stephen: 6 Newcomen Court, North Strand, D.

Hanniffy, John J: Tally House, Athenry, Galway.

Hanniffy, Michael: Tally-Ho, Athenry, Galway.

Hannigan, Thomas: 6 Gardiners Row, D.

Hannon, Arthur: 514 R Prescott Ave., Scranton, Pennsylvania, USA.

Hannon, James Joseph: 63 Charleville Ave., D.

Hanratty, Emily: 77 Eccles St., D.

Hanratty, Seámus: 9 Mill St., Dundalk, Louth.

Hansberry, Patrick: Castle Ellen, Athenry, Galway.

Harbourne, Eileen: Lios na Bruidhne, Butterfield Ave., Rathfarnham, D.

Harbourne, Seán: Lios na Bruidhne, Butterfield Ave., Rathfarnham, D.

Harmon, Bridget: 79 Rialto Buildings, South Circular Rd., D.

Harmon, Patrick Joseph: 32 Upr. Clanbrassil St., Harold's Cross, D.

Harnett, Alfred: Drimnagh Cottages, Inchicore, D.

Harris, Thomas: Caragh, Naas, Kildare.

Harte, William: Glanascaul, Oranmore, Galway.

Haughton, Christopher: 33 Sitric Rd., D.

Hawkins, Patrick: Moneymore, Galway.

Hawkins, Thomas: Rhin, Oranmore, Galway.

Hayes, Augustine: 16 Hume St., D.

Hayes, James Joseph: 31 Tolka Rd., Clonliffe Rd., D.

Hayes, Michael: 20 Brighton Square, Rathgar, D.

Hayes, Richard: Woodlands, Kill O' The Grange, Blackrock, D.

Hayes, Seán: 24 Kildare St., D.

Healy, Cathleen: 188 Phibsborough Rd., D.

Healy, Christopher: 188 Phibsboro Rd., D.

Healy, James: 16 Templeshannon, Enniscorthy.

Healy, John: 188 Phibsborough Rd., D.

Healy, Michael: Gloves Middle, Athenry, Galway.

Healy, Patrick: Mount Garrett, Monivea, Athenry, Galway.

Healy, Peadar: 158 Cabra Rd., D.

Healy, Richard: 151 Parnell St., D.

Healy, Thomas: 23 Lwr. Oriel St., D.

Hearne, May: 15 Ross Rd., Enniscorthy.

Hearne, Thomas: 15 Ross Rd., Enniscorthy.

Heavey, Thomas: 54 John St., Enniscorthy.

Heavey, William: Cloonkeen, Attymon, Galway.

Heery, James Michael: 29 Emoville Ave., South Circular Rd., D.

Heffernan, Michael: 7 St. Joseph's Place, Inchicore, D.

Henderson, Frank: 75 North Circular Rd., D.

Henderson, Leo James: Rosslea, Willbrook Rd., Rathfarnham, D.

Henderson, Thomas: 14 St. Kevin's Rd., South Circular Rd., D.

Hendley, Emily: 11 South Brown St., D.

Hendrick, Edward: 70 Collins Ave., Donnycarney, D.

Hendrick, James: 7 Hardwicke St., D.

Hendrick, John Joseph: 173 Emmet Rd., Inchicore, D.

Hendrick, Nicholas: 2 Weafer St., Enniscorthy.

Hendrick, William: 2 Weafer St., Enniscorthy.

Heneghan, Annie: 11 Lwr. Church St., Enniscorthy.

Henehan, Peter: Derrydonnell, Athenry, Galway.

Henry, Francis: 5 Fennells Cottages, Charlemont St., D.

Henry, Frederick: Rear of 92 Lwr. Mount St., D.

Henry, James: Collins Barracks, D.

Heron, Aine: Clonard, Ballawley, Dundrum.

Heron, James J.: Malahide Rd., Swords.

Hession, Michael: North Gate St., Athenry, Galway.

Heuston, George: 74 Parnell St., D.

Heuston, John: 20 Fontenoy St., D.

Hickey, Michael: 30 Lennox St., D.

Hickey, Richard: 28 Victoria St., South Circular Rd., D.

Higgins, Annie Gladys: 227 East 19th St., Manhattan, New York, USA.

Higgins, Daniel: Moneymore, Oranmore, Galway.

Higgins, Frederick Paul: 37 Seafield Rd. West, Clontarf, D.

Higgins, May: Cross St., Athenry, Galway.

Higgins, Michael: Moneymore, Oranmore, Galway.

Higgins, Michael Joseph: Cloonpark., Athenry, Galway.

Higgins, Patrick: Coshla, Athenry, Galway.

Higgins, Peter: 9 Horseman's Rd., Parnell St., D.

Higgins, Richard: Castlelambert, Athenry, Galway.

Hiney, William: 6 Hill View Terrace, Enniscorthy.

Hogan, Patrick Joseph: 1 Seafield Rd., Dollymount, D.

Hogan, William Conor: 48B Kimmage Rd., D.

Holahan, Patrick Hugh: 174 Oxmantown Rd., D.

Holbrook, Matthew: Templeshannon, Enniscorthy.

Holden, James Patrick: 32 Lwr. St. Columba's Rd., Drumcondra, D.

Holland, Daniel: 157 Inchicore Rd., Inchicore, D.

Holland, Francis Michael: 3 Russell St., off North Circular Rd., D.

Holland, Patrick: Ballinacourty, Oranmore, Galway.

Holland, Robert: 4 Reginald Square, D.

Holland, Thomas: Tawin, Oranmore, Galway.

Holland, Walter Leo: 157 Inchicore Rd., D.

Holmes, Denis: 17 Railway St., D.

Holohan, Colum: c/o Rev. L. Hoyne P.P., Tullaroan, Kilkenny.

Holohan, Gerard: 55 Botanic Ave., Glasnevin, D.

Holohan, Hugh Aloysius: c/o Newspaper Guild of New York, 62 West 45th St., New York, USA.

Horan, Daniel: 34 Hammond St., South Circular Rd., D.

Horan, John Joseph: 3 Prison Cottages, Ballymullen, Tralee, Kerry.

Hore, Martin: 1 Dean Swift Square, D.

Howard, George: 2 Flint St., North Ipswich, Queensland, Australia.

Howard, Seán: 26 Temple Cottages, Broadstone, D.

Howlett, Michael: 8 Grenville St., off Mountjoy Square, D.

Howley, Annie: Castlegar, Kilcolgan, Galway.

Howley, Michael Joseph: Oranmore, Galway.

Howley, Peter: Limepark, Peterswell, Loughrea, Galway.

Howlin, Patrick Joseph: 29 Slaney St., Enniscorthy.

Hughes, James: 3 West 101 St., New York, USA.

Hughes, James J.: 19 Iona Pk., Glasnevin, D.

Hughes, John: 6 New Range, Shannon, Enniscorthy.

Hughes, Patrick: 19 Pk. St., Dundalk, Louth.

Hughes, Patrick: 131 Foley St., D.

Hughes, Patrick J.: County Buildings, Galway.

Hughes, Thomas: 8 Summerhill, D.

Humphreys, Robert: 3 Aldborough Parade, North Strand Rd., D.

Hunter, James: 13 Sackville Ave., Ballybough Rd., D.

Hunter, Thomas: Glanworth, Cork.

Hurley, John: c/o Jury's Hotel, D.

Hurley, Seán: Moulagow, Drinagh, Dunmanway, Cork.

Hussey, William: Kilcolgan, Galway.

Hutchinson, Joseph: 15 Offaly Rd., Cabra, D.

Hyland, Christopher: 263 St Attracta Rd., Cabra, D.

Hyland, James: 15 St. Michael's Terrace, Blackpits, South Circular Rd., D.

Hyland, Joseph: Coolgarrow, Enniscorthy.

Hyland, Matthew: Drumgoold, Enniscorthy.

Hyland, Thomas: 11 Lwr. Bridge St., D.

Hynes, Francis: 149 Bandon Rd., Cork.

Hynes, John Frances: North Commons, Lusk, D.

Hynes, Martin: Railway View, Clifden, Galway.

Hynes, Michael: Monatigue, Craughwell, Galway.

Hynes, Seán: 4 Queen St., D.

Hynes, Thomas: 5 O'Donohoe's Terrace, Galway.

Hynes, Thomas: Ballinamana, Oranmore, Galway.

Hynes, Thomas: Lisduff, Craughwell, Galway.

Hynes, William: Oranbeg, Oranmore, Galway.

Irvine, George: 6 Mount Pleasant Square, Ranelagh, D.

Irwin, Samuel Patrick: Griffith Barracks, D.

Jackman, Nicholas: St. Enda's College, Rathfarnham, D.

Jackson, Joseph: 26 South King St., D.

Jackson, Peter: 83 D Block, New Bride St., D.

Jameson, Richard: 4 Bridge St., Dundalk, Louth.

Jenkinson, Margaret: 89 Church Rd., Fairview, D.

Jennings, Thomas Michael: 30 North William St., D.

Johnson, Patrick: Drumgoold, Enniscorthy.

Jones, Thomas: 15 Emmet St., Harold's Cross, D.

Jordan, James: Monbeg, Ballindaggin, Enniscorthy.

Jordan, Michael: 4 Market Square, Enniscorthy.

Jordan, Sara: 4 Market Square, Enniscorthy.

Jordan, Stephen: Davis St., Athenry, Galway.

Joyce, Brian: Sgoil Éanna, Rath Fearnáin, Baile Átha Cliath.

Joyce, Edward: c/o Miss Tutty, Newsagent, 10 High St., D.

Joyce, James: 51 Dominick St., D.

Joyce, John: Kilmore, Artane, D.

Joyce, John Vincent: General Headquarters, Parkgate, D.

Joyce, Joseph James: 15 Middle Mountjoy St., D.

Joyce, Margaret: 51 Lwr. Dominick St., D.

Joyce, Martin: Carnaun, Athenry, Galway.

Judge, John Patrick: Dromartin Hill, Dundrum, D.

Kain, Thomas: 15 Old Camden St., D.

Kavanagh, Daniel Joseph: 62 Tritonville Rd., Sandymount, D.

Kavanagh, Denis: 20 Oxmantown Rd., North Circular Rd., D.

Kavanagh, James: 16 Parnell Square, D.

Kavanagh, James: 8 Bishop St., D.

Kavanagh, James Joseph: 33 Lwr. Gardiner St., D.

Kavanagh, James Joseph: c/o Terenure College, D.

Kavanagh, John: 26 Greggs Hill, Arklow, Wicklow.

Kavanagh, Liam: 16 Wolseley St., South Circular Rd., D.

Kavanagh, Martin: 9 St Mary's Terrace, Inchicore, D.

Kavanagh, Mary: 33 St Mary's Rd., Church Rd., D.

Kavanagh, Michael J.: 9 Winton Ave., Rathgar, D.

Kavanagh, Patrick: 15 Victoria Ave., Donnybrook, D.

Kavanagh, Patrick: 33 St. John's St., Enniscorthy.

Kavanagh, Patrick: Russborough, Blessington, Wicklow.

Kavanagh, Patrick: 24 St Mary's Rd., Church Rd., D.

Kavanagh, Peter: 7 Oaklands Pk., Ballsbridge, D.

Kavanagh, Priscilla: 16 Wolseley St., South Circular Rd., D.

Kavanagh, Seamus: 302 Howth Rd., Killester, D.

Kavanagh, Seámus: 72 Russell Ave., Drumcondra, D.

Kavanagh, Thomas: Fire Station, Thomas St., D.

Kavanagh, William: Chapel St., Ferns, Wexford.

Keady, Thomas: Carnmore, Oranmore, Galway.

Kealy, John: Edmondstown, Rathfarnham, D.

Kealy, Sarah: 7 Shamrock Cottages, North Strand, D.

Keane, Denis: Ballycurraghan, Maynooth, Kildare.

Keane, James: Rockmore, Athenry, Galway.

Keane, John: Derrydonnell, Athenry, Galway.

Keane, John: Ballinacloughy, Oranmore, Galway.

Keane, Liam: 27 Palmerstown Rd., D.

Keane, Michael: Derrydonnell, Athenry, Galway.

Keane, Michael: Ballyclera, Kinvara, Galway.

Keane, Patrick: Gurrane, Maree, Oranmore, Galway.

Keane, Thomas: Gortnaglough, Kinvara, Galway.

Kearney, Francis: Tonroe, Oranmore, Galway.

Kearney, Hugh: 66 Dublin St., Dundalk, Louth.

Kearney, Michael: Cappamurragh, Dundrum, Tipperary.

Kearney, Peadar: 79 Mount Brown, D.

Kearney, Thaddeus: Ballinacourty, Oranmore, Galway.

Kearney, Thomas: 9 Killarney Ave., North Strand, D.

Kearns, Daniel: Oldcastle, Kiltulla, Athenry, Galway.

Kearns, Hugh: 13 St. Clement's Rd., Drumcondra, D.

Kearns, Joseph John: 13 St. Clement's Rd., Drumcondra, D.

Kearns, Patrick: 10 Daniel St., D.

Kearns, Sean: 13 St. Clement's Rd., Drumcondra, D.

Kearns, Thomas: 13 St Clements Rd., Drumcondra, D.

Keating, Cornelius: Renard, Caherciveen, Kerry.

Keating, Cornelius: 46 Richmond Rd., Drumcondra, D.

Keating, Mary Pauline: 28 Castlewood Ave., Rathmines, D.

Keeffe, Michael: Shannon Hill, Enniscorthy.

Keegan, Edward Laurence: 50 Casimir Rd., Harold's Cross, D.

Keegan, Ellen: 10 Irish St., Enniscorthy.

Keegan, Patrick: 10 Irish St., Enniscorthy.

Keegan, Teresa: 10 Irish St., Enniscorthy.

Keegan, Thomas: Wafer St., Enniscorthy, Wexford.

Keely, John: Ballyboden, Rathfarnham, D.

Keenan, Thomas Patrick: 14 Newmarket, D.

Kehoe, Josephine: Glencarrig, Enniscorthy.

Kehoe, Michael John: 71 Ranelagh Rd., Clonskea, D.

Kehoe, Patrick J.: Glencarrig, Enniscorthy.

Kehoe, Thomas: Rathduffmore, Hackettstown, Carlow.

Kelly, Annie: 220 Harold's Cross Rd., D.

Kelly, Clement: 28 Casino Rd., Croydon Pk., Marino, D.

Kelly, Edward: 45 Blessington St., D.

Kelly, Elizabeth: 34 Devenish Rd., Kimmage, D.

Kelly, Francis: 74 Marlborough St., D.

Kelly, Francis Matthew: Bun Avon, Boghall Rd., Bray, Wicklow.

Kelly, Hugh: 23 Synnott Place, D.

Kelly, James: Clonee, Camolin, Wexford.

Kelly, James: 39 Daniel St., South Circular Rd., D.

Kelly, James: 25 Newfoundland St., D.

Kelly, James: Mucklagh, Tullamore, Offaly.

Kelly, John: Tourkeel, Athenry, Galway.

Kelly, John: Commons West, Swords, D.

Kelly, John: 5 Swift's Row, D.

Kelly, John Emanuel: 7 Eckstein Rd., Clapham Junction, London SW11.

Kelly, John J.: Camolin Pk., Camolin, Wexford.

Kelly, John P.: Kilpierce, Enniscorthy.

Kelly, Joseph: 11 Upr. Dominick St., D.

Kelly, Joseph: 7 McGuinness Square, Pearse St., D.

Kelly, Joseph: 93 Lwr. Dorset St., D.

Kelly, Joseph Francis: 3 Chamber St., D.

Kelly, Joseph Patrick: Corduff, Lusk, D.

Kelly, Katie: Cashel, Connemara, Galway.

Kelly, Martin: 16 Kildare Rd., Kimmage, D.

Kelly, Mary: Liberty Hall, Beresford Place, D.

Kelly, Matthew: Corduff, Lusk, D.

Kelly, Michael: Two Mile Ditch, Galway.

Kelly, Michael: Castlelambert, Athenry, Galway.

Kelly, Michael: South Pk. Terrace, Galway.

Kelly, Michael J.: 6 Manor St., D.

Kelly, Patrick: Fahymactibbet, Craughwell,

Galway.

Kelly, Patrick: Caherlea, Claregalway, Galway.

Kelly, Patrick: The Square, Lusk, D.

Kelly, Patrick: Fire Station, Upr. Dorset St., D.

Kelly, Richard: 20 Howard St., Ringsend, D.

Kelly, Richard: Corduff, Lusk, D.

Kelly, Seán: 24 O'Curry Rd., South Circular Rd., D.

Kelly, Thomas Joseph: 1 Upr. Northbrook Ave., North Strand, D.

Kelly, William: 11 Donohue St., Inchicore, D.

Kelly, William: 9 Bishop St., D.

Kelly, William: Attymon, Athenry, Galway.

Kennan, Austin: 48 Vernon Ave., Clontarf.

Kennedy, James: 80 Aungier St., D.

Kennedy, John: 8 Coburg Place, off Seville Place, D.

Kennedy, John Joseph: Lecarrow, Athenry, Galway.

Kennedy, John L.: Cahercrin, Athenry, Galway.

Kennedy, Joseph: Raystown, Ashbourne, Meath.

Kennedy, Joseph: 'St Margarets', Stella Maris Rd., Sandymount, D.

Kennedy, Kathleen: Caheroyan, Athenry, Galway.

Kennedy, Luke: 58 Great Charles St., D.

Kennedy, Margaret: 117 Donore Terrace, South Circular Rd., D.

Kennedy, Martin: Lecarrow, Athenry, Galway.

Kennedy, Patrick: Caheroyan, Athenry, Galway.

Kennedy, Patrick: Slieverue, Athenry, Galway.

Kennedy, Seán: 22 Parnell St., D.

Kennedy, Thomas: Slieverue, Athenry, Galway.

Kennedy, Thomas: Carnaun, Athenry, Galway.

Kenny, Charles: 69 New St., D.

Kenny, Henry Vincent: Engineers Barracks, Curragh Camp, Kildare.

Kenny, James: High St., Belmont, Offaly.

Kenny, James: 5 Whitehall Cottages, Rathfarnham, D.

Kenny, James: 103 Rialto Buildings, D.

Kenny, James Joseph: 61 Fairview Strand, D.

Kenny, John: 56 Lwr. Gloucester St., D.

Kenny, John: 197 Clontarf Rd., D.

Kenny, John: 54 Ferguson Rd., Drumcondra, D.

Kenny, Kieran: Main St., Banagher, Offaly.

Kenny, Michael: 56 Lwr. Gloucester St., D.

Kenny, Patrick: Ballycarney P.O., Ferns, Wexford.

Kenny, Patrick: Caheroyan, Athenry, Galway.

Kent, Richard: Bawnard House, Castlelyons, Fermoy, Cork.

Kent, Thomas: Bawnard House, Castlelyons, Fermoy, Cork.

Keogh, Bernard Patrick: 2 Richmond Parade, North Circular Rd., D.

Keogh, Cyril Aloysius: 181 Beach 90th St., Rockaway Beach, Queens, New York, USA.

Keogh, Edward Patrick: 10 Pk. St., Inchicore, D.

Keogh, Gerald Anthony: 25 Elm Grove, Cullenswood, Ranelagh, D.

Keogh, James: 6 Hendrick St., D.

Keogh, John: 8 High St., D.

Keogh, Martin: 3 Raleigh Place, Dolphin's Barn, D.

Keogh, Patrick: 15 Dolphin's Barn St., D.

Keough, Joseph James: 33 Haverty Rd., Marino, D.

Kerr, John Patrick: Iveagh House, Bride Rd., D.

Kerr, Michael: 92 Harold's Cross Buildings, D.

Kerr, Neill: 1 Thornton Place, Dingle, Liverpool, England.

Kerrigan, Owen: 17 Oak Rd., Donnycarney, D.

Keys, John: 39 Thomas St., D.

Kieran, John: 11 Pk. St., Dundalk, Louth.

Kilcoyne, Thomas: 4 St Joseph's Terrace, Phibsborough Ave., D.

Kilgallon, John A.: 827 Dorian St., Far Rockaway, Long Island, New York, USA.

Kilkelly, John: Crushoa, Kinvara, Galway.

Kilkelly, Michael: Dooras Demense, Kinvara, Galway.

Killalea, John: 1 Flood St., Galway.

Killeen, Robert: 16 St. Joseph's Parade, Dorset St., D.

Killion, Patrick: 28 Great Western Villas, Phibsborough, D.

Kilmartin, Patrick: 23 Stoneybatter, D.

King, Daniel: 67 Aungier St., D.

King, George: 113 Home Farm Rd., Glasnevin, D.

King, John: 113 Home Farm Rd., Drumcondra, D.

King, John: Kiltulla, Oranmore, Galway.

King, Margaret: c/o Mental Hospital (employee), Enniscorthy.

King, Martin: 25 St. Ignatius Rd., Drumcondra, D.

King, Patrick: 4 Gulistan Terrace, Rathmines, D.

King, Patrick: Kiltulla, Oranmore, Galway.

King, Patrick: Kiltulla, Oranmore, Galway.

King, Peter: 3 Eglington Hill, Plumstead, London SE18.

King, Richard Francis: The Bungalow, Tinahask, Arklow, Wicklow.

King, Samuel: 25 St. Ignatius Rd., Drumcondra, D.

King, Sean Joseph Francis: 4 Effra Rd., Rathmines, D.

Kinsella, John: 45 Mountpleasant Square, Rathmines, D.

Kinsella, Peter: Summer Hill, Enniscorthy.

Kinsella, Robert: Tinnashrule, Ferns, Wexford.

Kirwan, Edward: 14 Old Camden St., D.

Kirwan, Michael: 27 Slaney St., Enniscorthy.

Kirwan, Patrick: Double Lane, Maynooth, Kildare.

Knightly, Michael: 65 St Laurence Rd., Clontarf, D.

Kyne, Martin: Kiltrogue, Claregalway, Galway.

Kyne, Nicholas: Palm Hill House, Claregalway, Galway.

Lacey, Philip: 10 Braithwaite St., D.

Lacy, James: 37 Hamilton St., Donore Ave., South Circular Rd., D.

Laffan, Nicholas: 8 Huxley Cres., Cork St., D.

Lafferty, John: Ballyvoy, Ballycastle, Antrim.

Lally, Frank: Rathgorgin, Craughwell, Galway.

Lally, Martin: Carnmore, Oranmore, Galway.

Lally, Michael: Carnmore, Oranmore, Galway.

Lalor, Eamon: 11 Newgrove Ave., Sandymount, D.

Lalor, Patrick Jospeh: 1 Coburgh Place, Seville Place, D.

Lamb, Patrick: 21 Ellesmere Ave., North Circular Rd., D.

Lane, Bridie: Killeely, Kilcolgan, Galway.

Lane, Edward: 170 North Strand, D.

Lanigan, Patrick: 7 Lindon's Flats, Lwr. Church St., D.

Lardner, Brigid: Church St., Athenry, Galway.

Lardner, John: Carnmore, Oranmore, Galway.

Lardner, Laurence: Church St., Athenry, Galway.

Largan, Michael: 9 Parnell St., D.

Larkin, Ita: 4 Armstrong's Range, Templeshannon, Enniscorthy.

Larkin, Stephen: c/o L. P. Lardner, Old Church St., Athenry, Galway.

Lavin, Andrew: Ballyfarnon, Carrick-on-Shannon, Roscommon.

Lawler, Patrick: 16 Fitzwilliam Lane, D.

Lawless, Colm: Saucerstown, Swords, D.

Lawless, Edward: Rathbeal, Swords, D.

Lawless, Eveleen: Saucerstown House, Swords, D.

Lawless, Frank J.: Saucerstown House, Swords, D.

Lawless, James Joseph: 20 First Ave., Saville Place, D.

Lawless, James Vincent: 148 North Strand Rd., D.

Lawless, Joseph Vincent: Glenview, Fardrum, Athlone, Westmeath.

Lawless, Michael: 20 First Ave., Seville Place, D.

Lawless, Monica: McDermott House, Curragh Camp, Kildare.

Lawless, Stephen: Lisnadrishna, Kiltulla, Galway.

Lawlor, Francis J.: Castleroe, Mageney, Kildare.

Lawlor, John: 18 Thomas Ashe St., D.

Lawlor, Laurence James: 29 Árd Rí Rd., Arbour Hill, D.

Lawlor, Mary: 29 Árd Rí Rd., Arbour Hill, D.

Leacy, James: 18 Ross Rd., Enniscorthy.

Leacy, John: 6 Trinity St., Wexford.

Leacy, Laurence: 13 John St., Enniscorthy.

Leacy, Owen: Duffry Gate, Enniscorthy.

Leahy, Denis: 17 Hill St., Dundalk, Louth.

Leahy, Thomas: 657 Dumbarton Rd., Partick West, Glasgow, Scotland.

Leddy, Peter: 14 Upr. Buckingham St., D.

Ledwith, Emily: 216 Kenilworth Rd., D.

Ledwith, Joseph: Laraghbryan, Maynooth, Kildare.

Ledwith, Peter: 65 Blessington St., D.

Lee, Hugh: 29 St Patrick's Cottages, Rathfarnham, D.

Lee, Joseph: 29 St. Patrick's Cottages, Rathfarnham, D.

Leggett, Robert: 30 Harmony Villas, Donnybrook, D.

Lemass, Noel: Office of the Minister of Supplies, D.

Lemass, Seán Francis: Churchtown Pk. House, Dundrum, D.

Lennon, Michael John: 11 Healthfield Rd., Terenure, D.

Lennon, Nicholas: 44 Beresford St., D.

Leonard, Edward: 277 Farranboley Cottages,

Windy Arbour, Dundrum, D.

Leonard, Joseph: 3 Lwr. Mountpleasant Ave., Rathmines, D.

Leonard, Margaret: 'Dunloe', Woonona Rd., Northbridge, Sydney, New South Wales, Australia.

Leonard, Patrick: Concrete, Milltown, D.

Levins, George: 5 North Temple St., D.

Linnane, Thomas: Stradbally, Kilcolgan, Galway.

Liston, Michael: 36 Bow Lane, James' St., D.

Litchfield, Henry: Falmore, Dundalk, Louth.

Little, James: 6 Charlemont Mall, Portobello, D.

Losty, Thomas: 39 Charleville Ave., North Strand, D.

Loughlin, James: Moneymore, Oranmore, Galway.

Love, Michael: 10 Bessborough Ave., North Strand Rd., D.

Lowe, Arnold: 33 Upr. Kevin St., D.

Lynch, Diarmuid: Goold's Hill, Mallow, Cork.

Lynch, Gilbert: 164 Crumlin Rd., D.

Lynch, John: 12 Shamrock Cottages, North Strand, D.

Lynch, Laurence: Flower Hill, Navan Rd., Cabra, D.

Lynch, Michael: 375 Clontarf Rd., D.

Lynch, Michael Joseph: 138 North Circular Rd., D.

Lynch, Patrick: North Cumberland St., D.

Lynch, Patrick: 29 Thomas St., D.

Lynch, Seán: Tigh Mhuire, Sutton, D.

Lynch, Sheila: 164 Crumlin Rd., Crumlin, D.

Lynch, Sheila: Flower Hill, Cabra, D.

Lynders, Thomasina: Turvey Hill, Donabate, D.

Lynskey, John: Clogher, Claregalway, Galway.

Lynskey, Patrick: Abbey Row, Athenry, Galway.

Lynskey, William: Clogher, Claregalway, Galway.

Lyons, Brigid: 4 Main St., Longford.

Lyons, Charles J.: 29 North Clarence St., D.

Lyons, Edward: 45 Croydon Pk. Ave., Marino, D.

Lyons, Edward: 22 Crampton Buildings, Temple Bar, D.

Lyons, George A.: Stationery Office, Beggars Bush, Barracks, D.

Lyons, John E.: 29 North Clarence St., D.

Lyons, Joseph: 38 Fairfield Ave., West Rd., D.

Mac Amhalghaidh, Mícheál Padraig: Árd Mhuire, 45 Whitehall Rd., Terenure, D.

Mac an Bhaird, Gilbert: 1 Bothar Chainneach,

Glasnaoidhean, D.

Mac Eochaidh, Micheál Seosaimh: Glynn, Wexford.

Mac Mahon, Bernard: Islandbridge Barracks, D.

MacBride, John: Roebuck House, Clonskeagh, D.

MacCarthy, Elizabeth: 1 Rehoboth Place, Dolphin's Barn, D.

MacCarthy, Thomas: 17 Iveagh Gardens, Crumlin Rd., D.

MacDermott, Joseph: 8 Emorville Ave., South Circular Rd., D.

MacDermott, Sean: Coranmore, Kiltyclogher, Leitrim.

MacDiarmada, Ruaidhrí: 1 Eaton Square, Monkstown, D.

MacDonagh, John: 46 Lwr. Leeson St., D.

MacDonagh, Joseph: 27 St Peter's Rd., Phibsborough, D.

MacDonagh, Thomas: c/o John MacDonagh, 51 Dame St., D.

MacDonnell, John Quinlan: 21 Croydon Green, Fairview, D.

MacDowell, Cathal: 10 Belgrave Rd., Rathmines, D.

MacEntee, Seán: 12 Herbert Pk., Ballsbridge, D.

MacGrait, Micéal: 34 Gardiners Place, D.

MacGrath, Peter Paul: Abbey Square, Enniscorthy.

Macken, Francis: Main St., Rathfarnham, D.

Macken, Patrick: 6 Dean Swift Square, Francis St., D.

Macken, Peter: 3 Redfern Terrace, Dolphin's Barn, D.

Mackey, Laurence: 2 Richmond Cres., North Circular Rd., D.

Mackey, Maura: 2334 Watling St. Rd., Fulwood, Preston, Lancashire, England.

Mackey, Michael: 23 North William St., D.

MacLaughlin, Daniel Aloysius: St Vincent's Hospital, St Stephen's Green, D.

MacMahon, Charles Eugene: 13 Millmount Place, Drumcondra, D.

MacMahon, Patrick: St Mary's, Portmarnock, D.

MacMahon, Sean: Portobello Barracks, D.

MacMathghamhna, Peadar: The Bungalow, Curragh Camp, Kildare.

MacNabb, Henry Russell: 147 Donegall St., Belfast, Antrim.

MacNeill, Dermot John: 4 Lwr. Fitzwilliam St., D.

MacNiamh, Liam: 9 Eaton Rd., Terenure, D.

MacSherry, Margaret Mary: 143 Townsend St., D.

MacWhinney (Kearns), Linda: 29 Gardiner's Place, D.

Madden, John: Griffith Barracks, D.

Magee, Michael: 20 Ostman Place, off Manor St., D.

Magee, Teresa: 185 Lwr. Kimmage Rd., D.

Maguire, James: Maree, Oranmore, D.

Maguire, James: 26 Irishtown Rd., D.

Maguire, James: 32 St. Michael's Terrace, Blackpits, D.

Maguire, John: 5 Dillon's Row, Maynooth, Kildare.

Maguire, Matthew: Brownstown, Dunboyne, Meath.

Maguire, Michael: 12 St. John St., Enniscorthy.

Maguire, Tomás: 3 Nugents Lane, Broadstone, D.

Maher, James: 3 Shannon, Enniscorthy.

Maher, Michael: 28 Island Rd., Enniscorthy.

Maher, William Joseph: 24 Lwr. Oriel St., D.

Mahon, John: 66 Monasterboice Rd., Crumlin, D.

Mahon, John: Loughauneenaughan, Monivea, Galway.

Mahon, John: Clarinbridge, Galway.

Mahon, Patrick: 37 Upr. Rathmines Rd., D.

Mahon, Patrick Joseph: Mahon's Printing Works, 2-3 Yarnhall St., D.

Mahon, Thomas: Kiltulla, Oranmore, Galway.

Mahon, Thomas Christopher: 'Carraig Uladh', Upr. Drumcondra, D.

Mahon, William: 61 Irish St., Enniscorthy.

Mahon, William: Cappananoole, Attymon, Athenry, Galway.

Mallin, Michael: 105 Ceannt's Fort, Mount Brown, D.

Mallon, James: 8 George's Quay, D.

Malone, Bridget: Grantstown, Waterford.

Malone, Jerome Joseph: 6 Wellington Terrace, Limerick.

Malone, Michael: 13 Grantham St., South Circular Rd., D.

Malone, Robert: Fire Brigade, Tara St., D.

Mangan, Thomas: 3 Leinster Cottages, Maynooth, Kildare.

Mannering, Edward: 10½ Cuffe St., D.

Manning, Henry: 19 Russell St., North Circular Rd., D.

Manning, Peter Paul: 4 Broadstone Ave., Royal Canal, D.

Manning, Tim: Ganty, Craughwell, Galway.

Mannion, Michael: Bresk, Kiltulla, Athenry, Galway.

Mapother, Máire: 18 Drumcondra Pk., D.

Marie, Louis: 15 Battalion, Curragh Camp, Kildare.

Markham, Thomas: 25 Windsor Ave., Fairview, D.

Marks, James: Barry's Pk., Swords, D.

Martin, Breeid: 5 Leeson Pk. Ave., D.

Martin, Christopher: 11A Boyne St., off Sandwith St., D.

Martin, Eamon: "Ferndale", Churchtown, Dundrum, D.

Martin, Frank: 64 Dublin St., Dundalk, Louth.

Martin, Joseph Patrick: Waterworks House, Kilcroney, Bray, Wicklow.

Martin, Kathleen: No.3 H Block, Arbour Hill, D.

Martin, Peter: Shannullagh, Louth.

Martyn, Peter: Gurrane, Oranmore, Galway.

Martyn, William: Roevagh, Kilcogan, Galway.

Mason, Frank: 22 High St., D.

Mason, Patrick: Ellenfield Lodge, Upr. Drumcondra, D.

Mason, Thomas: 26 Clonliffe Rd., D.

Masterson, James: Lusk, D.

Maxwell, Thomas: 9 Kingsland Parade, Portobello, D.

Mc Ardle, Thomas: North Commons, Lusk, D.

Mc Crea, Patrick: Baymount Cottage, Dollymount, D.

Mc Garry, Seán: 3 Charlemont Terrace, Dun Laoghaire, D.

Mc Mahon, Daniel: 20 Summerhill, D.

McAlerney, Lily: 613 - 32nd Ave., Seattle, Washington, USA.

McAllister, Bernard: Beaverstown, Donabate, D.

McAllister, Kathleen: North St., Swords, D.

McArdle, James: 10 North Portland Row, D.

McArdle, John: 45 Eccles St., D.

McArdle, Patrick: 4 North Portland Row, D.

McArdle, Peter: No. 2 Arnott St, South Circular Rd., D.

McAuliffe, Gearóid: Maiden St., Newcastle West, Limerick.

McBride, Patrick: 70 Croydon Pk. Ave., Fairview, D.

McCabe, Alasdair: Ballymote, Sligo.

McCabe, Frank: Fairford, Gloucestershire, England.

McCabe, John: 2 Prospect Villas, Crumlin Rd., D.

McCabe, Kevin Joseph: 93 Larkfield Grove, Kimmage, D.

McCabe, Michael: 2 Battalion, Royal West African Frontier Force, Ashante, Gold Coast Colony, British West Africa.

McCabe, Patrick: 93 Grove Pk., Rathmines, D.

McCabe, Peter: 9 Oakland Terrace, Terenure, D.

McCabe, William: 14 Brighton Ave., Rathgar, D.

McCabe, William A.: 4 Redmond's Cottages, Bath Ave., Ballsbridge, D.

McCann, Thomas Joseph: 51 Church Ave., Drumcondra, D.

McCarra, James: Rahoon House, Rahoon, Galway.

McCarthy, Bernard: 32 Penrose St., Ringsend, D.

McCarthy, Daniel: 4 Raleigh Place, Dolphin's Barn, D.

McCarthy, Daniel: West Green, Main St., Dunmanway, Cork.

McCarthy, Kathleen: 46 Brian Rd., Marino, Clontarf, D.

McCarthy, Michael: 157 Mountpleasant Buildings, Ranelagh, D.

McCormack, Bernard: Ardboro, Drumraney, Moate, Westmeath.

McCormack, Christopher: 76 Sean McDermott St., D.

McCormack, James: 13 Sutton Cottages, Sutton, D.

McCormack, James: River St., Athenry, Galway.

McCormack, John: 23 East Essex St., D.

McCormack, Thomas: 7 Elm Grove, Ranelagh, D.

McCormick, Richard: 31F St Michan's House, Mary's Lane, D.

McCrave, Thomas: Seatown, Dundalk, Louth.

McDermott, Louis Bernard: 16 Oaklands Terrace, Terenure, D.

McDermott, Owen: 3 Belgrave Terrace, Mountpleasant Ave., Rathmines, D.

McDermott, Patrick: Carrigans, Cloghboley, Sligo.

McDonagh, Joseph: 18 Station Rd., Baldoyle, D.

McDonald, John Bernard: 17 Lwr. Oriel St., D.

McDonald, Kathleen: 5 Ossory Rd., North Strand Rd., D.

McDonnell, Andrew: St. Therese, Glenayr Rd., Rathgar, D.

McDonnell, Denis: 27 Viking Rd., D.

McDonnell, Kathleen Keyes: Castlelack, Bandon, Cork.

McDonnell, Matthew: 12 Hardiman Rd., Drumcondra, D.

McDonnell, Michael: 310 Johnson Ave., Los Gatos, California, USA.

McDonnell, Patrick: 13 Nelson St., D.

McDonnell, Patrick: 11 Foyle Rd., Philipsburg Ave., D.

McDonnell, Thomas: 12 Hardiman Rd., Drumcondra, D.

McDonnell, William: 32 Mary St. South, Dundalk.

McDowell, Cathal: 53 Larkfield Grove, Kimmage, D.

McDowell, Maeve: 53 Larkfield Grove, Kimmage, D.

McDowell, Patrick: 2 Moyne Rd., Rathmines, D.

McDowell, William: 55 York St., D.

McElligott, James John: Oak Lodge, Southill Ave., Blackrock, D.

McEllistrim, Thomas: Ahane, Ballymacelligott, Kerry.

McElroy, Mairead: 20 Richmond Rd., Drumcondra, D.

McEntagert, John: 96 North King St., D.

McEvatt, Louis: 31 Ushers Quay, D.

McEvoy, Christopher: 40 Connolly Gardens, Inchicore, D.

McEvoy, Christopher: 7 Upr. Basin St., D.

McEvoy, Christopher James: 31 Darley's Terrace, Donore Ave., South Circular Rd., D.

McEvoy, James: 33 Lwr. Erne St., D.

McEvoy, Martin: Rooe, Craughwell, Galway.

McEvoy, Patrick: 33 Lwr. Erne St., D.

McEvoy, Thomas Richard: 1 Parkview Terrace, D.

McGaleagly, James: 799 Great Eastern Rd., Parkhead, Glasgow, Scotland.

McGallogly, John: 46 Eglington Rd., D.

McGarvey, Michael: 18 Gay St., New York, USA.

McGill, Joseph: 32 Darley St., Harold's Cross, D.

McGill, William Ewart: Castle St., Dunmore, Galway.

McGinley, Cormac: 56 Kenilworth Pk., Harold's Cross, D.

McGinley, Patrick: 29 Summer Place, Upr. Rutland St., D.

McGinley, William: 165 St. Attracta Rd., Cabra, D.

McGinn, Michael Conway: 131 Philipsburgh Ave., Fairview, D.

McGinty, Lillie: 36 Portland Row, North Strand, D.

McGlure, John: 1 Lwr. Gardiner St., D.

McGlynn, Seán: 35 Templeogue Rd., Terenure, D.

McGowan, Josephine: 97 Silvermore Rd., Crumlin, D.

McGowan, Seámus: 19 Hardiman Rd., Upr. Drumcondra, D.

McGrane, Christopher: 163 Crumlin Rd., Crumlin, D.

McGrane, Thomas: 7 Eaton Rd., Terenure, D.

McGrath, Daniel: 73 Fassaugh Rd., Cabra, D.

McGrath, Joseph: Seafort Lodge, Williamstown, D.

McGrath, Patrick: 13 Rutledge Terrace, Donore Ave., D.

McGrath, Patrick: 20 Kennedy's Villas, Bow Lane, James St., D.

McGrath, Patrick: 56 Haroldville Terrace, South Circular Rd., D.

McGrath, Patrick Joseph: 3 Upr. Northbrook Ave., North Strand, D.

McGrath, Patrick Joseph: 3 Upr. Northbrook Ave., North Strand, D.

McGrath, Sean: 116 Thomas St., D.

McGrath, Seán: Supply and Ordnance Sub-Department, Island Bridge Barracks.

McGrath, Thomas: 140 Parnell St., D.

McGuinness, Joseph: c/o Patrick Lyons, Garda Síochána, Rathfarnham, D.

McGuinness, Sean: 26 Linenhall St., D.

McGuire, John Joseph: 9 Drenon Square, Hayes, Middlesex, England.

McGuire, John Peter: North St., Swords, D.

McHugh, Alfred James: The Bungalow, Templemichael, Longford.

McHugh, Michael: 27 Hardwicke St., D.

McHugh, Patrick: 33 Barrow St., D.

McInerney, Thomas: 13 Cres. Ave., Limerick.

McKee, Richard: Finglas, D.

McKenna, Bernard: 24 Blackhall St., D.

McKenna, John: 134 Raglan St., Belfast, Antrim.

McKenna, John: 39 McCaffrey Estate, Mount Brown, D.

McKeon, Brigid: 26 Lwr. St Columba's Rd., Drumcondra, D.

McKeon, Peter: 7 St. Laurence Terrace, Mullingar, Westmeath.

McKeon, William: 134A Cork St., off Ardee St., D.

McKeown, Owen: 26 Lwr. Saint Columba's Rd., Drumcondra, D.

McLoughlin, Carrie: 33 Chesham Rd., Kemptown, Brighton, England.

McLoughlin, Mary: 57 Belton Pk. Rd., D.

McLoughlin, Seán: 77 Lees Hall Rd., Sheffield 8, Yorkshire, England.

McMahon, Daniel Joseph: 2 Richmond Row, Portobello, D.

McMahon, Seán: 1 Lwr. Dominick St., D.

McManus, Patrick: 172 North King St., D.

McMenamy, Francis Joseph: 83 Larkfield Grove, Kimmage, D.

McMenamy, Manus: 138 Parnell St., D.

McMullan, Bernard: 14 Pleasants St., South Circular Rd., D.

McNally, Francis: 1 O' Sullivan's Alley, Ballybough Rd., D.

McNally, John: Treen Hill, Lusk, D.

McNally, Peter: 21 Lwr. Leeson St., D.

McNamara, Delia: Ganty, Craughwell, Galway.

McNamara, James: 470 Concord Ave., The Bronx, New York, USA.

McNamara, John: 24 High St., D.

McNamara, Josephine: Connolly House, Mainguard St, Galway.

McNamara, Mary: 14 French Ville, Grattan Rd., Galway.

McNamara, Patrick J: 213-04, 50th Ave., Bayside, Long Island, New York, USA.

McNamara, Rose: 35 Upr. Ormond Quay, D.

McNamara, Sarah: 22 Capel St., D.

McNamee, Agnes: 2 Emerald Square, Cork St., D.

McNamee, James Kevin: Avondale, Fortfield Rd., Terenure, D.

McNestry, Patrick: 5 Enniskerry Rd., Phibsborough, D.

McNulty, Michael: 13 Sarsfield St., D.

McNulty, Peadar Joseph: 26 Connaught St., Phibsborough, D.

McParland, James: 74 Lwr. Mount St., D.

McPartlin, Francis: Osbourne Rd., Enniscorthy, Wexford.

McPartlin, Peter Celestine: 32 St. Joseph's Place, Dorset St., D.

McQuaid, John J.: 5 West St., Papakura, Auckland, New Zealand.

McQuaid, Thomas: 48 East Arran St., D.

McVeigh, James: 30 Cork St., D.

Meade, Daniel: The Hill, Malahide, D.

Meade, Henry: 16 City Quay, D.

Meade, Michael: 11 Upr. Oriel St., D.

Meade, Owen: 46 North Strand Rd., D.

Meade, Walter: 12 Bath Ave., Sandymount, D.

Meade, William Christopher: 23 Richmond Ave., Fairview, D.

Meagher, John William: 6 Richmond Place, Portobello, D.

Meagher, Michael: 27 Sandwith Terrace, D.

Meagher, Patrick: 98 Upr. Dorset St., D.

Meagher, Patrick: 1 Tudor Gardens, Barkingside, Essex, England.

Meagher, Thomas Francis: Post Office, Borrisoleigh, Thurles, Tipperary.

Meehan, William: 50 Foster Terrace, Ballybough, D.

Meldon, John: 33 Cherryfield Ave., Sandyford Rd., Ranelagh, D.

Meldon, Thomas J.: 45 Lwr. Gardiner St., D.

Mellows, Herbert Charles: 87 Dún Ceannt, Mount Brown, D.

Mellows, Liam: 21 Mountshannon Rd., D.

Melville, John: Raheen, Gort, Galway.

Melvinn, James: 163 Lwr. Drumcondra Rd., D.

Merrigan, Thomas: King St., D.

Merriman, Edward: 102 Crumlin Rd., D.

Merriman, Michael: 133 Pearse St., D.

Milroy, Seán: 25 Fitzwilliam Square, D.

Minahan, James: 142 South Circular Rd., Dolphins Barn.

Minahan, James: 1 Parnell Ave., Harold's Cross, D.

Mitchell, Patrick: Collins Barracks, D.

Molloy, Brian: Coolough, Castlegar, Galway.

Molloy, John: 17 Childers Terrace, Kilbirnie, Wellington, New Zealand.

Molloy, Joseph: The Rock, Coolattin, Carnew, Wicklow.

Molloy, Michael J.: 45 Bayview Ave., North Strand, D.

Molloy, Richard: 8 Cottage Place, North Circular Rd., D.

Molloy, Thomas Pat: Kileen, Castlegar, Galway.

Moloney, John: Grenage, Craughwell, Galway.

Moloney, John Joseph: 21 Langwood Ave., South Circular Rd., D.

Moloney, Martin: Raheen Pk., Athenry, Galway.

Moloney, Patrick: Greyfort, Leinster Square, Rathmines, D.

Molony, Helena: 51 Larkfield Grove, Kimmage.

Monahan, John: Knockbrack, Monivea, Athenry, Galway.

Monks, Andrew: 18 Oak Rd., Donnycarney, D.

Monroe, Thomas Joseph: 6 Annaly Rd., Cabra, D.

Monteith, Robert: 421 Fernhill Ave., Detroit, Michigan, USA.

Mooney, James: 17 Rutland Cottages, D.

Mooney, John Francis: River View Cottage, Castleknock, D.

Mooney, Patrick: 9 Lwr. Exchange St., D.

Mooney, Patrick: St Jude's, Clonsilla, D.

Moore, Brigid: 53 St John's Villas, Enniscorthy.

Moore, Edward John: New Rd., D.

Moore, John: 7 Youngs Cottages, Newfoundland St., North Wall, D.

Moore, John W: Rosbrien, Limerick.

Moore, Laurence: 18 Charlemont Mall, Portobello, D.

Moore, Patrick Thomas: 3 Rose Terrace, East Wall Rd., D.

Moran, Brigid Christina: Church St., Enniscorthy.

Moran, Christopher: Main St., Swords, D.

Moran, James Joseph: 7948 Drexel Ave., Chicago, Illinois, USA.

Moran, John: Lisheencoyle, Athenry, Galway.

Moran, John: 110 Bancroft Rd., Burlingame, California, USA.

Moran, John: Cloone, Claregalway, Galway.

Moran, Michael: Castle St., Enniscorthy.

Moran, Patrick: 5 Main St., Blackrock, D.

Moran, Patrick: Newtownblake, Peterswell, Loughrea, Galway.

Moran, Peter: Little Forest, Cloughran, D.

Moran, Sean: Church St., Enniscorthy, Wexford.

Moran, William: 9 Killala Rd., Cabra West, D.

Morcan, Eamon: General Headquarters, Parkgate St., D.

Morgan, John: 26 Castle Countess, Tralee, Kerry.

Morgan, John: Mooretown, Mulhuddart, D.

Morgan, John Eamon: 15 Hume St., D.

Morkan, Philomena: Strathmore, Willbrook Rd., Rathfarnham, D.

Morrissey, Gilbert: 75 Pk. St., Parkville, Melbourne, Victoria, Australia.

Morrissey, James E.: 14 Lwr. Garville Ave., Rathgar, D.

Morrissey, John: Monatigue, Athenry, Galway.

Morrissey, Martin: Monatigue, Athenry, Galway.

Morrissey, Patrick: Cahercrin, Athenry, Galway.

Morrissey, Patrick Stephen: 7 Gulistan Terrace, Rathmines, D.

Morrissey, Richard: Kingsland, Athenry, Galway.

Moughan, Henry: 2 Heuston's Cottages, Newfoundland St., North Wall, D.

Mulcahy, Mary Josephine: Lissenfield House, Rathmines Rd., D.

Mulcahy, Patrick: 24 Fitzwilliam Terrace, D.

Mulcahy, Richard: Lissonfield House, Rathmines Rd., D.

Muldowney, Patrick: Trumera, Mountrath, Laois.

Mulhall, Andrew J: 8 Lwr. Dominick St., D.

Mulholland, Patrick: Carrickrobin, Kilkerley, Dundalk, Louth.

Mulholland, Thomas: Carrickrobin, Dundalk, Louth.

Mulkerns, James Joseph: 21 St Catherine's Terrace, Phibsborough, D.

Mulkerns, Richard: Caheroyan, Athenry, Galway.

Mulkerrins, Michael: Caheroyan, Athenry, Galway.

Mullally, James: Woodpark, Dunboyne, Meath.

Mullally, Michael: 8 Cottage Place, Belvedere Ave., D.

Mullen, Martin: 16 Madden Rd., Fairbrothers Fields, D.

Mullen, Martin: 9 Emerald Terrace, Cork St., D.

Mullen, Patrick: 9 Emerald St., Cork St., D.

Mullen, Peter: 18 O'Curry Rd., South Circular Rd., D.

Mulligan, Andrew: 4 Willitt Place (off Rutland St.), D.

Mulligan, Margaret: 20 Cabra Rd., Phibsborough, D.

Mullin, Owen: Clarinbridge, Galway.

Mullin, Thomas: Derrydonnell, Athenry, Galway.

Mullins, Gretta: Hazelhill, Ballyhaunis, Mayo.

Mulroyan, Bartley: 1605 East Ohio St., Indianapolis, Indiana, USA.

Mulroyan, William: Kiltulla, Oranmore, Galway.

Mulroyan, William (Patrick): Kiltulla, Oranmore, Galway.

Mulvey, Dominick: 145 Harold's Cross Rd., D.

Mulvey, Stephen: 18 St. Brigid's Terrace, Dargle Rd., Bray, Wicklow.

Mulvey, William Robert: 28 St. Enda's Rd., Terenure, D.

Mulvihill, Michael: Ardoughter, Ballyduff, Lixnaw, Kerry.

Murnane, Liam: 63 Mount Prospect Ave., Clontarf, D.

Murnane, Margaret: 63 Mount Prospect, Clontarf, D.

Murphy, Bernard: 7 Inns Quay, D.

Murphy, Bridget: 12 Corporation St., D.

Murphy, Cait: Upr. Burgess, Killeagh, Cork.

Murphy, Christopher J: 40 Camden Row, D.

Murphy, Denis: 29 South Rd., Waterloo, Liverpool, England.

Murphy, Eamon: The Strand, Malahide, D.

Murphy, Edward: Cloneyburne, Newtownbarry, Wexford.

Murphy, Eileen: 19 Brighton Rd., Rathgar, D.

Murphy, Felix: St John's Villas, Enniscorthy.

Murphy, Felix: Crannaghmore, Athlone, Westmeath.

Murphy, Fintan Patrick: 9 Palmerston Rd., Rathmines, D.

Murphy, Francis: 1 Longwood Ave., South Circular Rd., D.

Murphy, Francis Ciaran: 226 Freshfield Rd., Brighton, Sussex, England.

Murphy, Frederick: 82 Lwr. Gardiner St., D.

Murphy, Frederick Charles: 23 Lwr. Stephen St., D.

Murphy, Gertrude: 129 Ferguson Rd., Drumcondra, D.

Murphy, Gregory: 119 South Circular Rd., Islandbridge, D.

Murphy, Hubert Joseph: 31 Ushers Quay, D.

Murphy, James: 10 St John St., Enniscorthy.

Murphy, James: Carley's Bridge, Enniscorthy.

Murphy, James (Junior): 15 Ross Rd., Enniscorthy.

Murphy, John: 4 Main St., Enniscorthy.

Murphy, John: 9 Leinster Ave., North Strand, D.

Murphy, John: 15 Ross Rd., Enniscorthy.

Murphy, John: Old Church St., Athenry, Galway.

Murphy, John Christopher: 5 Behan's Terrace, James's St., D.

Murphy, John J.: 1 Lwr. Clanbrassil St., D.

Murphy, John J.: 3 Back Lane, off High St., D.

Murphy, Kate: 1 O'Neills Terrace, Millpark, Enniscorthy.

Murphy, Kathleen: 20 Royal Terrace West, Dun Laoighaire, D.

Murphy, Liam P.: 35 South William St., D.

Murphy, Martha: 1 Leinster Ave., North Strand, D.

Murphy, Martin: Monivea, Athenry, Galway.

Murphy, Martin: 65 Blessington St., D.

Murphy, Martin: 19 Brighton Rd., Rathgar, D.

Murphy, Martin: Scoby, Enniscorthy.

Murphy, Matthew Joseph: Civic Guard Station, Stepaside, Sandyford, D.

Murphy, Michael: Church St., Athenry, Galway.

Murphy, Michael: 65 Ballybough Rd., D.

Murphy, Michael: 33 Homefarm Rd., Drumcondra, D.

Murphy, Michael: 12 Armstrong's Range, Shannon, Enniscorthy.

Murphy, Michael: 15 Vinegar Hill Terrace, Enniscorthy.

Murphy, Michael: 15 South Circular Rd., Portobello, D.

Murphy, Michael: Florence Villas, Drumcondra, D.

Murphy, Nicholas: Garda Siochana, Naas, Kildare.

Murphy, Patrick: Shroughmore, Ballycarney, Ferns, Wexford.

Murphy, Patrick: Chapel Lane, Ferns, Wexford.

Murphy, Patrick: Lydecan, Claregalway, Galway.

Murphy, Philip: 1 O'Neill's Terrace, Mill Park Rd., Enniscorthy.

Murphy, Philip: 9 High St., Galway.

Murphy, Richard: 35 South William St., D.

Murphy, Richard: Clarkes St., Athenry, Galway.

Murphy, Robert Joseph: 31 Ushers Quay, D.

Murphy, Seamus: 9 St. Mary's Rd., Ballsbridge, D.

Murphy, Stephen: 3A Old Church St., D.

Murphy, Thomas: Ring Terrace, Inchicore, D.

Murphy, Thomas: 76 Irish St., Enniscorthy.

Murphy, William: 21 Temple St., D.

Murphy, William: 57 Connolly Ave., Inchicore, D.

Murphy, William J.: Brew's Hill, Navan, Meath.

Murphy, Winifred: 12 Shannon Hill, Enniscorthy.

Murran, James Joseph: Military Barracks, Clonakilty, Cork.

Murray, Daniel: 35 Lwr. Mountpleasant Ave., Rathmines, D.

Murray, Edward Joseph: 32 Upr. Merrion St., D.

Murray, Eileen: 6 Killarney Parade, North Circular Rd., D.

Murray, Frank: 10 John St. West, D.

Murray, Henry S.: 2 Richmond Row, Portobello, D.

Murray, James: 708 First Ave., New York City, USA.

Murray, James: 4 Clarence Mangan Square (off John Dillon St.), D.

Murray, Joseph: 58 Upr. Drumcondra, D.

Murray, Joseph Michael: Verbena House, Saint Columba's Rd., Drumcondra, D.

Murray, May: 9 Montague Place, Wexford St., D.

Murray, Michael: 4 Hacketts Cottages, Milltown, D.

Murray, Patrick Joseph: 52 Lindsay Rd., D.

Murray, Thomas: 114 Newgrange Rd., Cabra, D.

Murtagh, Bernard: 63 Lombard St. West, South Circular Rd., D.

Murtagh, Francis Dominick: 29 Montpelier Hill, D.

Murtagh, Joseph: 5 Cecil Ave., Clontarf, D.

Murtagh, Laurence Joseph: 690 Hillside Cottages, St. Laurence, Chapelizod, D.

Murtagh, Patrick: 10 Ballybough Rd., D.

Musgrave, Denis Joseph: 208 Clontarf Rd., Clontarf, D.

Neary, Denis: 37 Blackpitts, D.

Neary, Joseph: 26 Staveley Ave., Hague Estate,

Stalybridge, Cheshire, England.

Neilan, Arthur James: 4 Mount Harold Terrace, Leinster Rd., D.

Neilan, Martin: Kilcolgan Castle, Galway.

Neilan, William: The Weir, Kilcolgan, Galway.

Nelly, Katie: George St., Gort, Galway.

Nelson, James: 9 Middle Gardiner St., D.

Nelson, Thomas: 34 North Great Georges St., D.

Nestor, Thomas: Stradbally, Kilcolgan, Galway.

Nevin, Patrick: 9 Lwr. Jane Place, off Oriel St., D.

Newell, Edward: 295 East 162nd St., Bronx, New York, USA.

Newell, James: 6554 South Bishop St., Chicago, Illinois, USA.

Newell, Martin: Caherdine, Craughwell, Galway.

Newell, Michael: Briarhill, Castlegar, Galway.

Newell, Thomas: Briarhill, Castlegar, Galway.

Newell, William: 516 West 134 St., New York City, USA.

Newman, John Patrick: The Cottage, Castle Ave., Clontarf, D.

Newport, Nicholas: Rathmacknee, Killinick, Wexford.

Ni Ceallaigh, Mairead: 49 Mespil Rd., D.

Nicholls, Henry: 70 Saint Stephen's Green, D.

Niland, William: Stradbally, Kilcolgan, Galway.

Noctor, Brigid: 70 Ross Rd., Enniscorthy, Wexford.

Nolan, Bartley: Renmore Rd., Galway.

Nolan, George Leo: 615 Water Pk., Kimmage, D.

Nolan, Michael: Burrowfield, Baldoyle, D.

Nolan, Michael: 3 Hospital Lane, Enniscorthy.

Nolan, Patrick: 171 Townsend St., D.

Nolan, Patrick: 3 Beaver St., D.

Nolan, Shaun: 13 Upr. Mayor St., Castleforbes Rd., North Wall, D.

Nolan, Thomas: 106 Cork St., D.

Nolan, Thomas Francis: 163 Templeogue Rd., Terenure, D.

Noonan, Christopher: 1 Haverty Rd., Fairview, D.

Noone, Ellen: 21 Church Gardens, Rathmines.

Norgrove, Alfred George: 15 Strandville Ave., North Strand, D.

Norgrove, Frederick: 26 St. Aidan's Pk., Marino, D.

Norton, James: 41 Parnell Square, D.

Norton, Joseph: Lispopple, Swords, D.

Norton, William: Lispopple, Swords, D.

Nugent, Christopher: Rathbeal Rd., Swords, D.

Nugent, John: 9 Fishamble St., D.

Nugent, Michael: 38 Aungier St., D.

Nugent, Patrick: 35 Fitzgibbon St., D.

Nunan, Ernest: Defence, Parkgate, D.

Nunan, Sean: Irish Legation, Washington D. C., USA.

Ó Braonáin, Éamonn: 39 Finglas Rd., D.

Ó Briain, Eoghan: "Naomh Gearáid", Bóthar Uacht na hAille, Beann Éadair, D.

Ó Briain, Seán: 42 Houghton Terrace, Arbour Hill, D.

Ó Broin, Liam: 7 St Catherine's Ave., Donore Ave., South Circular Rd., D.

Ó Broin, Pádraig: 21 Aungier St., D.

Ó Broin, Pádraig: 2 Alexander Terrace, Terenure, D.

Ó Broin, Proinsías: 6 Larkfield Gardens, Kimmage, D.

Ó Ceallaigh, Seán T.: 38 Anglesea Rd., D.

Ó Donnchadha, Tomás: c/o St. Therese, 8 Ferguson Rd., Drumcondra, D.

Ó Droighneáin, Mícheál: Furbough, Barna, Galway.

Ó Dubhghaill, Seámus: Baile Raincín, Sruth Airt, Fear na Mór, Wexford.

Ó Duibhir, Éamon: An Bealach, Crosaire an Ghúlaigh, Tipperary.

Ó Fathaig, Pádraig: Teach Enda, Tulladhraigh, Árd Rathain, Galway.

Ó Laoghaire, Seán: Spring Hill, Enniscorthy.

Ó Lóingsigh, Fionán: 11 Sunbury Gardens, Dartry Rd., D.

Ó Monacháin, Ailbhe: 63 Beaumont Rd., D.

Ó Muircheartaigh, Mícheál: Green St., Dingle, Kerry.

Ó Murchadha, Colm: Leinster House, Kildare St., D.

Ó Murchadha, Peadar: 13 Clonturk Park, Drumcondra, D.

O'Beirne, Mary Josephine: Abbey Row, Athenry, Galway.

O'Brennan, Francis Joseph: Derrygrogan, Ballycommon, Daingean, Offaly.

O'Brennan, Lily Mary: 44 Oakley Rd., D.

O'Breslin, Peadar: 7 Charleville Ave., North Strand, D.

O'Briain, Liam: Coill Tómair, Bóthar na hOllsgoile, Galway.

O'Brien, Annie: 16A Upr. Basin St., D.

O'Brien, Denis: 1 Greenville Parade, Blackpitts, D.

O'Brien, Denis: Pim St., D.

O'Brien, Denis: New St., Enniscorthy.

O'Brien, Eilis: Sean Costello St., Athlone, Westmeath.

O'Brien, Elizabeth: 24 St John St., Enniscorthy.

O'Brien, Francis: 11 Sydney Terrace, West Rd., D.

O'Brien, James: Main St., Rathdrum, Wicklow.

O'Brien, James: c/o Mental Hospital, Enniscorthy.

O'Brien, James: 63 Tullow St., Carlow.

O'Brien, John: B Company, 18 Infantry Battalion, Collins Barracks, Cork.

O'Brien, John: 49 Lwr. Dominick St., D.

O'Brien, John: 70 Hazel Rd., Donnycarney, D.

O'Brien, John: 452 North Circular Rd., D.

O'Brien, John Joseph: 8 St. Aidan's Villas, Enniscorthy.

O'Brien, Laurence: 230 Merrion Rd., D.

O'Brien, Liam: 11 Sydney Terrace, West Rd., D.

O'Brien, Liam: 114 Shelmartin Ave., Fairview, D.

O'Brien, Matthew: 2 Walkers Cottages, Mountpleasant, Ranelagh, D.

O'Brien, Michael: 63 Capel St., D.

O'Brien, Michael: Carnew, Wicklow.

O'Brien, Michael: 143 Harold's Cross Rd., D.

O'Brien, Patrick: 8 Pim St., D.

O'Brien, Patrick: Waterdale, Claregalway, Galway.

O'Brien, Patrick J: 36 Kirwan St., D.

O'Brien, Peadar: 1 Claremount Terrace, Dundrum, D.

O'Brien, Seamus: Morriscastle, Gorey, Wexford.

O'Brien, Stephen L.: 3 Tivoli Ave., Harold's Cross, D.

O'Brien, Thomas: 8 Ben Edar Rd., North Circular Rd., D.

O'Brien, Thomas: c/o Great Southern Railways, Macmine Station, Wexford.

O'Brien, Thomas: 14 Hendrick St., D.

O'Brien, William: 24 B Block, Marshalsea Barracks, Thomas St., D.

O'Brien, William Joseph: 50 Annamore Terrace, North Circular Rd., D.

O'Broin, Séamus: 42 St. Enda's Rd., Terenure, D.

O'Byrne, Hugh: 30 Killeen Rd., Rathmines, D.

O'Byrne, James: 44 Lwr. Mayor St., D.

O'Byrne, James: 56 Mary St., D.

O'Byrne, Joseph Michael: 55 Dartmouth Square, Ranelagh, D.

O'Byrne, Liam: 10 Convent Rd., Fairbrothers Fields, South Circular Rd., D.

O'Byrne, Patrick: 53 South Great George's St., D.

O'Byrne, Patrick Joseph: Mornington, Drogheda, Louth.

O'Byrne, Seán: The Ave., Gorey, Wexford.

O'Byrne, Thomas Joseph: Seaford Ave., Sandymount, D.

O'Callaghan, Denis: 85 St. Jarlath's Rd., Cabra, D.

O'Callaghan, Dominick: 9 Mountjoy Place, D.

O'Callaghan, John: Killmurry, Kenmare, Kerry.

O'Callaghan, Michael: 7 Dawson Villas, Tipperary.

O'Carroll, Annie: 17 St Jarlath's Rd., Cabra, D.

O'Carroll, James J.: 92 Manor St., D.

O'Carroll, Joseph: 28 Heytesbury St., South Circular Rd., D.

O'Carroll, Kevin: 74 Mobhi Rd., Glasnevin, D.

O'Carroll, Liam: 29 Annamoe Rd., D.

O'Carroll, Mary: 220 Darling St., Balmain, Sydney, Australia.

O'Carroll, Mary: 23 Arranmore Ave., Phibsborough, D.

O'Carroll, Michael: 2 Norseman Place, Arbour Hill, D.

O'Carroll, Peter James: 17 St Jarlath Rd., Cabra, D.

O'Carroll, Richard: Bricklayers Hall, 49 Cuffe St., D.

O'Carroll, Seán: 75 Manor St., D.

O'Ceallacáin, Seán: 20 Leinster St., Phibsborough, D.

O'Ceallaig, Sean T.: No Address.

O'Ceallaigh, Michael: 49 Mespil Rd., D.

O'Ceallaigh, Peadar: Rathbeal Rd., Swords, D.

O'Connaill, Mortimer: 34 Dartmouth Square, D.

O'Connell, Eilis: 23 Vernon Grove, Clontarf, D.

O'Connell, James: 9 Parnell Cottages, Malahide, D.

O'Connell, Patrick: 12 Chelmsford Rd., Ranelagh, D.

O'Connell, Richard Joseph: National Bank House, Cahirciveen, Kerry.

O'Connell, Seán: 147 Clonliffe Rd., D.

O'Connor, Aileen Mary: 164 Merrion Rd., D.

O'Connor, Bernard: 4 Eugene St., D.

O'Connor, Daniel: 4 Weafer St., Enniscorthy.

O'Connor, Dennis: 20 Incemore Rd., Mossley Hill, Liverpool, England.

O'Connor, Fergus: Lowell House, Herbert Ave., Merrion, D.

O'Connor, James: 37 Lwr. Prince's St., South Bank, Yorkshire, England.

O'Connor, James: 4 O'Donovan Rd., Fairbrothers Fields, South Circular Rd., D.

O'Connor, John: 18 Francis St., D.

O'Connor, John: Killthomas, Ferns, Wexford.

O'Connor, John Stephen: 19 Iona Drive, Glasnevin, D.

O'Connor, John Thomas: 5 Pleasants St., South Circular Rd., D.

O'Connor, Joseph: 32 O'Donovan Rd., South Circular Rd., D.

O'Connor, Joseph: 'Dunedin', 334 Harolds Cross Rd., D.

O'Connor, Michael: 26 St. John's St., Enniscorthy.

O'Connor, Patrick: Rathmore, Kerry.

O'Connor, Patrick: 3 Preston St., off Amiens St., D.

O'Connor, Patrick J.: 248 Harold's Cross Rd., D.

O'Connor, Peter: 212 Harold's Cross Rd., D.

O'Connor, Philip: 1 Lymington Rd., Enniscorthy.

O'Connor, Rory: St John's, Ardeenin, Dalkey, D.

O'Connor, Thomas: Lwr. Sherrard St., D.

O'Daly, Nora Margaret Mary: Cloncoora, Jobstown, Tallaght, D.

O'Daly, Patrick: 7 Belvue Terrace, Dollymount, D.

O'Dea, John: Mountain South, Athenry, Galway.

O'Dea, John: The Weir, Kilcolgan, Galway.

O'Dea, Michael: Drumcharley, Tulla, Clare.

O'Dea, Michael: 52 Spring St., Lynn, Massachusetts, USA.

O'Dea, Patrick: Caltra, Headford, Galway.

O'Dea, Thomas: Stradbally, Kilcolgan, Oranmore, Galway.

O'Dea, William: 40 St. Lawrence Rd., Clontarf, D.

O'Doherty, Florence J.: 44 Mountjoy St., D.

O'Doherty, Liam: 6 Sundrive Rd., Kimmage, D.

O'Doherty, Michael: 10 Lwr. Mayor St., D.

O'Donnell, Christopher: 28 Francis St., D.

O'Donnell, James: 28 Francis St., D.

O'Donnell, William: D Company, 15 Infantry Battalion, Curragh Camp, Kildare.

O'Donoghue, Denis: 7 Chaworth Terrace, Thomas St., D.

O'Donoghue, Henry Vincent: Aunascul, Kerry.

O'Donoghue, Patrick: Renard Rd., Cahirciveen, Kerry.

O'Donoghue, William: Killalongford, Clonmore, Hacketstown, Carlow.

O'Donovan, Cornelius: 50 Iona Cres., Glasnevin, D.

O'Dowd, Richard: 6 Murphy's Terrace, Castletown Rd., Dundalk.

O'Duffy, Brigid: 32 Mobhi Rd., Glasnevin, D.

O'Duffy, Patrick: 2 Preston St., D.

O'Duffy, Sean Martin: 7 Reuben Ave., D.

O'Dwyer, James: 76 Tolka Rd., Clonliffe Rd., D.

O'Dwyer, Peter: Tomalosset, Enniscorthy.

O'Flaherty, Martin: 22 Rialto St., South Circular Rd., D.

O'Flaherty, Seamus: 29 Mobhi Rd., Glasnevin, D.

O'Flaithbheartaigh, Liam: 364 Lwr. Kimmage Rd., D.

O'Flanagan, Francis: 30 Moore St., D.

O'Flanagan, George: 10 Patrick St., D.

O'Flanagan, Michael: 14A Wexford St., D.

O'Flanagan, Patrick Joseph: 11 Basin View Terrace, D.

O'Gorman, John Patrick: 9 Alexandra Terrace, Terenure, D.

O'Gorman, Joseph: Main St., Tallaght, D.

O'Gorman, Mary Christina: 16 Drumcondra Pk., D.

O'Grady, Charles Joseph: 27 Emerald Square, Dolphin's Barn, D.

O'Grady, John: 32 Lwr. Ormond Quay, D.

O'Grady, Michael: Old Church St., Athenry, Galway.

O'Hagan, Annie: 24 Prison Ave., Mountjoy, D.

O'Hagan, James: 39 Upr. Rathmines, D.

O'Halloran, Cornelius: Caherlohan, Tulla, Clare.

O'Hanlon, Bernard: 20 Prebend St., Broadstone, D.

O'Hanlon, Mollie: 7 Camac Place, Dolphins Barn, D.

O'Hanlon, Patrick: 31 Upr. Wellington St., D.

O'Hanlon, Seán: 60 Ferguson Rd., Drumcondra, D.

O'Hannigan, Donal: 95 St. Jarlath's Rd., Cabra.

O'Hanrahan, Edward: 149 North Strand Rd., D.

O'Hanrahan, Henry: 384 North Circular Rd., D.

O'Hanrahan, Joseph John: 149 North Strand, D.

O'Hanrahan, Mary: 149 North Strand Rd., D.

O'Hanrahan, Michael: 67 Connaught St., D.

O'Healy, Jeremiah: 506 North Circular Rd., D.

O'Hegarty, Diarmuid: 9 Brendan Rd., Donnybrook, D.

O'Higgins, James: 33 Ellesmere Ave., North Circular Rd., D.

O'Keeffe, Arthur: 4 O'Neill's Range, Shannon Hill, Enniscorthy.

O'Keeffe, John: 4 Wilson Place, Lwr. Mount St., D.

O'Keeffe, John Christopher: 26 Little Mary St., D.

O'Keeffe, Michael: 2 Bass Place, Denzille St., D.

O'Keeffe, Patrick: 6 Rathmines Terrace, Rathmines Rd., D.

O'Keeffe, Patrick: St Aidan's Villas, Enniscorthy.

O'Keeffe, William: 28 Forth Rd., East Wall Rd., D.

O'Kelly, Edward: 30 Oakley Square, London N.W.1.

O'Kelly, Fergus Francis: 26 Castle Ave., Clontarf, D.

O'Kelly, Joseph: Pine Hill, Vico Rd., Dalkey, D.

O'Kelly, Joseph Edward: Church St., Ballaghaderreen, Roscommon.

O'Kelly, Michael: Liberty Hall, Beresford Place, D.

O'Kelly, Patrick: 20 Seafield Rd., Clontarf Rd., D.

O'Kelly, Patrick Anthony: 5 St. Nicholas Place, D.

O'Kelly, Phyllis: 38 Anglesea Rd., D.

O'Kelly, Thomas: 25 St Aidan's Pk. Rd., Marino, D.

O'Leary, David: Fairview, Mount Ave., Dundalk, Louth.

O'Leary, Diarmuid Joseph: 54 Marlborough Rd., Donnybrook, D.

O'Leary, Liam: 8 Main St., Enniscorthy.

O'Leary, Michael: 17 Irish St., Enniscorthy.

O'Leary, Michael: Tarramuid, Kilcolgan, Galway.

O'Leary, Patrick Joseph: 36 East Essex St., D.

O'Leary, Philip: 4 Middle Gardiner St., D.

O'Leary, Simon: 9 Congress Terrace, Fethard, Tipperary.

O'Loughlin, Patrick: 18 Tirconaill St., Inchicore, D.

O'Mahony, Eamon Joseph: 108 Shelmartin Ave., Fairview, D.

O'Mahony, Matthew J.: 28 Church St., Skerries, D.

O'Mahony, Patrick C: Gort na Gréine, Oakpark, Tralee, Kerry.

O'Malley, Christopher Robert: 104 Seville Place, North Strand, D.

O'Malley, Ernest Bernard: c/o Hotel Victoria, 51 & Broadway, New York, USA.

O'Malley, Patrick: "Muintireoin", Ratoath, Meath.

Oman, George: 16 Kickham Rd., Inchicore, D.

Oman, Robert: 8 Daniel St., D.

Oman, William Edward: 8 Joyce Rd., Drumcondra.

O'Mara, Peter: 1 St. Nicholas Place, D.

O'Moore, Donough: 6 Lwr. St., Columbas Rd., Drumcondra, D.

O'Moore, Esther: 40 Philipsburg Terrace, Fairview, D.

O'Moore, Patrick Michael: City View Rd., Camphill S.E.2, Brisbane, Australia.

O'Moore, Seán: 40 Philipsburg Terrace, Fairview, D.

O'Neill, Aidan Mogue: 25 Shannon Hill, Vinegar Hill Terrace, Enniscorthy.

O'Neill, Andrew: 69 Marlborough St., D.

O'Neill, Annie: Hillview, Ferns Upr., Wexford.

O'Neill, Cecilia: Bawn Cottages, Malahide, D.

O'Neill, Charles: 358 East 138 St., Bronx, New York City, USA.

O'Neill, Edward: 14 Ring St., Inchicore, D.

O'Neill, Felix Aloysius: Benburb, St Mary's Rd., Dundalk, Louth.

O'Neill, James: 20 Dowth Ave., Cabra, D.

O'Neill, James: 187 Malahide Rd., D.

O'Neill, Jeremiah: 10 Main St., Enniscorthy.

O'Neill, John: 28 East Arran St., D.

O'Neill, John: 14 Grenville St., D.

O'Neill, John: 18 Irish St., Enniscorthy.

O'Neill, John: 61 Ballybough Rd., D.

O'Neill, John: 4 Pearse Rd., Enniscorthy.

O'Neill, Joseph: 11 Somerville Ave., Crumlin, D.

O'Neill, Joseph: 26 O'Neachtain Rd., Upr. Drumcondra, D.

O'Neill, Laurence: 59 Ross Rd., Enniscorthy.

O'Neill, Maura: 16 Lennon St., South Circular Rd., D.

O'Neill, Michael: 15 Irish St., Enniscorthy.

O'Neill, Michael: 4 St Mary's Terrace, Inchicore.

O'Neill, Michael Edward: 69 North King St., D.

O'Neill, Patrick: 45 Lwr. Dominick St., D.

O'Neill, Patrick: Drumgoold, Enniscorthy.

O'Neill, Patrick: 5 Old Church, Enniscorthy.

O'Neill, Patrick Francis: 65 Carleton Rd., Marino, D.

O'Neill, Patrick Joseph: 86-39 57 Rd., Elmhurst, Long Island, New York, USA.

O'Neill, Thomas: 10 Main St., Enniscorthy.

O'Neill, Thomas: 32 Braithwaite St., Pimlico, D.

O'Neill, Timothy: 33D Moss St., D.

O'Neill, William: 15 Upr. Jane Place, D.

O'Neill, William: 32 Duffry Gate, Enniscorthy.

O'Neill, William: 15 Faulkner Terrace, Old Kilmainham, D.

O'Reardon, Michael: 104 Lwr. Dorset St., D.

O'Regan, Liam: Climber Hall, Kells, Meath.

O'Reilly, Annie: 164 Merrion Rd., D.

O'Reilly, Christopher: 12 Sandwith Terrace, Sandwith St., D.

O'Reilly, Desmond: The Bungalow, Balkill Rd., Howth Summit.

O'Reilly, Eily: 67 Connaught St., D.

O'Reilly, Francis Thomas: 205 Griffiths Ave., Drumcondra, D.

O'Reilly, John: 30 Cork St., D.

O'Reilly, John: 12 Lwr. Gardiner St., D.

O'Reilly, John: 31A Spring Garden St., North Strand, D.

O'Reilly, John: 5E Ross Rd., D.

O'Reilly, John Joseph: Templeshannon, Enniscorthy.

O'Reilly, John Joseph: Raheenagurren, Gorey, Wexford.

O'Reilly, John Kevin: 12 Ranelagh Ave., Ranelagh, D.

O'Reilly, Joseph: Melrose, Lindsay Rd., Glasnevin, D.

O'Reilly, Joseph: 1 Cards Lane, Spring Garden St., North Strand, D.

O'Reilly, Joseph Lewis: Westpark, Glasnevin, D.

O'Reilly, Kevin: 171 Rathgar Rd., D.

O'Reilly, Luke: 20 Charlemont Place, D.

O'Reilly, Michael William: Moorfield, Roebuck, Dundrum, D.

O'Reilly, Nora: Society of Missionery Catechists, Huntington, Indiana, USA.

O'Reilly, Patrick: 43 Geraldine St., D.

O'Reilly, Patrick: 44 Reuben St., South Circular Rd., D.

O'Reilly, Paul: 403 Hastings St. East, Vancouver, Canada.

O'Reilly, Peter: 90 Aughrim St., D.

O'Reilly, Samuel Patrick: c/o Sean Nunan, Irish Consul General, New York, USA.

O'Reilly, Thomas: 43 Geraldine St., Berkley Rd., D.

O'Reilly, Thomas: 86 Elm Rd., Donnycarney, Malahide Rd., D.

O'Reilly, Thomas: 2 Sitric Place, Arbour Hill, D.

O'Reilly, Thomas: 283 Clontarf Rd., Dollymount, D.

O'Reilly, Thomas: 81 Mobhi Rd., Glasnevin, D.

O'Reilly, William Joseph: Vice Regal Lodge, Phoenix Park, D.

O'Riain, Seámus: Kindlestown House, Delgany, Wicklow.

O'Riordan, Michael: 19 Emmet Rd., Inchicore, D.

O'Rorke, Frederick: 29 Newbridge Ave., Sandymount, D.

O'Rorke, John: 16 Mannix Rd., Drumcondra, D.

O'Rorke, Joseph Francis: 29 Newbridge Ave., D.

O'Rourke, John: Maree, Oranmore, Galway.

O'Rourke, John Joseph: New Wapping St., D.

O'Rourke, Michael: 5 Battalion Engineers Barracks, Curragh Camp, Kildare.

O'Rourke, Patrick: 78 Marrowbone Lane, D.

O'Rourke, Richard: 23 St Aidan's Villas, Enniscorthy.

O'Rourke, William: 2 John Gates St., Wexford.

O'Shaughnessy, John: 81 Marrowbone Lane, D.

O'Shaughnessy, Theobald: 6 Mountain View, Grand Canal Harbour, James's St., D.

O'Shea, Dermot: Reenmeen, Glengariff, Cork.

O'Shea, James: 15 Joyce Rd., Drumcondra, D.

O'Shea, James: 46 Murtagh Rd., D.

O'Shea, John: Moran's Terrace, Ballyhaunis, Mayo.

O'Shea, John James: 102 South Lotts Rd., Ringsend, D.

O'Shea, Michael: 52 O'Connell Rd., Tipperary.

O'Shea, Robert: 52 Lwr. Mountpleasant Ave., Rathmines, D.

O'Suilleaváin, Gearóid: c/o Portobello Barracks, D.

O'Sullivan, Dorothy: Griffith House, South Circular Rd., D.

O'Sullivan, James J.: 22 Leinster St., Phibsborough, D.

O'Sullivan, John: 133 Roessler St., Monroe, Michigan, USA.

O'Toole, John: 15 Susanville Rd., Clonliffe Rd., Drumcondra, D.

O'Toole, William: 19 Hanover St. East, D.

O'Toole, William: 25 Leix Rd., Cabra, D.

Owens, John: 1 Coombe, D.

Parker, Bernard: 44 Aughrim St., D.

Parker, Ellen: 81 Brian Rd., Croydon Pk., Fairview, D.

Parker, Joseph Patrick: 109 South Circular Rd., Kilmainham, D.

Parnell, Matthew: 13 Wellington Place, Mountjoy St., D.

Parr, William George Francis: 49 Upr. Brook St., Stockport, England.

Partridge, William: 3 Patriotic Terrace, Brookfield Rd., Kilmainham, D.

Patton, Kathleen: 45 Warrington Cres., London W.9.

Pearle, Richard: 13 Cardiff Lane, South Wall, D.

Pearse, Patrick Henry: St. Enda's College, Rathfarnham, D.

Pearse, William: St. Enda's College, Rathfarnham, D.

Peate, Thomas: 22 Lwr. Dominick St., D.

Pedlar, Liam: c/o Irish Press Buildings, Burgh Quay, D.

Peelo, Denis: 27 Clarence Mangan Rd., South Circular Rd., D.

Pender, Bella: 4 Bellfield Terrace, Enniscorthy.

Pender, Henry: 94 Harold's Cross Rd., D.

Pender, James: Civic Guard Barracks, Kilcullen, Kildare.

Pender, Stephen: Milltown, Ferns, Wexford.

Peppard, Thomas: Cookstown Farm, Clondalkin, D.

Pepper, Aubrey George: 1 Devoy Rd., Kilmainham, D.

Perry, William Francis: 33 Gilford Pk., Sandymount, D.

Phelan, Michael: 173 Harold's Cross Rd., D.

Phelan, William: Bishop's Hill, Kilkenny.

Phillips, John: 9 South Brown St., D.

Phillips, Matthew: 48 Stephen's Rd., Inchicore, D.

Pierce, Patrick: Parnell Rd., Enniscorthy.

Plunkett, James P: Davis St., Athenry, Galway.

Plunkett, Joseph Mary: 8 Temple Villas, Palmerston Pk., D.

Pollard, Frank Dominic: 12 Valentia Parade, North Circular Rd., D.

Pollard, Louisa: 12 Valentia Parade, North Circular Rd., D.

Pollard, Stephen Patrick: 23 Zion Rd., Rathgar, D.

Poole, Christopher: 108 Walsh Rd., Drumcondra, D.

Poole, John: 43 James's St., D.

Poole, Patrick: 41 Upr. MacDermott St., D.

Poole, Vincent: 3 Ryders Row, D.

Porter, Eugene: 21 Warrenmount Place, D.

Pounch, James: 39 Synge St., D.

Power, Arthur: Bluebell, Inchicore, D.

Power, Joseph: 26 New Rd., Inchicore, D.

Power, William: 31 Camac Pk., Bluebell, Inchicore, D.

Prendergast, Seán: 213 Parnell St., D.

Price, Eamon: 15 Killarney Parade, North Circular Rd., D.

Price, Maire: 209 Griffith Ave., Whitehall, Drumcondra, D.

Price, Seán: 15 Killarney Parade, North Circular Rd., D.

Pugh, Thomas: 7 Charleville Mall, D.

Purcell, Charles: 35 Parliament St., D.

Purfield, James: 4 Leitrim Place, Grand Canal St., D.

Quigley, James: 33 Newfoundland St., North Wall, D.

Quinn, Charles: 13 Rialto Cottages, South Circular Rd., D.

Quinn, Charles: Cregboy, Claregalway, Galway.

Quinn, George J.: 2 Donore Ave., South Circular Rd., D.

Quinn, Hugh: Riverside House, Carginegh, Kilkeel, Down.

Quinn, James: 9 Rutland Place, Rutland Sq., D.

Quinn, James Joseph: 2 Hammond St., Blackpitts, D.

Quinn, John: 96 North Strand Rd., D.

Quinn, John: 26 Hanover St. East, D.

Quinn, John: 90 Railway St., Armagh.

Quinn, Margaret: 35 Lwr. Dorset St., D.

Quinn, Sean: 4 St. James Ave., Clonliffe Rd., D.

Quinn, William Joseph: 522 West 152 St., New York, USA.

Quirke, William: 25 Shannon Hill, Enniscorthy.

Rabbitt, Mary: Killeeneen, Craughwell, Galway.

Rabbitt, Patrick: Cahertymore, Athenry, Galway.

Rafferty, John: Garda Síochána, Leitrim Town, Carrick-on-Shannon.

Rafferty, Mary Josephine: 1 Eithne Rd., Cabra, D.

Rafferty, Thomas: Main St., Lusk, D.

Rafter, Seámus: Slaney Place, Enniscorthy.

Rafter, Thomas: Monalee, Ballindaggin, Wexford.

Raftis, Liam: Town Hall, Waterford.

Ramsbottom, Patrick Joseph: Sandbrook, Tullow, Carlow.

Rankin, Patrick: 25 O'Higgins Rd., Curragh Camp, Kildare.

Rath, Thomas: 12 Grand Canal Harbour, James's St., D.

Rawley, Albert Sylvester: 23 St Teresa Place, Glasnevin, D.

Reader, Seamus: 12 Rock Lane, Lwr. Baggott St., D.

Reardon, Daniel: Ferrybank, 13 Anglesea Rd., Ballsbridge, D.

Reardon, Laurence: 1 St Thomas Rd., Fairbrothers Fields, South Circular Rd., D.

Redican, Thomas Christopher: 5 Mountpleasant Buildings, Ranelagh, D.

Redmond, Andrew: 7 Camac Place, Dolphins Barn, D.

Redmond, Annie: 24 Charleville Ave., North Strand, D.

Redmond, Cathleen: 9 Upr. Sean McDermott St., D.

Redmond, Charles: Ballydonegan, Ferns, Wexford.

Redmond, Denis Joseph: 35 South William St., D.

Redmond, John: 8 Templeogue Rd., Terenure, D.

Redmond, Laurence: Castleannesley, Kilmuckridge, Gorey, Wexford.

Redmond, Owen Nicholas: Forties, Ferns, Wexford.

Redmond, Patrick: 24 Charleville Ave., North Strand, D.

Redmond, William J.: 148 Phibsborough Ave., Fairview, D.

Regan, Laurence: 13 Dorset Ave., Lwr. Dorset St., D.

Reid, John: 71 Amiens St., D.

Reid, John James: 52 Carleton Rd., Marino, D.

Reid, Patrick: 2 Reinhardt Buildings, Lombard St. East, D.

Reid, Seán Joseph: 2 Reinhardt Buildings, Lombard St. East, D.

Reidy, Thomas: Towna, Kinvara, Galway.

Reilly, Francis: Court View, Athenry, Galway.

Reilly, James: Rathmore, Dundalk, Louth.

Reilly, Matthew: 29 Lwr. Mountpleasant Ave., Rathmines, D.

Reynolds, Augustus Percival: 62 Fortfield Rd., Kimmage, D.

Reynolds, George: 1 Redmond's Hill, D.

Reynolds, John Arnold de Vere: 23 Clonmore Rd., D.

Reynolds, John Richard: An Cuan, Sutton, D.

Reynolds, Joseph Francis: 47 Donnellan Ave., Mount Brown, D.

Reynolds, Mary Catherine: Holme, Blind Lane, Navan Rd., D.

Reynolds, Peter Joseph: 64 North King St., D.

Riain, Aine: 25 Upr. Gardiner St., D.

Ríain, Bheronica: 1 Belan St., Baltinglass, Wicklow.

Richards, Bridie: 17 Kenmare Parade, North Circular Rd., D.

Richmond, John: 8 Shandon Pk., Phibsborough, D.

Rickard, James: Baldurgan, Donabate, D.

Ridgeway, Harry: 22 Sráid an Fheistighe, D.

Rigney, Patrick Joseph: 52 Westfield Rd., Harold's Cross, D.

Ring, Christopher: 5 Sackville Garden, D.

Ring, Joseph: 17 Clonmore Terrace, Ballybough Rd., D.

Ring, Leo: Sally Pk. House, Monasterevan, Kildare.

Ring, William: 32 Bóthar Ghort na Mara, Cluain Tarbh, D.

Riordan, James: Allora, Queensland, Australia.

Roach, Edward Joseph: 43 Arklow St., North Circular Rd., D.

Roban, Myles: St. John's Villas, Enniscorthy.

Robbins, Frank: 5 Fairview Terrace, Croydon Pk., D.

Robinson, John: 16 St. Teresa's Place, Glasnevin, D.

Robinson, Joseph: Frankford House, Dartry Rd., D.

Robinson, Seamus: 1 Lwr. Dodder Rd., Rathfarnham, D.

Roche, Joseph: 32 Arbour Place, D.

Roche, Julia: Rinamona, Kilnaboy, Corofin, Clare.

Roche, Michael: St. Leonards, Ballycullane, Wexford.

Roche, Seán Augustine: 23 Winetavern St., D.

Roche, Thomas: 55 Mountjoy St., D.

Roche, Thomas: Pearse Cottage, Ferns, Wexford.

Roche, Timothy: 8 Coburg Place, D.

Roche, William: 11 Emerald St., Seville Place, D.

Roe, Patrick Joseph: 142 Francis St., D.

Roe, Richard: 4 Granby Row, D.

Roe, William Charles: 114 Thomas St., D.

Rogan, Seán: 9 St. Kevin's Parade, D.

Rogers, Sarah: Crioch Mughdhorn, Cill Barrac, Sutton, D.

Ronan, Fenton Christopher: 52 Marlborough St., D.

Ronan, Patrick: Ferns, Wexford.

Ronan, William: 34 Fleming Rd., Walsh Rd., Drumcondra, D.

Rooney, Catherine: North Richmond St., D.

Rooney, Edward: Ratheny, Lusk, D.

Rooney, John: Cahercrin, Athenry, Galway.

Rooney, John J.: 36 Fairview Strand, Clontarf, D.

Ross, William: 15 Parnell Square, D.

Rossiter, Charles: 32A Sackville Ave., Ballybough, D.

Roughan, Bryan: Derrough, Tiaquin, Colemanstown, Ballinasloe, Galway.

Ruane, Bridget: St Jude's, Castlelambert, Athenry, Galway.

Ruane, James: Officer Commanding "A" Company, 4 Battalion, Westport.

Ruane, Martin: Castlelambert, Athenry, Galway.

Ruane, Michael: Glenascaul, Oranmore, Galway.

Ruane, Thomas: Carnmore, Oranmore, Galway.

Russell, James: Ballymadun, Ashbourne, Meath.

Rutherford, Albert: 6 Camac Place, Dolphin's Barn, D.

Ryan, Cornelius: 48 York St., D.

Ryan, Desmond: 76 Lwr. Drumcondra Rd., D.

Ryan, Frederick: 3 High St., D.

Ryan, Gabriel V.: 8 Cabra Rd., D.

Ryan, Gilbert: Roscam, Rosshill, Galway.

Ryan, James: 16 Peter St., D.

Ryan, John: Castlegar, Galway.

Ryan, Laurence: 79 Derby Rd., Seedley, Manchester, England.

Ryan, Martin: Abbey Row, Athenry, Galway.

Ryan, Maureen: Kindlestown House, Delgany, Wicklow.

Ryan, Oliver: 5 Erris Rd., Cabra, D.

Ryan, Patrick Joseph: Collinstown, Cloghran, D.

Ryan, William: 14 Aldboro Place, North Strand, D.

Ryan, William: 30 Oulton Rd., Clontarf, D.

Ryder, John: 21 Harrington St., D.

Ryder, Michael: Ballinamana, Oranmore, Galway.

Ryder, Patrick: Carrowmonish, Oranmore, Galway.

Ryder, William: 19 Elizabeth St., Moston, Manchester, England.

Sally, James Joseph: 458 Pulaski St., Brooklyn, New York City, USA.

Saul, John: 9 Suir Rd., Kilmainham, D.

Saunders, Michael: 26 Daleview, Ballybrack, D.

Saurin, Charles James: 3 Seafield Rd., Dollymount, Clontarf, D.

Savage, Martin: Streamstown, Ballisodare, Sligo.

Schweppe, Frederick: 35 Mountjoy Square, D.

Scollan, John Joseph: 18 Saint Joseph's Ave., Drumcondra, D.

Scott, William John: 7 New Rd., Inchicore, D.

Scullin, Francis: 26 Annamoe Drive, Cabra, D.

Scullin, Leo Patrick: 27A Upr. Glengarriffe Parade, North Circular Rd., D.

Scully, Michael: 39 Keogh Square, Inchicore, D.

Scully, Thomas: 2 Baggott Court, D.

Scully, William: 103 Merchant's Rd., Wharf Rd., D.

Sears, David: 74 Leinster Rd., Rathmines, D.

Seaver, Thomas: 4 South Circular Rd., Rialto, D.

Seely, Patrick Joseph: 4 Strand Cottages, Rathfarnham, D.

Seery, James: 15A Corporation Place, D.

Seery, John: 2 Beresford Place, D.

Seville, James: 17 Findlater Place, D.

Sexton, James: 2 Tolka Rd., Ballybough, D.

Sexton, Michael: 4 O'Daly Rd., Drumcondra, D.

Shanahan, Jane: 71 Larkfield Grove, Kimmage, D.

Shanahan, Philip: Foremacduff, Hollyford, Tipperary.

Shannon, Martin Joseph: 1 Emerald St., Seville Place, D.

Shaughnessy, Michael: Cregboy, Claregalway, Galway.

Shaughnessy, Michael: Ballylinn East, Craughwell, Galway.

Shaw, John: Mary's Lane, D.

Sheehan, Daniel: Ballintubrid, Newcastle West, Limerick.

Sheehan, Patrick: Rafter St., Enniscorthy.

Sheerin, Thomas: 50 Seville Place, D.

Sheils, James: General Headquarters, Parkgate, D.

Shelly, Charles: 20 Lwr. Stephen St., D.

Shelly, Denis: 2 Upr. Oriel St., D.

Shelly, Thomas: 22 Melrose Ave., Fairview, D.

Sheridan, Frank: 5 Castle View Terrace, Rathfarnham, D.

Sheridan, James: 5A Carters Lane, D.

Sheridan, James: 6 Mountain View Ave., Harold's Cross, D.

Sheridan, John: 49 Bridgefoot St., D.

Sheridan, Michael J.: 6 Coote St., Portlaoise.

Sherwin, Patrick: 23 Harold Rd., Arbour Hill, D.

Shiel, Martin J.: 30 Slaney St., Enniscorthy.

Shiel, Thomas: 36 Moyelta Rd., West Rd., North Strand, D.

Shields, Arthur: 50 Sandymount Ave., Ballsbridge, D.

Shiels, Henry: 19 Upr. Sherrard St., D.

Shortall, Alicia: 8 Hill View Terrace, Enniscorthy.

Shortall, Seán: 58 Phibsborough Rd., Cabra, D.

Shortall, William: 17 Charlemont Place, Ranelagh, D.

Shortis, Patrick: Ballybunion, Kerry.

Shouldice, Frank: 307 Clontarf Rd., D.

Shouldice, John Francis: 19 Inverness Rd., Fairview, D.

Simpson, Matilda: Upton Cottage, Goose Green, Drumcondra, D.

Simpson, Terence: Upton Cottage, Goose Green, Drumcondra, D.

Sinnott, Patrick: 138 Faythe, Wexford.

Sinnott, Patrick: Mary St., Enniscorthy.

Sinnott, Patrick: 10 St. Ibar's Villas, Wexford.

Sinnott, Thomas D.: Carraig Ruadh, Clonard, Wexford.

Skinnider, Margaret: 31 Waverley Ave., Fairview, D.

Slater, Bridie: 38 Offaly Rd., Cabra, D.

Slater, Michael: 33 Foyle Rd., Fairview, D.

Slater, Thomas: 38 Offaly Rd., Cabra.

Slater, William: 6 Sandford Gardens, South Circular Rd., D.

Slattery, James Joseph: Bodyke, Clare.

Slattery, Peter: Virginia, Cavan.

Smart, Thomas: Fire Station, Buckingham St., D.

Smith, Albert: 15 Charlemont Mall, Portobello, D.

Smith, Charles: 43 Foley St., D.

Smith, Loftus Herbert: Screen, Castlebridge, Wexford.

Smith, Michael: 1 Park View, Rathmines Ave., D.

Smyth, Michael: 56 Botanic Ave., Drumcondra, D.

Smyth, Peter: 10 Rafter St., Enniscorthy.

Somers, Daniel Charles: 11 Merton Rd., Rathmines, D.

Somers, Moses: 125 Griffith Ave., Drumcondra, D.

Somerville, Winifred: 16 Susan Terrace, Donore Ave., D.

Spelman, Thomas: Oranmore, Galway.

Spelman, William: Oranmore, Galway.

Stafford, Edward: The Green, Swords, D.

Stafford, John: Royal Oak, Santry, D.

Stafford, Mathew: 23 Lwr. Drumcondra Rd., D.

Staines, Henry Vincent: 8 Proby Square, Blackrock, D.

Staines, James: 8 Proby Square, Blackrock, D.

Staines, Michael: 235 North Circular Rd., D.

Staines, William F.: 63 Murtagh Rd., North Circular Rd., D.

Stanley, Joseph Michael: An Stad, Clogherhead, Louth.

Stanley, Liam T.: 157 Kildare Rd., Crumlin, D.

Stapleton, William James: 3 St. Patrick's Terrace,

Russell St., D.

Steinmayer, Charles Joseph: 5 Williams Park, Rathmines, D.

Stephenson, Patrick Joseph: 80 Manor St., D.

Stokes, John Joseph: 34 Lwr. Leeson St., D.

Stokes, Patrick Francis: 65 Whitfield Lane, Heswall, Wirral, Cheshire, England.

Stokes, Richard: Blaney Lodge, Skerries, D.

Stokes, Thomas J.: Cathedral St., Enniscorthy, Wexford.

Stynes, Ellen: 17 Farranboley Cottages, Windy Arbour, Dundrum, D.

Stynes, James: 95 Morehampton Rd., Donnybrook, D.

Sunderland, John: Milltown, Ferns, Wexford.

Supple, Patrick: 19 Auburn Ave., Donnybrook, D.

Sutton, Michael: 22 Wexford Rd., Arklow, Wicklow.

Sutton, Thomas: 1 St. Brigid's Terrace, Dargle Rd., Bray, Wicklow.

Swan, Anthony: 15 Belvedere Ave., North Circular Rd., D.

Swan, Patrick Joseph: 15 Belvedere Ave., North Circular Rd., D.

Swanzy, Patrick: 3 Mountjoy Square, D.

Sweeney, James: 1 Butterfield Ave., Rathfarnham, D.

Sweeney, James Joseph: 12 Lwr. Dominick St., D.

Sweeney, Joseph Aloysius: Burtonport, Donegal.

Sweeney, Michael: 14 Grove Park, Rathmines, D.

Sweeney, Patrick: 1 Butterfield Ave., Rathfarnham, D.

Sweeney, Patrick Emmet: 16 Cadogan Rd., Clontarf, D.

Tallon, Christopher: 10 Saint Killian's Cres., Carlow.

Tallon, James: 36 Grace Pk. Gardens, Drumcondra, D.

Tallon, Joseph: 51 Leinster Rd., Rathmines, D.

Tannam, Michael Aloysius: 3A Wilton Terrace, Lwr. Leeson St., D.

Tannam, William: 165 Harold's Cross Rd., D.

Taylor, Joseph: Main St., Swords, D.

Taylor, Thomas: Coolock, D.

Thompson, Alexander: 1 Plás Tige Laigean, D.

Thompson, William: Ardrahan, Galway.

Thornton, Francis Joseph: 88 Phibsborough Rd., D.

Thornton, Hugh: 84 Donnelly's Orchard, Clonliffe Rd., D.

Thornton, Nora: 29 Lwr. Leeson St., D.

Thornton, Patrick: New Ireland Assurances Co. Ltd, 12 Dawson St., D.

Thorpe, William: 8 Shannon Hill, Enniscorthy.

Thunder, Joseph F.: 207 Mount Prospect Ave., Dollymount, D.

Tierney, Sadie: Bridge St., Swords, D.

Timmons, Margaret: St Anne's, 183 Crumlin Rd., D.

Tobin, Liam: 24 Munster St., Phibsborough, D.

Tobin, Margaret: 5 Market Square, 18 Parnell Ave., Enniscorthy.

Tobin, Michael: Bohreen, Hill, Enniscorthy, Wexford.

Tobin, Patrick: Bohreen Hill, Enniscorthy.

Tóibín, Pádraic: Bohreen Hill, Enniscorthy.

Tomkins, Patrick: Ballycarney, Ferns, Wexford.

Toole, Daniel: Toolle, Oranmore, Galway.

Toole, Martin: Oranbeg, Oranmore, Galway.

Toole, Michael: 4836 Hutchinson St., Chicago, Illinois, USA.

Toomey, John Charles: 88 Phibsboro Rd., D.

Toomey, Joseph: 38 Clonturk Pk., Drumcondra, D.

Tracey, John: 164 Shelbourne Rd., Ballsbridge, D.

Travers, Edward: 134A Parnell St., D.

Trayers, Denis: Maree, Oranmore, Galway.

Trayers, Michael Joseph: Labour League Club, Adelaide St., Brisbane, Australia.

Traynor, John: 8 Ceannt's Fort, Mount Brown, D.

Traynor, Oscar: c/o Fodhla Printing Works, 2 Rutland Place, D.

Traynor, Thomas: 142 McCaffrey's Estate, Mount Brown, D.

Treacy, Michael: Blackpark, Athenry, Galway.

Treanor, Thomas: Courthouse, Gorey, Wexford.

Treston, Catherine: Glen Aulinn, Lwr. Glenageary Rd., Dun Laoghaire, D.

Trimble, Joseph George: 47 Pearse Square, D.

Troy, Daniel: 179 Emmet Rd., Inchicore, D.

Tuite, Daniel: 1 Murphy's Terrace, Castletown Rd., Dundalk, Louth.

Tuke, Edward: 35 Fairview Strand, D.

Tully, George: Gloucester Place, D.

Tumbleton, Patrick: Mary St., Enniscorthy.

Tuohy, Patrick Colman: 73 Bride St., D.

Turner, Cormac: 'Glenlion', Baily, D.

Turner, Francis: 11 Summerhill, D.

Turner, Henry: 21 Annally Rd., Cabra, D.

Turner, John: 106 Foley St., D.

Turner, Joseph: 97 Annamoe Drive, Cabra, D.

Twamley, John Joseph: 6 St Thomas's Rd., South Circular Rd., D.

Twomey, Eileen: Maymount, Granabraher, Cork.

Tynan, Daniel: 16 St. Teresa's Place, Glasnevin, D.

Tyrell, Patrick: 10 Duffry Gate, Enniscorthy.

Tyrrell, Timothy: Crewhill, Maynooth, Kildare.

Vaughan, John: 3 Church Lane, Galway.

Venables, Thomas: 17H Iveagh Buildings, Old Bride St., D.

Viant, Margaret: 'Lorraine', Eleanor Cres., Mill Hill, London N.W.7.

Vize, Joseph Edward: Portobello Barracks, D.

Wade, Michael: 41 Mountjoy Square, D.

Wafer, Patrick: Shannon Hill, Enniscorthy.

Waldron, John: Mulpit, Athenry, Galway.

Walker, Charles: 20 North Great Georges St., D.

Walker, John: 3 St. James's Terrace, Sandymount, D.

Walker, Matthew Joseph: 28 Joyce Rd., Drumcondra, D.

Walker, Michael: 136 Morehampton Rd., Donnybrook, D.

Wall, James: 12 Staff Barracks, Boherbee, Tralee, Kerry.

Wall, John Pat: Kiltulla, Oranmore, Galway.

Walpole, Leo: 11 Donore Ave., South Circular Rd., D.

Walpole, Robert Henry: 3 Ranelagh Rd., D.

Walsh, Christopher: 19 Synnott Place, D.

Walsh, Edward: 3 Ryder's Row, D.

Walsh, Helena: 7 Russell St., North Circular Rd., D.

Walsh, J. J.: Ailesbury House, Ailesbury Rd., D.

Walsh, James: 4 East James's St., D.

Walsh, James: 89 Tolka Rd., off Clonliffe Rd., D.

Walsh, James: 317 Lwr. Kimmage Rd., Rathgar, D.

Walsh, James: 17 Rafter St., Enniscorthy.

Walsh, James: 6 Westview Terrace, Bray, Wicklow.

Walsh, James Joseph: 6 Holles St., D.

Walsh, John: Old Church, Athenry, Galway.

Walsh, John: Carnmore, Oranmore, Galway.

Walsh, John Peter: 2 Sutton Cross, Sutton, D.

Walsh, Joseph: Lymington Terrace, Enniscorthy.

Walsh, Mark William: 14 Courtney Place, Ballybough Rd., D.

Walsh, Martin: Old Church St., Athenry, Galway.

Walsh, Michael: Old Church St., Athenry, Galway.

Walsh, Patrick: Court St., Enniscorthy.

Walsh, Patrick: Kilbrogan Hill, Bandon, Cork.

Walsh, Patrick: 13 Irish St., Enniscorthy.

Walsh, Patrick: 25 Court St., Enniscorthy.

Walsh, Patrick Joseph: 47 Grove Pk., Rathmines, D.

Walsh, Philip: 43 Manor Place, D.

Walsh, Thomas: 23 Cuffe St., D.

Walsh, Thomas: Summit Hotel, Howth, D.

Walsh, Thomas: 27 Derrynane Gardens, Sandymount, D.

Walsh, Walter: Great Down, The Downs, Mullingar, Westmeath.

Walsh, William: Rockwell, Killconly, Tuam, Galway.

Ward, Christina: 12 Monck St., Wexford.

Ward, George: 24 Annamoe Terrace, off North Circular Rd., D.

Ward, James: 4 Abbey Lane, Galway.

Ward, Nicholas: Dunmore, Victoria Rd., Clontarf, D.

Ward, Patrick: 73 Stella Gardens, Sandymount, D.

Ward, Patrick: 130 Grace Pk. Rd., Whitehall, D.

Ward, Patrick Joseph: 46 Herberton Rd., Dolphin's Barn, D.

Ward, Peter: 5 O'Curry Ave., Tenters, D.

Ward, Sean: 1 Wigan Rd., Drumcondra, D.

Wardick, James: 23 Russell Ave., Dromcondra, D.

Waters, James: 11 Ranelagh Rd., D.

Weafer, John Joseph: Mulgrave St., Limerick.

Weafer, Patrick: 7 St. John's Ave., Limerick.

Weafer, Thomas Joseph: 87 Saint Ignatius Rd., D.

Webster, John: Shannon, Enniscorthy.

Weston, Bartholomew: Turvey Hill, Donabate, D.

Weston, Charles: Turvey Hill, Donabate, D.

Weston, Mary Julia: Turvey Hill, Donabate, D.

Weston, Thomas: 15 Roman St., Cork.

Wheatley, Thomas: 8 North William St., D.

Whelan, George: 19 Russell St., D.

Whelan, James: 6 Bellefield Terrace, Enniscorthy.

Whelan, James: Towna, Kinvara, Galway.

Whelan, John: Askasilla, Blackwater, Wexford.

Whelan, John: St Senan's, Old Church Rd., Templeshannon, Enniscorthy.

Whelan, John: 24 Glorney's Buildings, Gloucester St., D.

Whelan, Joseph: 92 Lwr. Gardiner St., D.

Whelan, Kathleen: Court House, Enniscorthy.

Whelan, Laurence: 15 Clarence St., North Strand, D.

Whelan, Maurice: 3 Grosvenor Villas, Bray, Wicklow.

Whelan, Michael: 61 Upr. Dorset St., D.

Whelan, Patrick: 28 Pembroke Cottages, Ringsend, D.

Whelan, Patrick: Woodlands, Ferns, Wexford.

Whelan, Richard: Lwr. Church St., Enniscorthy.

Whelan, Thomas: Lodgewood, Ferns, Wexford.

Whelan, William: 12 Lwr. Northbrook Ave., North Strand, D.

Whelehan, Christopher John: Irishtown, Mullingar, Westmeath.

White, John: Alma Mansions, Brent Green, Hendon, London NW4.

White, Mary: Prospect, Enniscorthy.

White, Michael: 34 Pk. St., Inchicore, D.

White, Michael: 20 Upr. Sherrard St., D.

Whyte, Charles: Caheroyan, Athenry, Galway.

Whyte, Patrick: Knockroe, Attymon, Athenry, Galway.

Wildes, Myles: 56 St Aidan's Villas, Enniscorthy.

Williams, Henry Joseph: 27 Lwr. Pembroke St., D.

Williams, John Joseph: 2 Lwr. Wellington St., D.

Williams, Patrick: 24 Stafford St., D.

Williams, Peter: 8 Coombe, D.

Williams, Walter: 169 Galtymore Rd., North Crumlin, D.

Willis, Henry Christopher: 56 St. Mobhi Rd., Glasnevin, D.

Willis, James: 3 Hill View Terrace, Enniscorthy.

Wilson, Edward: 10 Francis Row, Enniscorthy.

Wilson, James: Balheary, Swords, D.

Wilson, Joseph: 2 Hospital Lane, Enniscorthy.

Wilson, Mark: 1 Post Office Hill, Curragh, Kildare.

Wilson, Owen: 4 Hospital Lane, Enniscorthy.

Wilson, Peter: North St., Swords, D.

Wilson, Peter: North St., Swords, D.

Wilson, Robert: 10 Francis Row, Enniscorthy.

Wilson, William: Balheary, Swords, D.

Windrim, Samuel W.: 16 Rossas Ave., Limerick.

Winstanley, Henry: 30 Millmount Cottages, Windy Arbour, Dundrum, D.

Wisely, May: 30 Strandville Ave., North Strand.

Woodcock, William Joseph: 5 Grantham Place, D.

Woods, Annie: The Priory, Walmer, Port Elizabeth, South Africa.

Wren, James: 163 Malahide Rd., D.

Young, Eamon Christopher: 37 Hamilton St., South Circular Rd., D.

Young, Patrick John: 37 Hamilton St., Donore Ave., South Circular Rd., D.

Young, Robert Martin: 17 Sandford Ave., Donore Ave., South Circular Rd., D.

Young, Thomas Lawrence: 37 Hamilton St., D.

Yourell, Thomas: 96 Devinish Rd., Kimmage, D.

Notes

SECTION TWO

1. O'Brolchain, Honor, *16Lives: Joseph Plunkett,* The O'Brien Press, Dublin, 2012, pp364–66.
2. Surrey House was the home of Countess Markievicz.
3. Lynch, Diarmuid, *The IRB and the 1916 Rising,* Mercier, Cork, 1957, pp76–77.
4. BMH WS 705 Christopher Brady.
5. Ed. Helen Litton, *Kathleen Clarke: Revolutionary Woman, My Fight for Ireland's Freedom,* The O'Brien Press, Dublin, 1991, pp69–70.
6. BMH WS 541 Dr Nancy Wyse-Power.
7. BMH WS 705 Christopher Brady.
8. BMH WS 268 Liam T Cosgrave.
9. BMH WS 716 Michael J Molloy.
10. The author measured one Proclamation as 29 ¾ by 20 ⅛ inches.
11. BMH WS 705 Christopher Brady.
12. Ibid.
13. BMH WS 716 Michael J Molloy.
14. Kindly donated by the McCrossan family in March 2006.
15. Kathleen Clarke donated her copy of the Proclamation.
16. NLI (Ms. 15,453), author's transcription.

SECTION THREE

1. Amongst the shipment landed at Larne in April 1914 were thousands of Austrian Mannlicher rifles, German Model 1888 'Commission' rifles and Italian Vetterli-Vitali rifles. Bruno Spiro, who was Jewish, was arrested by the Gestapo in July 1916 and committed suicide on 29 September 1936 while imprisoned in the concentration camp at Fuhlsbüttel near Hamburg.
2. Moritz Magnus, persecuted for being Jewish, fled to Belgium in 1938 but was deported to Auschwitz in 1942, where he subsequently died.
3. BMH WS 310 James Grace.
4. BMH WS 208 Seamus Kavanagh.

5. BMH WS 147 Bernard McAllister.

6. BMH WS 288 Charles Saurin.

7. BMH WS 242 Liam Tannam.

8. BMH WS 304 James Coughlan.

9. BMH WS 188 Seán O'Keeffe.

10. BMH WS 833 Michael Knightly.

11. The nickname comes from the Siege of Sidney Street, in which Peter Piatkov, a Latvian anarchist known as Peter the Painter, escaped from the London police with the help of his C96.

12. BMH WS 161 Donal O'Hannigan.

13. BMH WS 304 James Coughlan.

14. BMH WS 751 Colm O'Lochlainn.

15. BMH WS 638 Patrick Caldwell.

16. Collins, Lorcan, *16Lives: James Connolly*, The O'Brien Press, Dublin, 2012, p263.

17. *Sinn Féin Rebellion Handbook*, *The Irish Times*, Dublin, 1917, p19.

18. Military Archives; the BMH Photo (BMH P) series; P19 A.

19. After Michael Collins, who was killed at Béal na mBláth on 22 August 1922.

20. After Comdt. Gen. Tom Keogh, who was killed in an ambush on 11 September 1922.

21. Cathal Brugha was shot on O'Connell Street on 5 July 1922 at the beginning of the Civil War. He died of his wounds two days later.

22. After Arthur Griffith, founder of Sinn Féin, who died on 12 August 1922.

23. After Dick McKee, one of three men murdered in Dublin Castle on 21 November 1920. Peadar Clancy and Conor Clune were the other two.

SECTION FOUR

1. Ring, Jim, *Erskine Childers*, John Murray Publishers, London, 1996, p95.

2. Monteith, Robert, Franz von Papen and Sean O'Casey, *Casement's Last Adventure*, M.F. Moynihan, Dublin, 1953.

3. Clayton, Xander, *Aud*, GAC, Plymouth, 2007.

4. Clayton, Xander, *Aud*, GAC, Plymouth, 2007, p781.

5. For the Maxim Machine guns.

6. For the Howth Mausers.

7. de Courcy Ireland, John, *The Sea and the Easter Rising*, Maritime Institute, Dublin, 1966, p30.

8. The RMS *Lusitania*, a passenger liner that was carrying munitions bound for

Liverpool, was sunk on 7 May 1915 and was a major contributing factor to the US entering the War in 1917, as 128 Americans were among the 1,198 dead.

9. Mitchell, Angus, *16Lives: Roger Casement*, The O'Brien Press, Dublin, 2013, p263.

10. The *U-19*'s dinghy is on loan from the Department of Defence and is usually on show in the North Kerry Museum. The Museum has kindly offered to return it to Dublin as part of the centennial celebrations in 2016. (Conversation with North Kerry Museum Curator Seán Quinlan, 25 July 2015.)

11. Mitchell, Angus, *16Lives: Roger Casement*, The O'Brien Press, Dublin, 2013, p269.

12. Joyce, Lar, *History Ireland*, March–April 2010.

13. In 1907 a first *Helga* was sold and renamed *Constance*, so some people refer to this second *Helga* as *Helga II*.

14. *Sinn Féin Rebellion Handbook*, *The Irish Times*, Dublin, 1917, p20.

15. de Courcy Ireland, John, *The Sea and the Easter Rising*, Maritime Institute, Dublin, 1966, p49.

SECTION FIVE

1. Martin, F.X. (ed.), *The Irish Volunteers 1913–1915*, Duffy & Co., Dublin, 1963, p15.

2. Lynch, Diarmuid, *The IRB and the 1916 Rising*, Mercier, Cork, 1957, p28.

3. Bulmer Hobson version.

4. Bulmer Hobson had founded the first version of the Fianna on 26 June 1902, but they wore no uniform nor was there any provision for drilling or military training.

5. BMH WS 31 Bulmer Hobson.

6. 1912 Fianna Éireann Consitution.

7. Military Archives, Fianna Éireann, Dublin Brigade FE/2.

8. Eamon Martin, IRB.

9. Garry Houlihan, IRB.

10. Herbert Barney Mellows.

11. Military Archives, Fianna Éireann Nominal Rolls Ref: FE 2 Dublin Brigade.

12. Eamon Martin.

13. Seán Heuston, Commandant of Mendicity Institute in 1916.

14. Herbert Barney Mellows, IRB.

15. O'Cathasaigh, Seán (Sean O'Casey), *The Story of the Irish Citizen Army*, Maunsel, Dublin, 1919, p17.

16. Military Archives; IRA Nominal Rolls; Irish Citizen Army (RO/10A).

17. Christopher Poole, who drew up the list, stated it was Thomas Jackson, but it was Peter Jackson.

18. Martin, F.X. (ed.), *The Irish Volunteers 1913–1915*, Duffy & Co., Dublin, 1963, p169.

19. Ibid, p182.

20. Ibid, pp202–3.

21. Matthews, Ann, *Renegades*, Mercier, Dublin, 2010, p115.

22. O'Donnell, Ruan (ed.), *The Impact of the 1916 Rising*, IAP, Dublin, 2008: Matthews, Ann, 'Vanguard of the Revolution? The Irish Citizen Army, 1916'.

23. Collins, Lorcan, *16Lives: James Connolly*, The O'Brien Press, Dublin, 2012, p243.

24. Ibid, p265.

25. Lynch, Diarmuid, *The IRB and the 1916 Rising*, Mercier, Cork, 1957, p158. Also BMH WS 510 Frank Thornton.

26. BMH WS 284 Michael Staines.

27. Connell, Joseph, *Dublin in Rebellion: A Directory 1913–1923*, Lilliput, Dublin, 2009, p328.

28. BMH WS 355 Kitty O'Doherty.

29. BMH WS 497 Eamon Bulfin.

30. BMH WS 370 Fintan Murphy.

31. O'Casey wrote years later that it was blue. He had in his possession Megahy's original watercolour design of the flag, so he may have based his memory on the drawing. He also suggested there may have been one blue flag and one green flag. The Starry Plough in the National Museum is green. They also have the original watercolour, which is blue. See Hayes-McCoy, G.A., *A History of Irish Flags from Earliest Times*, Academy Press, Dublin, 1979, p216.

32. Collins, Lorcan, *16Lives: James Connolly,* The O'Brien Press, Dublin, 2012, p227.

33. BMH WS 510 Frank Thornton.

34. BMH WS 120 Diarmuid Lynch.

35. BMH WS 201 Nicolas Laffan.

36. BMH WS 4 Diarmuid Lynch.

37. BMH WS 1,768 Andrew McDonnell.

38. BMH WS 242 Liam Tannam.

39. BMH WS 120 Diarmuid Lynch.

40. BMH WS 813 Padraig O'Connor.

41. BMH WS 120 Diarmuid Lynch.

42. BMH WS 290 Sean McLoughlin.

43. BMH WS 120 Diarmuid Lynch.

44. BMH WS 120 Diarmuid Lynch.

45. Wimborne was a first cousin of Winston Churchill.

SECTION SIX

1. Seán Heuston worked for the GSWR in Kingsbridge Train Station. See Gibney, John, *16Lives: Seán Heuston*, The O'Brien Press, Dublin, 2013, p62.

SECTION SEVEN

1. The Military Archive Pension Records were consulted for all the women who received a medal. Where applicable, the Military Archive Witness Statements were also used for this list. This list would not have been possible to complete without the tremendous work undertaken by the archivists and historians in the Military Archives and the Department of Defence.

2. Founded St. Ultan's Children's Hospital with Dr. Kathleen Lynn, who was her partner. In order to counter the male-dominated world of most Irish hospitals, St. Ultan's was run by an entirely female staff.

3. Born in Mayo and studied medicine in the Royal University and the US. Had a GP practice in Rathmines. Established St. Ultan's Children's Hospital on Charlemont Street with her friend Madeleine ffrench-Mullen.

4. Constance Gore-Booth, 1868–1927. Born in London, raised in Lissadell House, Sligo. Married a Polish count, Casimir Markievicz. Founded Na Fianna in 1909.

5. Elizabeth O'Farrell was not air-brushed out of the surrender photograph in 1916. She was mostly hidden by Patrick Pearse, and in fact she said that she 'stood back' while the image was being taken. If she was air-brushed, her feet and skirt would have been removed from the picture as well. However, much later the image was 'cleaned up' and her skirt and boots were removed, thus starting the urban legend that the British (or Irish) had air-brushed her out of history. She also delivered the Surrender Order to Boland's, Jacob's, the Four Courts and St. Stephen's Green. She worked as a midwife in Holles Street. O'Farrell's name is conspicuously absent from the 1936 Roll of Honour, but a park on City Quay, Dublin, was dedicated to her in 2003.

6. Raised a green flag above Liberty Hall on 16 April 1916.

7. Matthews, Ann, *Renegades, Irish Republican Women 1900–1922*, Mercier, Cork, 2010, p158.

8. Ibid, p147.

9. Sincere thanks to Mícheál Ó Doibhilín of Kilmainham Tales and Ann Matthews for help in identifying the women. If any are incorrect, it is my fault.

SECTION EIGHT

1. Connell, Joseph, *Who's Who in the Dublin Rising 1916*, Wordwell, Dublin, 2015. Joe Connell has undertaken the most extensive research on the numbers who fought with the Dublin Brigade. Thanks and respect to Joe for permission to use his research. Figures are inclusive of women and also include anyone who spent even a small amount of time with each Battalion.

2. Gibney, John, *16Lives: Seán Heuston,* The O'Brien Press, Dublin, 2013, p102.

3. At the start of the Rising it was a man named P. Begley, but O'Connor replaced him: 'From Thursday I was the Vice-Commandant of the Battalion.' BMH WS 157 Joseph O'Connor. However Joseph did not claim to be V/C in his pension record for 1916 but was O/C of the Third Battalion 1917–22.

4. O'Callaghan, John, *16Lives: Con Colbert,* The O'Brien Press, Dublin, 2015.

5. This was William Jameson's, which closed in the 1920s. Once a thriving distillery producing 900,000 gallons per annum and occupying thirteen acres around Marrowbone Lane, the business folded due in the main to the Civil War, Prohibition and the trade war with Britain. This Jameson's should not be confused with John Jameson's or the Old Jameson Distillery.

6. Collins, Lorcan, *16Lives: James Connolly*, The O'Brien Press, Dublin, 2012, p259.

7. Kenna, Shane, *16Lives: Thomas MacDonagh*, The O'Brien Press, Dublin, 2014, pp186–192.

8. O'Rahilly, Aodogán, *Winding the Clock: O'Rahilly and the 1916 Rising*, Lilliput Press, Dublin, 1991.

9. Lynch, Diarmuid, *The IRB and the 1916 Rising*, Mercier, Cork, p158.

10. Ryan, Desmond, *The Rising: The Complete Story of Easter Week*, Golden Eagle, Dublin, 1949, p125.

11. Lynch, Diarmuid, *The IRB and the 1916 Rising*, Mercier, Cork, p164.

12. Collins, Lorcan, *16Lives: James Connolly*, The O'Brien Press, Dublin, 2012, p337.

SECTION NINE

1. Glasnevin Cemetery was opened in 1832. There is a 'Republican Plot' for those who fought or contributed to the cause of Irish freedom. This should not be confused with the '1916 Plot' which is in St. Paul's, across the road from Glasnevin Cemetery.

2. Bateson, Ray, *They Died by Pearse's Side*, Irish Graves Publications, Dublin, 2010.

3. Ibid.

4. Ibid.

5. Ibid.

6. Ibid.

7. Ibid.

8. Ibid.

9. Of the sixteen men executed, Roger Casement was the only one to be hanged. The rest were shot by firing squad. Those executed in Kilmainham were interred in Arbour Hill Cemetery.

10. Buried Cork Detention Barracks. Reinterred 18 September 2015, Castlelyons, Cork, after a state funeral.

11. Reinterred 1 August 1965 in Glasnevin Cemetery after a state funeral.

12. There were also four children (two ICA and two Fianna) killed in the Rising. They are included in the list of republicans and socialists killed. See also Neville Fryday, who was shot in his Canadian Army uniform and is included in the list of British Army killed. With thanks to Ann Matthews, Joe Duffy and Ray Bateson for the work they have done in this area.

13. An unidentified boy and an infant were buried from the city morgue. The death certificates stated that they were killed by gunfire. See Duffy, Joe, *Children of the Rising*, Hachette, Dublin, 2015, p152.

14. The *Independent* reported that he was found with his throat cut in the Castle and died in Jervis Street Hospital. An inquest found that he committed suicide whilst temporarily insane. See Bateson, Ray, *The Rising Dead, RIC & DMP,* Irish Graves Publications, Dublin, 2012 p64–6.

15. BMH WS 152 Arthur Agnew.

16. *The Automobile*, December 1985, and correspondence with Patrick Collins, National Motor Museum, England.

SECTION TEN

1. The signatures for Roe's Distillery were not collected until 1948.

SECTION ELEVEN

1. For many of the prisoner lists, the total released by the British does not tally with the number of entries on the list. For example, in this first list, it was noted that there were 200 prisoners moved – but there are only 198 names on the list released.

SECTION TWELVE

1. Lynch, Diarmuid, *The IRB and the 1916 Rising*, Mercier, Cork, 1957, p49.

2. Ibid, pp152–53.

3. Ryan, Desmond, *The Rising*, Golden Eagle, Dublin, 1949, p250.

4. BMH WS 1046 Patrick J Ramsbottom.

5. Fleming, Jim and Brendan (eds), *1916 in Laois*, 1916 Commemoration Committee, Laois, 1996.

6. BMH WS 298 Ailbhe O Monachain (Alf Monaghan).

7. BMH WS 342 Michael Newell.

8. Liam Mellows was executed alongside three other republicans, Rory O'Connor, Dick Barrett and Joe McKelvey, on 8 December 1922 by Free State forces.

9. BMH WS 298 Ailbhe O Monachain (Alf Monaghan).

10. Mac Curtain, as Lord Mayor of Cork, was murdered by the RIC on 20 March 1920 in front of his wife and son. MacSwiney replaced him as Mayor but was later arrested and sent to Brixton Prison, where he died after 74 days of hunger strike on 25 October 1920.

11. Castlelyons is nearly four miles south of Fermoy.

12. Bateson, Ray, *The Rising Dead, RIC & DMP*, Irish Graves Publications, Dublin, 2012, p110.

13. BMH WS 226 William J Kelly (Senior).

14. BMH WS 224 John Shields.

SECTION THIRTEEN

1. Collins, Lorcan, *16Lives: James Connolly*, The O'Brien Press, Dublin, 2012, p304.

2. Litton, Helen, *16Lives: Thomas Clarke*, The O'Brien Press, Dublin, 2014, p208.

3. dh.tcd.ie/letters1916/diyhistory/items/show/158.

4. Feeney, Brian, *16Lives: Seán MacDiarmada*, The O'Brien Press, Dublin, 2014, p303.

5. dh.tcd.ie/letters1916/diyhistory/items/show/1030.

6. O'Brolchain, Honor, *16Lives: Joseph Plunkett*, The O'Brien Press, Dublin, p399.

SECTION FOURTEEN

1. Bureau Military Archives, Military Service Pension Collection.

Index